Charlotte
Spirit of the New South

Also by Mary Norton Kratt

The Only Thing I Fear Is a Cow and a Drunken Man
A Bird in the House
A Little Charlotte Scrapbook
My Dear Miss Eva
Southern Is . . .
The Imaginative Spirit:
    Literary Heritage of
    Charlotte and Mecklenburg County
Legacy: The Myers Park Story
Spirit Going Barefoot
Marney

North Tryon Street looking north from the Square, c. 1890s

Charlotte
Spirit of the New South

*Mary
Norton
Kratt*

 *John F. Blair, Publisher
Winston-Salem, North Carolina*

Book design by Debra Long Hampton
Printed and bound by R. R. Donnelley & Sons
Photograph on page i courtesy of Carolina Photo Group, Charlotte, North Carolina

Library of Congress Cataloging-in-Publication Data

Kratt, Mary Norton.
Charlotte, spirit of the new South / by Mary Norton Kratt.
p.   cm.
Includes bibliographical references and index.
ISBN 0-89587-095-9
1. Charlotte (N.C.)—History. I. Title.
F264.C4K7 1992
975.6'76—dc20   92-25020

Contents

Acknowledgments vii
My Charlotte 1

A River and a Path 3
A Town on the Trading Path 11
A Spirit of Independence 19
The Lure of the Earth 39
Confederate Mecklenburg 62
Boom-Town Beginnings 75
A Sure-Enough City 131
Depression Too Well Remembered 183
The Road to Independence 217
Tracing the City's Growth 239

Selected Resources 283
Index 286

Members of the W. A. Frye family surround Charlotte's first wrecker, called an auto ambulance.

Courtesy of W. G. Frye

Acknowledgments

I am particularly indebted to my family and to Margaret Couch, Jack Claiborne, the family of Mildred Morse McEwen, Claire Trexler, W. G. Frye, Dan and Mary Lynn Morrill, Tom Hanchett, Jack Boyte, Ed Smith, Ron Green, Don Hunter, Jim Lockman, Katherine Wooten Springs, Stewart Lillard, Robin Brabham, Pat Ryckman and the staff at the Carolina Room of the Public Library of Charlotte and Mecklenburg County, Dennis Lawson of Duke Power Archives, Frank Thies, Jr., and Knight Publishing Company. I continue to be grateful to the memory of Henrietta Wilkinson and Elizabeth Williams for their assistance with the first edition of this book, and to all those who have chronicled events and tales of Charlotte and Mecklenburg County.

*Summer trolley
to North Charlotte*

Charlotte
Landmarks
Commission

*Cars and wagons travel
Beatties Ford Road, c. 1940s.*

Courtesy of Pat Morgan

My Charlotte

Charlotte is no longer the town I knew. We were a Studebaker family, and like most other folks who were lucky enough to buy a car, we owned a sturdy one, conservatively colored and dependable because it would have to last a very long time.

Charlotte in the forties and fifties was the kind of town she had always been—no nonsense and plenty of grit. She respected character, freedom, money, and trees. She was practical and determined. Almost everybody went to church and wore a hat. There were so many relatives around I had no choice but to behave.

Those were the days people came from afar to ride Efird's amazing escalator, weigh themselves at the S&W Cafeteria and toss a penny into its wishing fountain, or walk through the Carnegie Library.

When we walked along South Boulevard or Morehead and were in a hurry, we hiked the railroad tracks to town. Uptown was ours. Like everybody else in the county, we did our serious shopping there. Quail hunting was good in fields that now are suburbs of saltbox houses, shops, and expressways.

The circling communities of Newell, Davidson, and Pineville were far country. Those days before air conditioning and television may have been uncomfortable or a little boring, but nobody talked about it much. An airplane flying over was an event.

People still knew then why roads were called Sardis, Sharon, Carmel, and Providence—those old biblical names of our churches and the roads that led to them. It was mostly a Protestant town where any preacher who had a Scottish brogue was well-beloved no matter what he said.

Charlotte was a town with few heroes. FDR seemed permanently holy, then Eisenhower, but the real ones were gone, though well remembered—Abraham Lincoln, Stonewall Jackson, Robert E. Lee, and, further back, Hezekiah Alexander and his peers. Hezekiah's house was in disrepair, but we knew the story and had seen what we thought must surely be the bullet holes of redcoats at the Ezekiel Wallace rock house on Albemarle Road. Somehow as children, we knew we had something special to be proud of here, even if we could not always explain.

The city has changed a great deal and not at all. The land welcomed spirited settlers during the eras of gold, cotton, machinery, education, medicine, communication, and finance. Now, her people are immigrants again, many of them recognizing what natives know—that Charlotte is a good place. It always has been. The river meanders west of a city and county of over five hundred thousand people. The fertile land glistens with lakes, creeks, spires, and highways. The story of this place is about these people—where they came from, who they are.

A River and a Path

Before the settlers or the town, there was the river. Before the land had a name, the river meandered and roiled and greedily climbed banks to fill the soil with itself and then withdrew, clear and fish-filled between the forests, the rolling shoulders of tall grasses stretching as far as sight.

Thickets of tender cane drew occasional herds of buffalo. Deer grazed, and bears startled wild turkeys. In winter, great flocks of pigeons flying overhead darkened the entire sky.

Eswa Taroa — "the great river" — the Indians called it. And to those living among the wild pea vines of its eastern banks was given the name Catawba, "the people of the river."

They had not always dwelled there. Once, they lived toward the river's headland, near Old Fort at the foot of the mountain, and before that, according to legend, "Where the sun sleeps, our forefathers came thence." Their ancestors had in ancient time, some believe, come across a landmass of the Bering Strait. Some current scholars believe the Catawbas and their ancestors did not come in recent times from the north and northwest, but had lived in the area many centuries, actually holding sway over a large part of the Carolinas. The Catawba villages gathered a strong remnant estranged from northern tribes of Sioux and later cut off from their Indian neighbors. The name Catawba — also Katahba or Kadapau — resembles the Choctaw word for separated or divided.

And if their river, the Catawba, lacked the wide grandeur of the great western river or the immensity of the eastern sea, it did not concern them. This water and its rich land were known and plentiful.

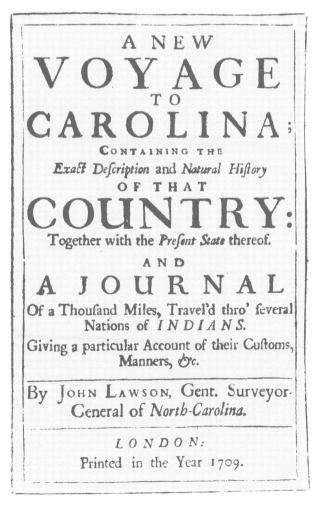

Title page of a classic

North Carolina Collection, UNC Library, Chapel Hill

A NEW

VOYAGE
TO
CAROLINA;

CONTAINING THE

Exact Description and *Natural History*

OF THAT

COUNTRY:

Together with the *Present State* thereof.

AND

A JOURNAL

Of a Thousand Miles, Travel'd thro' several Nations of *INDIANS*.

Giving a particular Account of their Customs, Manners, &c.

By JOHN LAWSON, Gent. Surveyor-General of *North-Carolina*.

LONDON:

Printed in the Year 1709.

A People of the Land

At least six Indian villages sprawled along a twenty-mile stretch of Catawba riverbank in 1700, their cornfields tended by women, their bark-covered houses near a thatched council house. Their principal village, Nawvasa, was by the headwaters of Sugar Creek—Soogaw or Sugau, meaning "group of huts."

Before white travelers found them, they lived well by their fertile river land, but not in peace. The Catawbas were tribes of Sioux squeezed between two branches of their ancient enemies from the north. These Iroquois enemies were called Cherokees to the west and Tuscaroras to the east. The vigorous Catawbas skirmished often with their Indian neighbors. In the legendary battle around 1650 at Nation's Ford, the Cherokees lost eleven hundred warriors and the Catawbas a thousand in a single day. There was no victory that night in any campfire. Their truce drew the Broad River as a dividing line; the land between the Broad and the Catawba rivers became neutral hunting grounds. Tribal enemies of the Catawbas vowed continued revenge, legend has it, "whilst the grass grew and the waters ran."

The Catawba nation at the height of its strength was a loosely organized confederation of villages along the river's eastern banks. These were the Indians whom English traveler John Lawson visited in 1700 on his thousand-mile trek inland.

King Charles II of England had awarded the land south of Virginia and westward to the "South Seas" to eight prominent men who helped restore him to power. These men, the Lords Proprietors, were looking for wealth beyond the early settlement. They appointed John Lawson to survey and observe the Carolina interior. He was an exceptionally gifted man who kept a remarkable journal.

There were no charts of the area. Spanish explorers Hernando De Soto and Juan Pardo

Opposite and below:
The Catawba River
The water level changed rapidly according to the season.

Opposite photo courtesy of Eleanor Brawley

had made earlier incursions into the territory, but the only maps were in the minds of the Indians or the solitary, illiterate traders or sailors who learned the paths between the villages.

Lawson's Indian guide led the small party (which included Lawson's spaniel dog) upriver from Charleston, village by village. Up the Santee, the Wateree, the Catawba they went, over to the Waxhaws, through the Uwharries to the muddy Yadkin. Lawson was an educated scientist and gentleman with a keen eye for social custom, wildlife, the colors of earth and rock. By the time he arrived near what later became Hillsborough, he realized that the Indians "had the finest part of Carolina while the English were enjoying only the fag end."

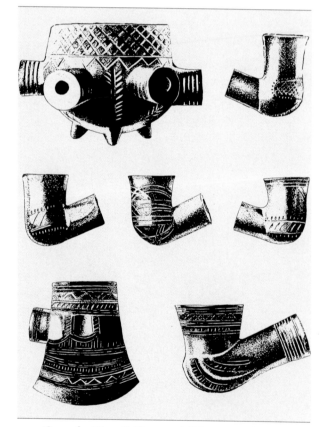

Catawba River Indians etched decorative designs on tribal peace pipes and smoking pipes.

American Philosophical Society
and the University of South Carolina Press

Lawson noticed dogwood blooming, loose rocks like marble, "well tasted water," and "the land hereabouts which is a Marl soil as red as blood."

He described the Catawbas as "a very large nation, containing many thousand people." One Indian woman in the tribe in the Waxhaws "was the cleanliest I ever saw amongst the Heathens of America, washing her hands before she under-took to do any Cookery; and repeated this unusual decency very often in a day. She made us White-Bread as any English could have done, and was full as neat, and expeditious in her Affairs." Very likely, she was cooking venison and fowl in the Indian fashion—with skin and fur and feathers together in a bubbling pot.

In January 1701, Lawson described how the Indians killed pigeons so numerous a traveler glimpsed millions in each flock. These pigeons "sometime split off the Limbs of Stout-Oaks, and other Trees, upon which they rest 'o Nights. . . . The Indians take a Light, and go among them in the Night, and bring away some thousands, killing them with long Poles, as they roost in the Trees. At this time of the Year, the Flocks, as they pass by, in great measure, obstruct the Light of the day."

The Catawba women were excellent basket weavers and potters who formed pots from cylindrical strips of local clay with stamped designs. These containers were used to store grain or hold roasted acorns or hot stew. In their clay pipes, the men and women smoked tobacco.

These peaceful riverside villages with cornfields and dogs were deceptive. Here also lived the Catawba men widely known as warriors and hunters. As Sioux, they had long been followers of the buffalo. Daily, they tracked the deer and led war parties against the Cherokees. Survival among hostile neighbors made the Catawbas ever watchful for marauding Indians. From the beginning, however, they remained friendly to white men, trustful and hospitable.

Lawson was hardly the first of the white strangers, nor would he be the last. With their main village near the mouth of Sugar Creek, the Catawbas were on the Indian highway, one of the oldest routes in America. This great "Trading Path" was known by all who traveled in the New World. Nation's Ford, the ancient river crossing close by the great path, was named for its proximity to the Catawba Indian nation.

The great Trading Path probably began as a buffalo trail or the track of migrating animals seeking the shortest route along high ground to water, food, and shelter. Revering the wisdom of animals, the Indians used the path for travel between the Great Lakes and the Carolinas and beyond to the Savannah River.

The Catawbas living beside their river were on a boulevard that was to alter their lives forever. Since it was the most traversable

Catawba River Indians living along the riverbank decorated this pottery with a pattern of curves.

Smithsonian Institution

Indian route, it became the logical path of the foreign adventurers who trafficked among the Indians trading furs and skins for profit.

Only the courageous traveled that path, for along it lay piles of stones that were the burial cairns of Indians who died in battle or ambush. Passing Indians added stones. Many white men lay dead, lost and nameless in the leaf-strewn forests.

These traders often stayed with friendly tribes such as the Catawbas, sleeping with their generous women, sharing their houses, learning the essentials of the language, and returning for lodging and company whenever they took the great path again.

Traders brought fascinating and sometimes useful trinkets; Lawson found an iron pot in one remote Carolina village. But they also brought smallpox and other diseases, as well as liquor. And these combined to wipe out the Catawbas as surely as the encroaching fur

The great and the small
The colonial journal of John Lawson included his sketches of Carolina buffalo and opossum.

North Carolina Collection, UNC Library, Chapel Hill

traders did. Later, the settlers eliminated the vast herds of slow-moving buffalo.

The buffalo that Lawson sighted in Carolina were probably smaller than those of the western plains. Due to their strange appearance, he published a drawing as evidence. In 1728, Colonel William Byrd described seeing in Carolina and Virginia this "American Behemoth. His body is vastly deep from the shoulders to the Brisket, sometimes 6 feet in those that are full grown. The portly figure of this animal is disgrac'd by a Shabby little Tail, not above 12 inches long. This he cocks up on end whenever he's in a Passion, and instead of lowing or bellowing, grunts with no better grace than a Hog."

Historian Douglas Rights told the story of a visitor to Buffalo Ford on the banks of the Catawba in 1857. The visitor's elderly host for the night remembered asking his own grandfather how Buffalo Ford got its name. "His grandfather told him that when he was a boy, the buffalo crossed there, and when the rocks in the river were bare, they would eat the moss that grew on them." There are still twenty-four separate Buffalo Creeks in North Carolina, not to mention the Buffalo Fords. At least one is marked in Mecklenburg County.

Three other creatures noticed by Lawson still frequent the area. "The Possum is found nowhere but in America. He is the Wonder of all the Land-Animals," he wrote. "The wren is the same as in Europe, yet I never heard any Note she has in Carolina." One kind of owl was "as big as a middling Goose, and has a prodigious head. They make a fearful Hollowing in the Nighttime, like a Man, whereby they often make strangers lose their way in the Woods."

The Catawba Indians, unlike the Tuscaroras, continued their long friendship with traders, then with settlers. They fought beside the newcomers in their wars, led by their colorful chieftain, whom the English called King Hagler. King Hagler was a powerful ally, much respected among the Piedmont tribes and wisely courted by the early officials.

Thomas Dryden Spratt, in his family *Recollections* (1875), told of a French dancing master who traveled briefly in Catawba country along the Trading Path in 1760. He was murdered for his violin. The tribes' white friend, the author's ancestor Thomas Spratt (called "Kanawha"), hastened with a group of irate white settlers to call on King Hagler. They found him hunting near Hagler Creek, and he assured them of apt punishment.

> Then requesting the white men to seat themselves around, [he] sought the highest pinnacle for himself, took his stand upon it, and taking up his handsome, silver mounted rifle, put in fresh priming, blew a piercing blast on his hunting horn, and with the air of a king and eye of an eagle, watched the approaches on every side. In a few moments, an Indian came in view, toiling up the ascent with a fine buck on his back. As soon as the Indian king descried him, he [Hagler] raised his piece to his shoulder, fell on his knee, took a rest, deliberate aim, and fired. The unerring rifle did its work, the victim of the savage monarch's justice fell dead, and the royal marksman turned to Spratt and his associates, extended his hand in turn for each to shake, in token of further amity between them.

Immediately, King Hagler invited the visitors to dine on roast venison and sweet potatoes served on pieces of pine bark.

Hagler led the Catawbas as allies of the English against the French and their Indian allies at Fort Duquesne. Repeatedly, the Catawbas defended settlers from the Cherokee marauders. He was an advocate for his people at Salisbury, and in the *Colonial Records of North Carolina* (1756) issued a promise and possibly one of the state's earliest temperance speeches: "Mine is a small Nation yet they are brave men, and will be fast friends to their Brothers and White people as long as the sun endures. . . . I desire a stop may be put to the selling of strong Liquors by the White people to my people especially near the Indian Nation. If the White people make strong drink, let them sell it to one another or drink it in their own Families. This will avoid a great deal of mischief which otherwise will

happen from my people getting drunk and quarreling with the White people."

And finally, Hagler asked the chief justice what to do with a white woman he had captured from the Cherokees. The chief justice indicated she was an indentured servant. Hagler agreed to return her to her owner in Virginia, adding wistfully, "I am always sorry to lose a Woman. The loss of one Woman may be the loss of many lives because one Woman may be the mother of many children."

Liquor sales to the Indians continued, and

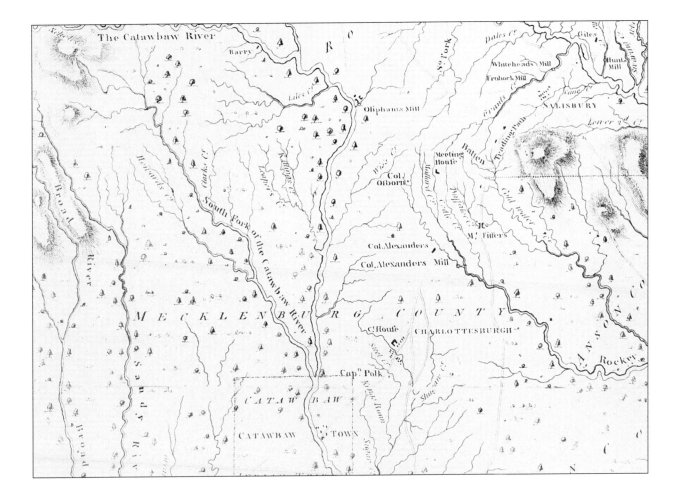

A 1770 map created for King George III of England
This detail shows the location of the Catawba Indian nation,
the village the cartographer called Charlottesburgh, and Salisbury.

North Carolina Division of Archives and History

Hagler watched his tribes diminish. Worried about his people's destiny, Hagler in 1761 brought his grandson before Lieutenant Governor William Bull. "I am an old Man and I have no Son, but a Grand Son, whom I have brought hither to see your Honour. He will succeed me and I have recommended to him to love the English the same as I have done and I hope he will do so."

Hagler continued to negotiate for lands to guarantee against inroads of the settlers until the day in 1763 when he was ambushed and murdered by the bullets of seven Shawnees.

After his death, the land agreement he had so long pursued was finalized. A tract fifteen miles square covering 144,000 acres was set aside for the Catawbas. King Hagler's name was put on the document, since it accomplished what he had persistently sought.

Hagler's burial—five years before Charlotte was incorporated—marked the end of an era along the Catawba River and among the Indian nation. In 1775, James Adair, Irish traveler, writer, and trader, wrote, "The Katahba are now reduced to very few above one hundred fighting men."

Detail of Catawba pottery

A Town on the Trading Path

Charles II, king of England

Down the Indians' well-trodden path, close behind the traders, came hordes of white settlers. First a few, then large numbers packed the path into a muddy wagon road. "That bad road," it was called. Frequent rains mired wagon wheels at the edge of the frontier.

Once the forest along the path began to resound with the rhythm of axes felling trees and the tossing of rocks in piles for homes instead of Indian burial cairns, a new kind of life burgeoned in the wilderness of central Carolina.

Few of these settlers came from the near sea, from the genteel plantations of Albemarle, Bath, Edenton, and New Bern. The eastern rivers of Carolina were not conducive to traditional movement inland from the coastline. Instead, the Trading Path from the north and the rivers up from Charles Town opened wide the side doors of Carolina, and a different kind of people began to arrive in their wagons, on horseback, or walking alone.

These were Germans, French Huguenots, Swiss, and Highland Scots. But the overwhelming majority were Scotch-Irish Presbyterians. To all of them, this new land smelled of freedom. In great numbers, they settled near the rivers and streams, drawn like a magnet to the fertile woodland that reminded them of other fond terrain or the country of a dream.

Early trails often followed a ridge or river.

The Scotch-Irish Migration

The Scotch-Irish never were Irish. The term does not denote bloodlines; it was a geographical heritage. These Scotch-Irish were descendants of Scottish parents who had fled the harsh Scottish Low Country for Ireland at the suggestion of James I, the Scottish king of England. He offered them new life in Ulster, an English "plantation" in Northern Ireland, just twenty miles across the north channel of the Irish Sea. James had hoped to solve two problems—to lift the Lowland Scots out of poverty, filth, plagues, and poor soil, and to control Ireland by peaceful means.

The experiment succeeded initially far beyond the hopes of King James. In 1634, ten thousand immigrants crossed the north channel to colonize Ulster. Attracted by the long leases on the land, they at last saw a new reward for their hard work and an escape from destructive border wars with the English. Their skill and industry literally transformed Ulster; however, in 150 years, the Ulster Scots and the Irish seldom intermarried. The Ulster Scots cultivated their land and plowed a Reformation zeal into their independent, imported Kirk, or church. An excitement born of religious freedom under John Knox came with the Scots to Ulster. And when James, and later Charles II, tried to impose an Episcopal order on their Presbyterian souls, it was a denial of their church and their freedom.

"Tyranny," they cried, "a threat of popery!" Indeed, England's Test Act of 1703 excluded Presbyterians from teaching in the schools of

Ulster, forbade their practice of law, and denied them other religious rights, such as the authority of Kirk ministers to perform marriages.

That added insult to the oppressive Woolen Act, in which England levied a tax to thwart the vigorous Scotch-Irish wool trade. When combined with harsh rents from landlords and Irish famines of the 1720s and 1740s, these tragic forces propelled the Scotch-Irish into what became the great migration. It was a cruel departure—forced out because of astounding success, not failure.

Records indicate that between 1725 and 1760, from three thousand to six thousand persons left Northern Ireland each year, nearly three hundred thousand altogether. Many of these became indentured servants to obtain ship passage to America, facing years of servitude ahead in the new land. Behind them in Ulster, whole villages lay empty. Boatloads of Scotch-Irish arrived at the ports of Philadelphia, Chester, and Newcastle in response to fantastic reports of fertile land in

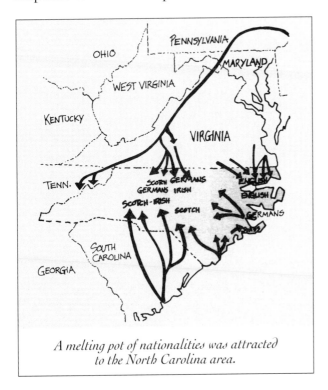

A melting pot of nationalities was attracted to the North Carolina area.

Pennsylvania. James Logan, provincial secretary of Pennsylvania, wrote that "it looks as if Ireland is to send all her inhabitants hither, for last week not less than 6 ships arrived, and every day 2 or 3 arrive also. The Common fear is that if they continue to come, they will make themselves proprietors of the province."

Many lingered in Pennsylvania and Maryland and settled there. Frequently, they moved several times. Then their children and grandchildren ventured forth to look for new land. After British King George II regained the Carolinas from the mismanagement of the Lords Proprietors, the Scotch-Irish and others heard that fertile land which was free or cheap lay to the south. They traveled onto the pioneer highway, the Great Wagon Road down the Shenandoah Valley of Virginia to the Haw River, and merged with the old Trading Path coming into John Lawson's "delicious country" between the Yadkin and the Catawba rivers.

Most Scotch-Irish were farmers, few of them letter writers, and fewer still had the energy left to record their journey. Moravian Bishop August Gottleib Spangenberg traveled with German immigrants via Pennsylvania in a similar search for religious and personal freedom. In his journal, he gave Carolinians his precise observations. In 1752, he reached the Catawba River along the Trading Path and described coming across at least one house each day along the road, which gradually led into the wilderness. Such stretches of loneliness must have been what Thomas Polk of Cumberland, Pennsylvania, saw as he chose for his home the ridge at the Trading Path crossroads. In 1755, he followed and married Susannah, daughter of Thomas Spratt of Pennsylvania. Her family is believed to have been the first to drive a wagon into the land between the Yadkin and the Catawba.

A Notch on the Trail

Another, lesser trail crossed the Trading Path on the ridge where Tom Polk and his bride settled. From the beginning, enterprising surveyor Tom Polk chose to be where things were happening. Not much occurred, but this solitary place was the intersection of what was to become the center of Charlotte Town, as it was called by some, with his modest home on the southeast corner of Trade and Tryon streets. The farm of Thomas Spratt, Polk's father-in-law, lay near what is now Caswell Road and Randolph. Polk's claim to the land was the felled trees, the notched rough logs of his cabin. And it was the same with the others who joined him.

Within a few years, a small scattering of cabins sat at Thomas Polk's crossroads near the Trading Path. When Henry McCulloch, agent for Lord Selwyn, who actually owned the land, sent surveyors, he learned that marauding, pilfering Indians were considerably more welcome than his ominous English-men. According to state records, the surveyors came because "on November 1, 1763, George Augustus Selwyn, an English Gentleman who owned large bodies of land in North Carolina, appointed as his Agents and Attorneys in Fact, to sell and execute Deeds for his said lands." One of these agents was Henry Eustace McCulloch of North Carolina.

The surveyors barely escaped with their measurements and their lives, such was the ire of the Scotch-Irish. These backwoodsmen had come to escape the English Crown, the tax, and all accompanying constrictions. These English-employed men were a sharp reminder of what the wary settlers had so recently fled. They attacked the surveyors, breaking their instruments and measuring chains. McCulloch knew the reputation of the Piedmont settlers near Sugar and Reedy creeks. Governor Dobbs received a communication about them in 1762. "No officer or Justice . . . dare meddle with them, their number rendering them formidable. . . . [They] unite together to repel what they call an injury offered any one of them."

Early settlers' log house shows the fruits of hard labor.

North Carolina Collection, UNC Library, Chapel Hill

Only Tom Polk's intervention saved the surveyors from the incensed upcountry ruffians. Selwyn was paid ninety pounds for the land. On January 15, 1767, Selwyn, by a deed executed by Henry McCulloch as agent, conveyed to Abraham Alexander and Thomas Polk of Mecklenburg and John Frohock of Rowan County, and their successors as trustees and directors, a tract of land "in Mecklenburg County, on the waters of Neale's and Garrison's creeks, being part of my tract of 100,000 acres of land known by the name of the Tract No. 3, and bounded as follows: to wit: BEGINNING at White Oak about 150 yards from Thomas Polk's line running thence North 40 West 240 poles to a Pine; thence South 40 West 240 poles to a Hickory; then South 40 East 240 poles to a Black Oak Sapling; thence to the BEGINNING, *including the Cross Roads* and containing by survey 360 acres of land."

A Spiritual Leader

As soon as the predominantly Scotch-Irish settlers built their early one-room cabins, they moved their modest goods from the wagons, where they had camped in the interim. Their next concern was always a church. Until the families had a building, they convened in an agreed-upon central spot for preaching—a home, a grove of trees, or beneath a large, patriarchal oak, their horses hitched to saplings and their lunches tucked under the wagon seat.

The Scotch-Irish brought with them the very serious conviction that education makes the man and the family. To that end, a spiritual leader was sought to teach them. Families often settled within several miles of each other in order to attract a preacher. When— and if—he came (for preachers were scarce), he was the exhorter, the academic and catechistic teacher of children and youth as well as adults, a one-man cultural resource—no small task even for this era of extraordinary men and women. The community fed on interminable sermons, read Scripture as literature, and used the Bible to teach reading and writing. In the *Colonial Records of North Carolina*, Governor Dobbs reported seeing a

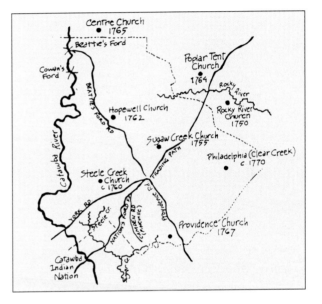

Religious influence
Map shows early Scotch-Irish settlers'
original churches, which were also primary
social and political centers.

settlement of Scotch-Irish at Rocky River. "I sett out the 17th of June to view my lands," he wrote. He saw between thirty and forty families and "except two there was not less than 5 or 6 to ten children in each family, each going barefooted in their shifts in the warm weather, no woman wearing more than a shift and one thin petticoat. They are a colony from Ireland removed from Pennsylvania of what we call Scotch-Irish Presbyterians who with others in the neighboring Tracts settled together in order to have a teacher of their opinion and choice."

To such eager, serious souls as these at Rocky River came Alexander Craighead in 1758, a lightning bolt of a man. He was a revivalist (a "New-sider" as they were called), and by preaching civil liberty, he altered the early county as no one else had done. Some call him the area's "father of independence."

Craighead swayed stones and Presbyterians and an occasional Tory with his fervent rhetoric. A Scotch-Irish immigrant from County Donegal in Ulster, he came to Boston with his parents in 1715. He preached in Pennsylvania until he wrote a political pamphlet unfriendly to the Crown and was no longer welcome.

In 1758, Craighead was called to Rocky River Church, which had begun ten years earlier. His contentious spirit matched well the spirit of the fiercely independent Scotch-Irish as he settled into a ministry that continually made sparks fly. His specialty, as described by William Henry Foote, was to "preach sermons peculiarly calculated to awaken careless sinners."

Soon he was preaching at Sugaw Creek Church, where he flaunted his fierce love of liberty, encouraging the congregation to resist oppression at all costs. He echoed the tenets of John Knox, who wrote, "If princes exceed their bounds, they may be resisted by force." Tradition says Craighead preached occasionally in the lower part of the county, too, shouting from atop the tall stones by the roadside across from what soon became Providence Presbyterian Church.

As more settlers poured into Anson County (established 1750), Rowan (1753) and Mecklenburg (1762) were cut off into separate counties. Mecklenburg also embraced what are now Lincoln, Gaston, and about half of Cabarrus and Union counties. A circle of sister churches sprang up, forming a loop of Presbyterian meeting houses—Rocky River

Pioneer preacher makes his house calls.

North Carolina Collection, UNC Library, Chapel Hill

(c. 1750), Sugaw Creek (1755), Steele Creek (1760), Hopewell (1762), Poplar Tent (1764), Centre (1765), and Providence (1767). From these emerged the county leaders.

Poplar Tent gatherings originally began in a stand of large poplar trees. A hand-fashioned brush arbor—raised poles with leafy boughs laid across for shade—covered the preaching stand as well as some of the listeners and was called a "tent."

Those hardy folk thought nothing of riding horseback ten or fifteen miles to church. They sang familiar psalms together. They exchanged news of neighbors' crops and weddings, as well as the vital events in Boston and New Bern.

By this time, Polk's village was ringed by a wide scattering of homesteads that clung to each other by tenacity and the knowledge of each other's presence. Food was abundant if the families were frugal and energetic. Infrequent travelers made life interesting and were ever welcome.

Queen Charlotte of Mecklenburg-Strelitz, Germany

Queens College

A Charter and a Courthouse

Without Polk's energies, the village might have remained inconsiderable. In 1762, the new county cut off from the larger Anson County was named after the birthplace of the new bride of King George III of England. She was from Mecklenburg-Strelitz, Germany. News of the royal wedding must have captured the backwoodsmen's imagination as well as that of their wives and daughters. Only seventeen, the queen looked pale and genteel as ten bridesmaids carried her ermine-lined purple train. To honor her — a fragile newcomer in a strange land — settlers named their village Charlotte in the county of Mecklenburg. Despite their displeasure with His Majesty's colonial officers, the villagers thought it a pleasant name for a town. Possibly, such a name might bring political advantage as well.

In 1768, Charlotte Town with her honor-

This sketch was based on descriptions of Charlotte's earliest courthouse, which sat in the center of the crossroads at what are now Trade and Tryon streets. The ground level served as a village market. The courthouse was often used for public meetings and for preaching when a clergyman came to town.

Courtesy of Aaron Boggs

able new name was officially established as a town. The act stipulated a courthouse, prison, stocks, and lots. General assembly member Polk wanted Charlotte to be the county seat. But Martin Phifer, the county's other state assemblyman, vigorously sought the honor for his more populous eastern settlement of Rocky River.

The General Assembly of North Carolina met in March 1774 in New Bern and acted on matters concerning Mecklenburg. Charlotte was chosen as permanent county seat, but only because Tom Polk and others had built a courthouse at their own expense at the crossroads shortly after its establishment in 1768. They were determined to keep court meeting

in Charlotte past the seven years originally stipulated by law. When assemblymen learned a courthouse already existed, the act of 1774 went into law, stating that "the said courthouse already built in Charlotte Town be, continue, and remain the said courthouse of the County of Mecklenburg." This important political decision made a vast difference throughout all of Charlotte's future. It was also typical of the astute maneuvering employed to effect legislation favorable to Mecklenburg.

With a charter and a courthouse, Charlotte firmly straddled the Trading Path, her spartan courthouse not on a corner, but square in the middle of the crossroads.

A Spirit of Independence

The Trading Path ran a lifeline through the town and county. It marked a boundary of the land Martha Spratt sold in 1761; the deed cites its beginning at a corner "on the South of the Indian path that leads from the Widow Pickins to the Catawba Nation."

Taverns sprung up all along the path, where travelers stopped between Salisbury and Charles Town (Charleston) to sample local whiskey. Spirits were an essential of Scotch-Irish life, just as they had been in Ireland. A Mecklenburg farm of any size produced its own spirits; whiskey from grain, wine from grapes, and brandy from local peaches were traded in Charlotte Town or carried to Charles Town or Philadelphia to be exchanged for salt, spices, and other household goods. Spirited refreshments were commonly served at funerals and weddings. Even Preacher Craighead's estate inventory noted a punch bowl among his effects.

Each farm of any size was largely self-sufficient, producing its own food, yarn, cloth, and shoe leather. Currency remained in such short supply that anything desirable was often traded for goods and services. Homesteaders traded tallow, butter, cheese, and leather from their cattle for such items as a piece of window glass, a pottery bowl, an iron skillet, or cutlery.

Muddy travel along Carolina highways

North Carolina Collection, UNC Library, Chapel Hill

A Hard Road to Travel

Most farmers and craftsmen were poor when they arrived. As their energies and those of their wives and children quickly yielded results, they needed help with their expanding fields of corn and cattle. They sent or journeyed to Charles Town to purchase slaves who had arrived by ship, often from the West Indies.

Most Mecklenburgers stayed close to home, but some—whose education and trading and property interests gave them a wider view—took the trouble to describe the terrain and conditions of travel.

Thomas Dryden Spratt's grandfather leased forty-seven hundred acres for ninety-nine years from the Catawbas in the middle of the 1700s. He traveled the Trading Path and struck an agreement with friendly Catawbas whom he met by his campfire. He recalled the colonial thoroughfare near Nation's Ford, where he settled and his descendants remain:

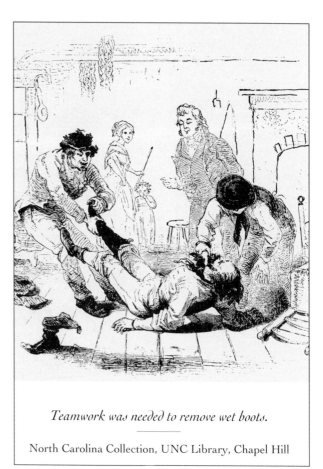

Teamwork was needed to remove wet boots.

North Carolina Collection, UNC Library, Chapel Hill

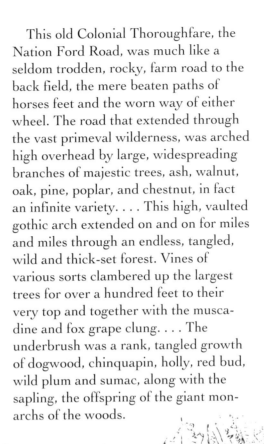

This old Colonial Thoroughfare, the Nation Ford Road, was much like a seldom trodden, rocky, farm road to the back field, the mere beaten paths of horses feet and the worn way of either wheel. The road that extended through the vast primeval wilderness, was arched high overhead by large, widespreading branches of majestic trees, ash, walnut, oak, pine, poplar, and chestnut, in fact an infinite variety. . . . This high, vaulted gothic arch extended on and on for miles and miles through an endless, tangled, wild and thick-set forest. Vines of various sorts clambered up the largest trees for over a hundred feet to their very top and together with the muscadine and fox grape clung. . . . The underbrush was a rank, tangled growth of dogwood, chinquapin, holly, red bud, wild plum and sumac, along with the sapling, the offspring of the giant monarchs of the woods.

The perils of early travel

North Carolina Collection, UNC Library, Chapel Hill

William Alexander, the son of blacksmith-planter-magistrate Hezekiah Alexander, was apparently a trusted regional trader. William knew well the road and its ordinaries, or tavern inns. He carried a wagon train full of goods, especially furs and skins, north to Hillsborough, to Virginia, and farther. Merchandise he received in trade for these furs included a rifle, a Barcelona handkerchief, pairs of silver shoe buckles, and writing paper, which he brought home to Carolinians.

His account book and diary of his trade journeys from 1776 to 1778 recorded that he paid two shillings and four pence for one "quart rum, paid three shillings for ferryage at Yadkin where a pretty young Virginia woman ferry'd us over from thence." He purchased and delivered for his uncle, John McKnitt Alexander, one brass kettle holding thirty-two gallons. His uncle also ordered one large ivory fan. And for his own family, he was urged to remember "one pattern for gown Calico for Easter."

Waightstill Avery, a Princeton graduate and Charlotte's first lawyer, lived in the home of Hezekiah Alexander for a time. Avery was another frequent traveler. Sometimes, he stayed along the road at the homes of friends or well-to-do acquaintances. But often these homes were not conveniently spaced for the end of a hard day's journey on horseback, so that meant spending the night in an ordinary, such as the one recorded in Avery's diary in February 1769. Riding west of Halifax near Hillsborough, Avery "after 30 m. came up late with one private and found him and one of his neighbors drunken and their being but one Room in the House, he reel'd and stagger'd from side to side, fought and kept up the roar-rearum til morning. Thus I watch'd carefully all night to keep them from falling over and spewing upon me. Thus without shutting my Eye to sleep, I set out at Day break. And happy that I had escaped, continu'd my Journey."

A subsequent day's ride put Avery in more amenable company. "In the evening after 30 m. ride arriv'd at Doctor Cathcart's whom I found to be a Gent. of extraordinary fine sense and great reading. I improv'd by his company."

Avery, a Quaker whose name, Waightstill, was said to be taken from the biblical "Wait still upon the Lord," was sometimes beset by the natural elements. Often, he had to cross a rain-swollen creek or river. On one such occasion, he noted, "The waters were deep, dashing and rushing with great noise engulf'd. But haply I got hold of the verge of the bank a little above the great fall, and with difficulty saved myself and my horse."

The elements and drunken settlers were not the only hazards of the road. Colonial records tell of persistent "out-rages" by Indians—some petty thievery and gory killings. All Indians looked alike to the settlers—Tuscaroras, Catawbas, Cherokees. To frugal householders, the theft of an iron pot, a tool, or food was serious and threatening. But to the Catawba it was his due, since he was a warrior fighting in the white man's wars defending him against the Cherokees. To

Travelers ford a stream.

North Carolina Collection, UNC Library, Chapel Hill

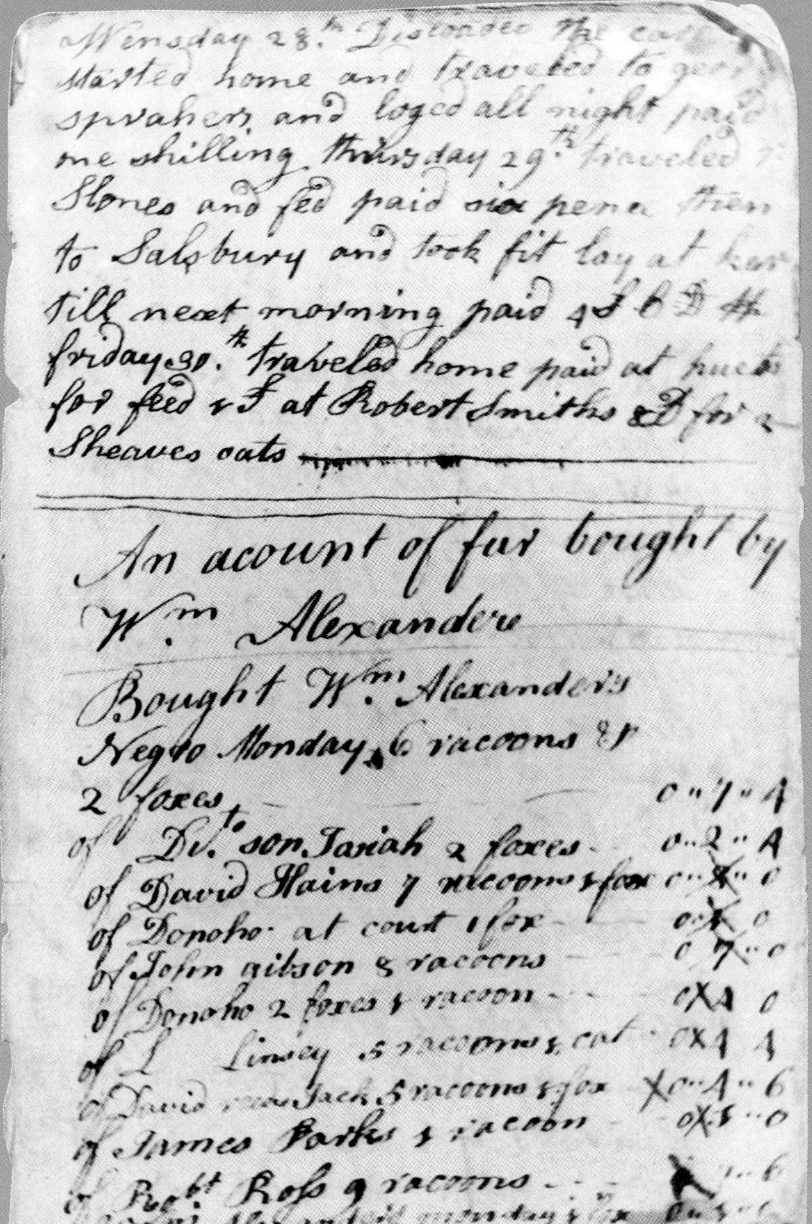

Wensday 28.th Disloaded the cat
started home and traveled to geor
sprakers and loged all night paid
me shilling thursday 29.th traveled t
Stones and fed paid six pence then
to Salsbury and took fit lay at har
till next morning paid 4 S 6 D 4
friday 30.th traveled home paid at hues
for feed & S at Robert Smiths D for
Sheaves oats

An acount of fur bought by
W.m Alexander

Bought W.m Alexander's
Negro Monday 6 racoons 8 t
2 foxes ——————————— 0 " 7 " 4
of D.t son Jariah 2 foxes ———— 0 " 2 " A
of David Hains 7 racoons 3 fox 0 " A " 0
of Donoho at cout 1 fox ——— 0 " X " 0
of John gibson 8 racoons ——— 0 " 7 " 0
of Donoho 2 foxes & racoon ——— 0 X A 0
of L   Linsey 5 racoons & cat 0 X A A
of David   Jack 5 racoons 3 fox X " A " 6
of James Parks 4 racoon ——— 0 X S " 0
of Rob.t Ross 9 racoons ——— " " 6
of W.m Alexand.r monday 4 fox
of D.to son Josias 4 fox
of D.to John Alexander ck

Diary page of trader William Alexander, 1776–78

Courtesy of Osmond L. Barringer, Jr.

other Indians traveling through the territory, any food was fair forage, any obstacle a threat. Coexistence of such disparate ways of life was impossible, and the settlers and white travelers in growing numbers knew who would survive.

If the exigencies of the road made travelers uneasy, so did the rumblings that they and the British governors sensed throughout the new land.

The hornets' nest historic marker commemorates the feisty spirit of the Mecklenburg Declaration of Independence, declaring to British oppressors, "Let us alone."

More Hostile to England Than Any

Trouble overflowed in eastern and central North Carolina in 1771. Royal Governor Tryon's officers, charged with corruption and extortion, met open, ragged rebellion in the shape of testy Regulators. The cost of Tryon's elegant palace in New Bern outraged the farmers and tradesmen in the back country. Near Concord, rebellion surfaced when nine young men blackened their faces and set fire to Tryon's powder wagons.

Charlotte was also ripe for revolt. Its much-desired Queens College, incorporated early in 1771 for young men, had hardly begun two blocks down Tryon Street from the courthouse when King George III refused to approve its charter. A classical academy or high school had long been in operation at Sugar Creek and other churches. Some of Mecklenburg's leaders—themselves educated at the College of New Jersey (Princeton)—desired higher education for their sons. Colonial records state that funding was to come not from the province but from "a duty of six pence per gallon on all rum brought into and disposed of in Mecklenburg County for ten years following the passage of the act."

Even after amendments that included changing the school's name to Queens Museum, the charter was still refused by the Crown. In defiance, Queens Museum operated without a charter and was the first college in North Carolina. The denial of a charter was a slap to the people who believed education as essential as food or shelter. They were convinced an uneducated people would remain a servile people, and they had no such intention. Under Governor Josiah Martin, conditions deteriorated, and news from Boston was no comfort.

The community regularly held militia muster, where able-bodied men assembled to organize for defense against any dangers to the settlements. Usually, it was a social time of visiting, celebration, and news gathering. But in 1774 and 1775, eighteen counties and four towns in North Carolina set up committees of public safety in response to the growing inequities of British rule.

Colonel Thomas Polk, as commander of the county militia, sent word in 1775 instructing citizens in each militia district to elect two representatives to assemble at the Charlotte courthouse on May 19. The delegates gathered and were considering steps to protect their personal liberty when a courier rode in with astounding news. The redcoats had fired on Americans on the village green at Lexington, Massachusetts, a month before. Incensed, the delegates—among them nine Presbyterian elders and one minister—omitted all tactful phrasing, and in their combined written statement declared themselves a free and independent people.

"My grandfather and several of the Catawbas rode up the old National road to Charlotte," recalled Thomas Dryden Spratt, "where a much heralded event was to occur on the 20th day of May, 1775—the signing of the Mecklenburg Declaration of Independence." However, Thomas "Kanawha" Spratt did not himself sign this famous paper, because instead of dipping into an inkwell, he dipped into a gallon jug.

But Old Kanawha was among those who "threw up their hats" and ardently approved the signing. In fact, he became so excited that an officer of the law put him in "the county jail, which was a small building boarded up and down, depot fashion, the heavy, thick oak planks being spiked to the sills and to the plates," according to Thomas Dryden Spratt.

John McKnitt Alexander of Hopewell was a delegate and the secretary to the meeting that day. A surveyor-statesman who was also a tailor, a magistrate, and a member of the North Carolina Provincial Assembly, he remembered his feelings as the messenger told the incredible news: "Soon afterwards we *smelt* and *felt the blood* and carnage of Lexington which raised all the passions into fury and revenge which was the immediate cause of abjuring Great Britain on May 19, 1775, as before related."

The proclamation was read the next day, May 20, on the courthouse steps. Thirteen-year-old Susan (or Susannah) Barnett stood in the crowd watching the wild excitement of her tiny village. Susan "was present with everyone else able to get there," wrote J. B. Alexander, "and bore witness to the crowd in 'throwing up hats'. . . many of which fell on the roof of the courthouse."

Eleven days later, the same delegates formulated and passed a list of resolves. These outlined a system of government under which Mecklenburg would operate independently. They dissolved all Crown commissions and laws, invested power in the provincial congress of each province under the great Continental Congress, and set out the manner in which selectmen would be chosen and empowered, debts paid and collected, and militia companies armed and readied.

A messenger, Captain James Jack, took

the packet containing the declaration and the resolves and mounted his fastest horse to deliver them to North Carolina's delegates at the Second Continental Congress.

When he delivered the packet in Philadelphia, the Congress was still in hopes of successful negotiation with the Crown. A movement toward independence was judged to be premature and incendiary, and the papers were not presented.

In 1800, fire destroyed the home of John McKnitt Alexander, secretary to the convention and custodian of the records. Although the originals were burned, the notes he had made from them for his own use survived and are extant. These notes include the six resolutions passed May 20, 1775, which constituted the Mecklenburg Declaration of Independence. At the conclusion of the notes, he stated, "The foregoing extracted from the old minutes & c." The declaration as reprinted below is taken from *The Hornet's Nest: The Story of Charlotte and Mecklenburg County*, by Legette Blythe and Charles Brockman.

Meticulous Moravians recorded in the *Salem Diary* that a Mecklenburg messenger returned from the Congress in Philadelphia on July 7, 1775, bearing news. The Moravian merchant Traugotte Bagge of Salem wrote in his accounts, "I cannot leave unmentioned at the end of the 1775th year that already in the summer of this year, that is in May, June or July, the County of Mecklenburg, in North

Carolina, declared itself free and independent of England, and made such arrangements for the administration of the laws among themselves as the Continental Congress later made for all. This Congress, however, considered the proceedings premature."

The audacity of a year-early backwoods Declaration of Independence and the lack of an original document have left historians dubious. But notes of the May 19–20 meeting and supporting papers remain, creating Mecklenburg's lively controversy. The authenticity of the resolves is unquestioned. They were published in the *Cape Fear Mercury* in August 1775, and an outraged Governor Martin sent a copy to England. Not to be overlooked is the staunch character of these early civic forefathers and the affectionate, determined manner in which the declaration has been continually celebrated for more than two hundred years with grand balls, United States presidents' visits, and weekends of parades and hoopla far exceeding attention paid the Fourth of July. The date May 20, 1775, appears on the state flag.

Given the times, the impetuous Scotch-Irish temperament, their arduous odyssey into Carolina, and their fearless liberal spirit, such a declaration was not only logical but entirely in character for the followers of Calvin, Knox, and Craighead. It would be more dubious if they had done nothing.

Mecklenburg Declaration of Independence
May 20, 1775

1. That whosoever directly or indirectly abetted or in any way, form or manner countenanced the unchartered & dangerous invasion of our rights as claimed by G. Britain is an enemy to this County—to America & to the inherent & inaliable rights of man.

2. We the Citizens of Mecklenburg County do hereby desolve the political bands which have connected us to the Mother Country & hereby absolve ourselves from all allegiance to the British

crown & abjure all political connection, contract or association with that nation who have wantonly trampled on our rights & liberties & inhumanely shed the innocent blood of American patriots at Lexington.

3. We do hereby declare ourselves a free and independent people—are & of right ought to be a sovereign & self-governing association, under the controul of no power other than that of our God & the general government of the congress, to the maintainence of which independence civil & religious we solemnly pledge to each other our mutual cooperation, our lives, our fortunes & our most sacred honor.

4. As we now acknowledge the existence & controul of no law or legal officers, civil or military, within this County, we do hereby ordain & adopt as a rule of life, all, each & every of our former laws—wherein nevertheless the crown of great britain never can be considered as holding rights, privileges, immunities, or authority therein.

5. It is also further decreed that all, each & every military officer in this County is hereby reinstated in his former command & authority, he acting conformably to these regulations. And that every member present of this delegation shall henceforth be a civil officer, viz. a Justice of the peace in the character of a 'Committee-man' to issue process, hear & determine all matters of controversy according to sd. adopted laws—to preserve peace, union & harmony in sd. County & to use every exertion to spread the love of country & fire of freedom throughout America untill a more general & organized government be established in this province. A selection from the members present shall constitute a Committee of public safety for sd. County.

6. That a copy of these resolutions be transmitted by express to the President of the Continental Congress assembled in Philadelphia, to be laid before that body.

Ephraim Brevard   Matthew McClure
Hezekiah J. Balch   Neil Morrison
John Phifer   Robert Irwin
James Harris   John Flennegin
William Kennon   David Reese
John Foard   William Graham
Richard Barry   John Queary
Henry Downs   Hezekiah Alexander
Ezra Alexander   Adam Alexander
Charles Alexander   John Davidson
Zaccheus Wilson   Richard Harris
Waightstill Avery   Thomas Polk
Benjamin Patton   Abraham Alexander
                    John McKnitt Alexander

Mecklenburg Resolves
Charlotte Town, Mecklenburg County, May 31, 1775.

This day the Committee of this County met, and passed the following RESOLVES:

WHEREAS by an Address presented to his Majesty by both Houses of Parliament in February last, the American Colonies are declared to be in a state of actual Rebellion, we conceive that all Laws and Commissions confirmed by, or derived from the Authority of the king or Parliament, are annulled and vacated, and the former civil Constitution of these Colonies for the present wholly suspended. To provide in some Degree for the Exigencies of the County in the present alarming Period, we deem it proper and necessary to pass the following resolves, viz.

1. That all Commissions, civil and military, heretofore granted by the Crown, to be exercised in these Colonies, are null and void, and the Constitution of each particular Colony wholly suspended.

2. That the Provincial Congress of each Province, under the Direction of the Great Continental Congress, is invested with all legislative and executive Powers within their respective Provinces; and that no other Legislative or Executive does or can exist, at this Time, in any of these Colonies.

3. As all former Laws are now suspended in this Province, and the Congress have not yet provided others, we judge it necessary, for the better Preservation of good Order, to form certain Rules and Regulations for the internal Government of this County, until Laws shall be provided for us by the Congress.

4. That the Inhabitants of this County do meet on a certain Day appointed by this Committee, and having formed themselves into nine Companies, *to wit*, eight for the County and one for the Town of *Charlotte*, do choose a Colonel, and other miliary Officers, who shall hold and exercise their several Powers by Virtue of this Choice, and independent of *Great Britain*, and former Constitution of this Province.

5. That for the better Preservation of the Peace, and Administration of Justice, each of these Companies do choose from their own Body two discreet Freeholders, who shall be impowered each by himself, and singly, to decide and determine all Matters of Controversy arising within the said Company under the Sum of Twenty Shillings, and jointly and together all Controversies under the Sum of Forty Shillings, yet so as their Decisions may admit of Appeals to the Convention of the Select Men of the whole County; and also, that any one of these shall have power to examine, and commit to Confinement, Persons accused of Petit Larceny.

6. That those two Select Men, thus chosen, do, jointly and together, choose from the Body of their particular Company two Persons, properly qualified to serve as Constables, who may assist them in the execution of the Office.

7. That upon the Complaint of any Person to either of these Select Men, he do issue his Warrant, directed to the Constable, commanding him to bring the Aggressor before him or them to answer the said Complaint.

8. That these Eighteen Select Men, thus appointed, do meet every third *Tuesday* in *January*, *April*, and *October*, at the Court-House in *Charlotte* to hear and determine all Matters of Controversy for Sums exceeding Forty Shillings; also Appeals: And in Cases of Felony, to commit the Person or Persons convicted thereof to close Confinement, until the Provincial Congress shall provide and establish Laws and Modes of Proceeding in Such Cases.

9. That these Eighteen Select Men, thus convened, do choose a Clerk to record the Transactions of the said Convention; and that the said Clerk, upon the Application of any Person or Persons aggrieved, do issue his Warrant to one of the Constables, to summons and warn the said Offender to appear before the Convention at their next sitting, to answer the aforesaid Complaint.

10. That any Person making Complaint upon Oath to the Clerk, or any Member of the Convention, that he has Reason to suspect that any Person or Persons indebted to him in a Sum

above Forty Shillings, do intend clandestinely to withdraw from the County without paying such Debt; the Clerk, or such Member, shall issue his Warrant to the Constable, commanding him to take the said Person or Persons into safe Custody, until the next sitting of the Convention.

11. That when a Debtor for a Sum below Forty Shillings shall abscond and leave the County, the Warrant granted as aforesaid shall extend to any Goods or Chattels of the said Debtor as may be found, and such Goods or Chattels be seized and held in Custody by the Constable for the space of Thirty Days; in which Term if the Debtor fails to return and Discharge the Debt, the Constable shall return the Warrant to one of the Select Men of the Company where the Goods and Chattels were found, who shall issue Orders to the Constable to sell such a part of the said Goods as shall amount to the Sum due; that when the Debt exceeds Forty Shillings, the Return shall be made to the Convention, who shall issue the Orders for Sale.

12. The Receivers and Collectors of Quitrents, Public and County Taxes, do pay the same into the Hands of the Chairman of this Committee, to be by them disbursed as the public Exigencies may require. And that such Receivers and Collectors proceed no farther in their Office until they be approved of by, and have given to this Committee good and sufficient Security for a faithful return of such Monies when collected.

13. That the Committee be accountable to the County for the Application of all Monies received from such Officers.

14. That all these Officers hold their Commissions during the Pleasure of their respective Constituents.

15. That this Committee will sustain all Damages that may ever hereafter accrue to all or any of these Officers thus appointed, and thus acting, on Account of their Obedience and Conformity to these Resolves.

16. That whatever Person shall hereafter receive a Commission from the Crown, or attempt to exercise any such Commission hereto fore received, shall be deemed an Enemy to his Country; and upon Information being made to the Captain of the Company where he resides the said Captain shall cause him to be apprehended, and conveyed before the two Select Men of the said Company, who, upon Proof of the Fact, shall commit him the said Offender into safe Custody, until the next sitting of the Convention, who shall deal with him as Prudence may direct.

17. That any Person refusing to yield Obedience to the above Resolves shall be deemed equally criminal, and liable to the same Punishments as the Offenders above last mentioned.

18. That these Resolves be in full Force and Virtue, until Instructions from the General Congress of this Province, regulating the Jurisprudence of this Province, shall provide otherwise, or the Legislative Body of Great-Britain resign its unjust and arbitrary Pretentions with Respect to America.

19. That the several Militia Companies in this county do provide themselves with proper arms and accoutrements, and hold themselves in constant Readiness to execute the commands and Directions of the Provincial Congress, and of this committee.

20. That this committee do appoint Colonel Thomas Polk, and Doctor Joseph Kennedy, to purchase 300 lb. of Powder, 600 lb. of Lead, and 1000 Flints; and deposit the same in some safe place, hereafter to be appointed by the committee.

EPH. BREVARD,
Clerk of the Committee.
Signed by Order of the Committee.

The Revolution Moves South

The American Revolution may have begun in Boston, Concord, and Lexington, but the war eventually moved south. Some contend that the end of the Revolution began in Mecklenburg County.

Stung by their defeat at Saratoga, New York, the British looked south for victory. First, they captured Savannah, and their strategy revealed that Lord Charles Cornwallis would hold Georgia and South Carolina, then conquer North Carolina and Virginia. His victories and Loyalist support would, the British hoped, send the upstart patriots trembling to their knees.

But Mecklenburg's patriot sons did not wait at home for the British troops to come. Some, including William Lee Davidson, had spent the harsh winter of 1777–78 in the snows of Valley Forge with General George Washington. The British moving south soon found Southerners were sharply divided between Loyalists (Tories) and Whigs. The generals had hoped for help with food and communications. But they received little aid in Mecklenburg, according to an announcement in the *South Carolina and American General Gazette* in 1776:

> The young ladies of the best families of Mecklenburg County, North Carolina, have entered into a voluntary association that they will not receive the address of any young gentleman of that place except the brave volunteers who served in the expedition to South Carolina and assisted in subduing the Scovalite (loyalist) insurgents. The ladies being of the opinion, that such persons as stay loitering at home, when the important calls of the country demand their military services abroad, must certainly be destitute of that nobleness of sentiment, that brave, manly spirit which would qualify them to be defenders and guardians of the fair sex.

Not until Lord Cornwallis, British commander in the South, approached Charlotte from Camden, South Carolina, in September 1780 did Charlotte confront the redcoats on the red clay of Mecklenburg, where patriots turned the mud, the bees, and the river into allies.

Lord Cornwallis had routed the American army at Camden and was in no hurry as his army foraged north toward Charlotte, where he knew there were gristmills and food on prosperous farms. He was pestered along the way by partisans led by lawyer-soldier William R. Davie and Mecklenburg's favored military sons, William Lee Davidson and Joseph Graham.

Cornwallis rode in at noon on September 26 on Trade Street. The belligerent reception Charlotte gave him and Banastre Tarleton should have been an omen.

A handful of Davie's men waited in the village of twenty houses, hiding behind corners and the base of the courthouse, which was used as a street-level market. They fired on Cornwallis's advance troops and held them at bay until Cornwallis came from the rear to taunt his men forward against the upstarts. The rebels were delighted to have halted the redcoats even for a moment. On October 3, Governor Martin presumptuously pronounced victory for Britain in North Carolina and restoration of royal rule.

In Charlotte, Cornwallis occupied Tom Polk's house, made his headquarters across the street, and found food and Tory supporters hard to come by. Cornwallis soon saw the unhappy evidence of the frontiersmen's skill with the long rifle. (Charlotte housed one of America's few early rifle factories.) Owners burned barns rather than supply the British

Lord Charles Cornwallis,
British commander in the South

North Carolina Collection, UNC Library, Chapel Hill

Colonel Tarleton, one of Cornwallis's star subordinates, a cocky cavalry officer, told of one large foraging party of three hundred men who went to McIntyre's farm, seven miles toward the river at Beattie's Ford. Neighboring farmers gathered in the woods and fired on the soldiers and their sixty wagons. "A British captain was killed with others, several wounded," Tarleton noted. "The detachment returned to town disappointed of their forage, and reported to Lord Cornwallis that 'every bush concealed a rebel.'" This was the "Battle of the Bees," in which farmer McIntyre's beehives were knocked over in the rout. The bees zealously attacked the redcoats as they stole chickens and pigs. Tarleton reported that "the town and environs abounded with inveterate enemies." Cornwallis called it "a hornet's nest." The *Pennsylvania Packet* subsequently reported the event.

Most messengers Cornwallis sent to outlying troops never got out of town. Communiques seldom entered. Tarleton reported, "The vigilance and animosity . . . destroyed all communications between the King's troops

with grain and hay for their horses. Patriot riders raced ahead to warn of enemy foragers. Farmers drove livestock deep into the woods.

Among those approached by the British was Susannah Barnett Smart, who had witnessed the "throwing up of hats" earlier. When the British tried to bridle a family horse, according to an account in *Godey's Lady's Book* (1856), Susannah pulled off the bridle, even though they threatened to kill her. When they brought a crock of milk from her cellar to drink, she deliberately turned it over, spilling the milk. They swore they would cut her to pieces. "Do it if you dare!" said Susannah with an air of haughty defiance. "You will be shot at from every bush in the county." They wisely left her with her horse and milk and rode away to find provisions elsewhere.

McIntyre Cabin,
site of the "Battle of the Bees" in 1780

Public Library of Charlotte and Mecklenburg County

and loyalists." Cornwallis wrote Sir Henry Clinton, "Charlotte is an agreeable village but in a damn rebellious country." Tarleton later wrote, "The counties of Mecklenburg and Rowan were more hostile to England than any in America."

During Cornwallis's occupation of Charlotte, the war turned upside down.

Kings Mountain

View at Kings Mountain battleground

North Carolina Collection, UNC Library, Chapel Hill

Colonel Patrick "Bull Dog" Ferguson, inventor of the Ferguson flintlock rifle and son of a Scottish laird, commanded the British left-flank army while Cornwallis camped in Charlotte. Had his troops been supplied with his rifles instead of the less accurate muskets, history might have been different.

In Rutherford County, Ferguson sent out the word ordering the mountain men to lay down their arms or else he would march his forces over the mountains, hang their leaders, and lay waste to their country with fire and sword. As a Scotsman, he should have known better. The American Scotch-Irish tucked into remote settlements in the Tennessee, South Carolina, and North Carolina mountains knew a personal threat when they heard it. It was their back-country homes he threatened. Swiftly, they gathered at Sycamore Shoals. These "Overmountain Men"—long rifles in hand, wearing skin breeches, homespun shirts, and moccasins, a thousand proud but motley men—listened as preacher Samuel

Doak thundered how the Lord saved Israel when Gideon slew the Midianites. With their battle cry, "The Sword of the Lord and of Gideon," they rode toward Ferguson. More rugged men with knives in their belts and long rifles joined them at Quaker Meadows and still more at Cowpens. They were eighteen hundred strong. They camped on the plain where cattle traders pastured and penned cows for market. From the group, nine hundred were chosen to march toward Ferguson, who wore a silver whistle and clean, checkered jacket on the promontory of Kings Mountain.

Ferguson felt secure in his high camp overlooking the surrounding countryside, and he said, "Here is a place God Almighty cannot drive us from."

The lean patriots left their horses, shinnied up the mountain tree to tree, aiming at redcoats instead of the usual squirrels or panthers. Ferguson is still on the mountain, under a cairn of stones, with a female camp follower buried beside him at Kings Mountain National Military Park.

The amazing victory, the colonials' first in the Southern campaign, turned the tide of the war by encouraging the patriots to believe

British map of Mecklenburg in 1780

Courtesy of Aaron Boggs

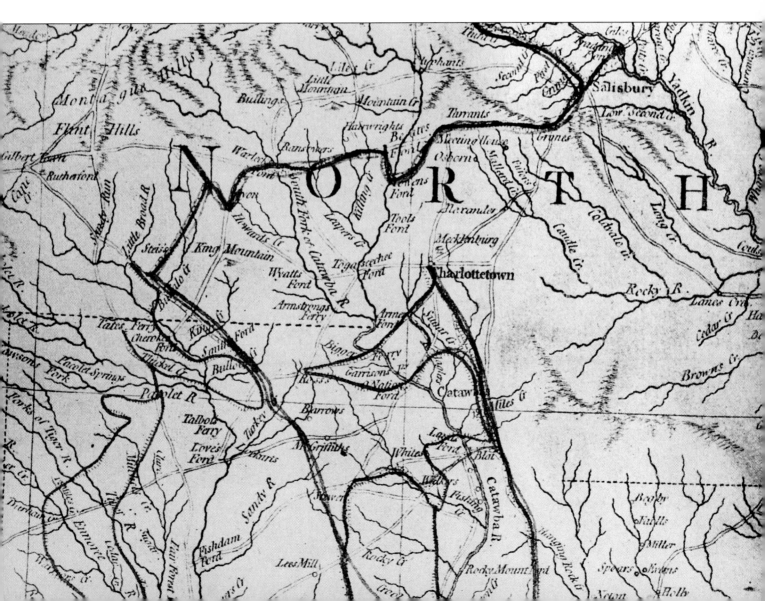

that the impossible was possible after all. Cornwallis was stunned. Washington was overjoyed. Three days after the battle, a jubilant Tom Polk wrote to the North Carolina Board of War:

Camp Yadkin River
October 11, 1780

Gentlemen:
    I have the pleasure to inform you that on Saturday last the noted Col. Ferguson, with 150 men, fell on Kings Mountain; 800 taken prisoners, with 150 stand of arms. Cleveland and Campbell commanded. Glorious affair. In a few days doubt not we shall be in Charlotte, and I will take possession of my house and his lordship take the woods.
    I am gentlemen, with respect,

Your humble servant,
Thomas Polk

Supplies from the battle at Kings Mountain
Kings Mountain Military Park

Kings Mountain
North Carolina Collection, UNC Library, Chapel Hill

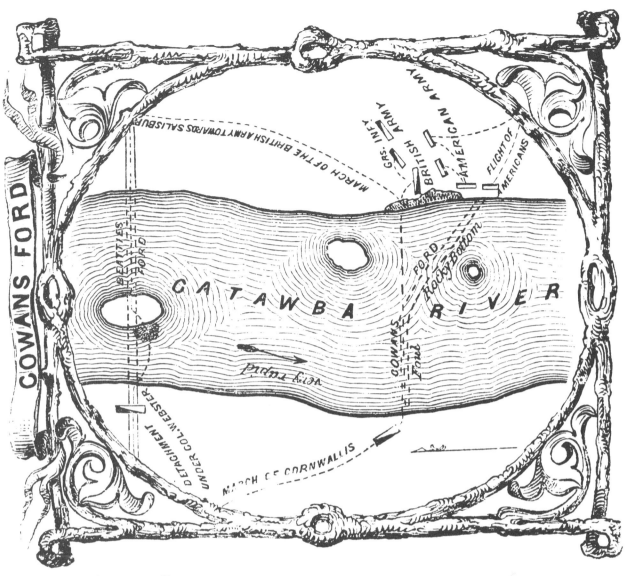

COWANS FORD

MARCH OF THE BRITISH ARMY TOWARDS SALISBU...

GRS. INFY
BRITISH ARMY
AMERICAN ARMY
FLIGHT OF AMERICANS

BEATTIES FORD

CATAWBA RIVER

Rocky Bottom
COWANS FORD

very rapid

DETACHMENT UNDER COL. WEBSTER

MARCH OF CORNWALLIS

Cowan's Ford

Drawing of the river battle at Cowan's Ford on the Catawba

North Carolina Collection, UNC Library, Chapel Hill

After the loss at Kings Mountain, Cornwallis left the inhospitable country, crossed the Catawba River into South Carolina, and wintered there several months. Into Mecklenburg came General Nathanael Greene in December 1780, sent by Washington to head the American army of the South. There was not much army to head, but Greene's task was to recruit, organize, and train men and keep Cornwallis far from supplies and aid.

An American victory by Daniel Morgan against Tarleton at Cowpens sent Cornwallis north to recross the Catawba chasing him. The cunning Morgan, who had been only an army teamster during the French and Indian War, cannily put the swollen Catawba River between them. It was impassable. The Americans were wise in the ways of their Piedmont rivers.

General Greene, that Quaker blacksmith-farmer from Rhode Island, assisted Mecklenburg's popular William Lee Davidson of the North Carolina militia, who mustered troops, scouted the river, and lay in wait for Cornwallis to choose his time and

Nathanael Greene,
patriot general sent to harass Cornwallis
and organize defense

North Carolina Collection, UNC Library, Chapel Hill

place.

Several wagon and horse fords, or crossing places, marked the Catawba. But after heavy rains, the tawny Catawba widened, obscuring passages and making crossing difficult at best. Horses, losing their footing, disappeared in the tumbling current.

Davidson arranged guards at the obvious fords Cornwallis might choose—Tuckasegee, Tool's, Cowan's, Beattie's. The main Southern army, now under Greene, advanced to Salisbury, leaving Graham's cavalry and William Polk's infantry to assist Davidson's militia, mustered from church meetings and plantation fields for temporary duty.

During the night of February 1, 1781, noises of horses revealed Cornwallis was crossing at Cowan's Ford. The American cavalry began to fire, and early in the attack General Davidson fell suddenly and silently from his horse. Cornwallis crossed as the leaderless Whigs fled in panic.

Later that day, Davidson's body was found stripped naked near the river's ford, a rifle ball near his heart. The young general had fallen in his home county. A kinsman, David Wilson, carried his body on horseback to a neighbor's. Davidson's body was dressed in a borrowed suit and buried by torchlight in the Hopewell churchyard.

Since the British used only muskets, not rifles, it has been conjectured that Davidson was shot by a Mecklenburg Tory guiding the British across the river. The place where Davidson fell is now covered by deep waters behind the Cowan's Ford dam. A marker near the site honors General Davidson. Davidson College (established by Presbyterians in 1837), the town of Davidson, and Davidson County are named for him.

Before the battle of Cowan's Ford, the general spent a night at Major John Davidson's nearby plantation, according to Dr. Chalmers G. Davidson, historian and descendant of General Davidson. Slaves recounted strange noises heard in the darkness and recalled he mounted his horse the next morning under a low-boughed elm, an omen of certain doom.

Mecklenburg's Oldest Dwellings

H ezekiah Alexander, a man of wide community influence, built what is now the oldest dwelling still standing in Mecklenburg County. It sits on a tract of land purchased from his brother, John McKnitt Alexander. Completed in 1774, the house is fashioned of stone quarried from nearby hillsides. It resembles early houses in Maryland and Pennsylvania, where Alexander lived before settling in the Piedmont. A cool stream still trickles down the sylvan creek bed below the house and flows under the stone springhouse, which was used to keep butter, cheese, and milk cool. The six-hundred-acre plantation had numerous cattle and a dairy, and in 1790 supported thirteen slaves.

There are many Alexanders in Mecklenburg, but residents refer fondly and personally to this frugal, industrious, acquisitive Scotch-Irish landowner, calling him Hezekiah, as though he rode by yesterday. Citizens trace the travels and fortunes of his ten children and know that his wife, Mary Sample, could read and met hard times after his death. Hezekiah was a justice of the peace, a founding trustee and later treasurer of Queens College, an elder at Sugaw Creek Presbyterian Church, and a signer of the Mecklenburg Declaration of Independence. He served as a delegate to the Fifth Provincial Congress as well as on the committee that drafted the North Carolina State Constitution and Bill of Rights. Hezekiah and Mary Alexander's "Rock House" is listed on the National Register of Historic Places and has been designated a Charlotte-Mecklenburg Historic Site.

Another immigrant to early Mecklenburg was Hugh Torance, whose log residence from the 1770s survives. Torance arrived in America bearing a letter of character reference dated 1763 from his clergyman in County Tyrone, Ireland. It declared Torance to be "an unmarried person descended from honest and reputable parents . . . [who has] always behaved himself orderly and supported a very fair character." He purchased land on McDowell Creek in 1779 and, before becoming a soldier, traveled as a peddler. He subsequently sold goods in his log house in north Mecklenburg. The Hugh Torance House and Store on Gilead Road is a Charlotte-Mecklenburg Historic Site.

Closeup of the cornerstone of
Hezekiah Alexander Homesite

Hezekiah Alexander's springhouse

Basket-weave door of
Hugh Torance House and Store, 1770s

The Lure of the Earth

George Washington

North Carolina Collection,
UNC Library, Chapel Hill

In 1791, George Washington paid Charlotte a social call. America had finally sorted out her early constitutional squabbles and happily elected him president. After a year in office, Washington set out to see the people, all those backwoods politicians, settlers, and Indians. On the way, he squinted across revolutionary battlegrounds of Cornwallis, Greene, and Gates, imagining military flanks across that ridge or sloshing this "impenetrable swamp." In some settlements, he wiped his muddy boots, adjusted his properly powdered wig, and strode into a parlor to take tea with the ladies.

He must have come up from Camden by way of Providence Road, but as he crossed from South Carolina where the Trading Path follows the boundary, Washington recorded, "I was met by some of the chiefs of the Catawba nation who seemed under apprehension that some attempts were making, or would be made, to deprive them of part of the 40,000 Acres wch. was secured to them by Treaty and wch. is bounded by this Road."

Concerned with agriculture as much as politics or battlefields, he studied the soil along the roadside. "Suddenly," he wrote, "the piney and sandy lands took quite a different complexion, here they began to assume a very rich look." Journeying from the home of one prominent roadside resident to another, he slept at the Crawfords', breakfasted at the Harrisons', and in Charlotte "dined with General [Thomas] Polk and a small party invited by him, at a Table prepared for the purpose. . . .

"Charlotte is a trifling place, though the Court of Mecklenburg is held in it. There is a School called a College [Queens Museum-Liberty Hall] in it, at which, at times there has been 50 or 60 boys."

Riding on to Salisbury, he noted the lands between that town and Charlotte were "very fine, of a reddish cast and well timbered, with very little underwood . . . the first meadows I have seen on the Road since I left Virg[inia]." He was more impressed with Salisbury, a town of tradesmen and "about three hundred souls," where he had tea and a public dinner.

The Iron Age

Washington was not the only one to admire Salisbury's prospects even though Charlotte had about the same number of townspeople. In 1790, there was not much reason to go to Charlotte unless the journeyer was curious or thirsty. Travelers often bypassed the town, taking a fork south near present-day Concord. More often, they headed west toward Lincolnton, perhaps stopping at Beattie's Ford, then on to Vesuvius Furnace, where there was good reason to tarry.

When trade with Britain ceased after the Revolution, Americans quickly felt the loss of commercial income and wares. Iron products, such as pots, rifles, and cannonballs, were in great demand, so the state encouraged iron manufacture by offering bounty lands (free, tax-exempt lands from which iron could be produced).

In 1791, the year of Washington's visit, Alexander Brevard, John Davidson, and Joseph Graham bought an interest in Peter Forney's Big Ore Bank in Lincoln County, which dug local iron ore and used it in manufacture. Their success with three large iron furnaces was immediate. Vesuvius Furnace, Mount Tirzah Forge, and Rehoboth Furnace became a center where western merchants brought their wagons loaded with wool, flax, hams, and cloth in exchange for iron implements. Waiting their turns at loading, they often camped overnight in wide pastures on the owner's adjacent iron plantation in the area of Iron Station, near Lincolnton. Vesuvius Furnace, the home and business of General Joseph Graham, was right on the road in front of his gracious family residence and was a bustling center of daily traffic. The casual overnight visitors brought news.

By 1810, there were at least six iron "bloomeries" straddling the iron deposits that

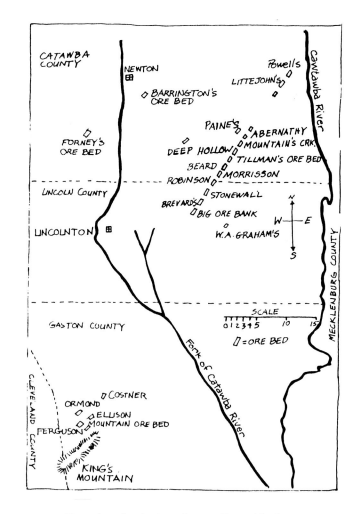

Map of ore banks in and around Mecklenburg County when mining was at its peak

stretched north from Kings Mountain. During the trade war with Britain (1812–14), the area's main involvement was sending soldiers and cannonballs. The iron balls, like other iron products, were sometimes loaded at Beattie's Ford onto flatboats and shipped river-fashion to Charleston.

The Home as Castle

Among the early iron plantations, John Davidson's Rural Hill was outstanding.

It consisted of five thousand acres on the Catawba River. The house burned in 1886, but the ghostly columns remain. In 1817, Daniel Forney built Ingleside (Scottish, meaning "many hearths") in Lincoln County for his beautiful bride, Harriet Brevard. She had said she would marry the man who would build her the finest house. It still stands in Lincoln County. It was so expensive to build, Forney could not afford to live there long.

Throughout northern Mecklenburg, there were an astounding number of other plantations whose families' investments were their only connection with iron. These many-acred estates boasted large homes and rich lands that, until the invention of the cotton gin in 1793, had raised cotton mainly for home clothing needs.

From this prosperous period following the cotton gin's arrival came one of the handsomest houses in Charlotte. Near the historic Sugaw Creek Presbyterian Church stands the graceful and elegant plantation home of tax collector Archibald Frew. Its scale and sophistication, in comparison with other local houses, many still built of logs, caused neighbors to dub it "Frew's Folly." The home's proudest features are the living room's original Adam woodwork, a third-floor ballroom for formal celebrations, and an elegant formal garden. Research architects date it 1815 because of the home's Federal design and because a newspaper from that time bearing Frew's name was found behind the warming chimney during restoration. Renamed Rosedale, in 1819 it became the home of William Davidson, a state senator and United States congressman. It remained in the Davidson family until 1987, when means were found for its restoration and preservation as a historic site. Rosedale located out North Tryon Street three miles from the village Square, was on the main colonial and

Rosedale,
the early-1800s plantation home once called "Frew's Folly"

Cotton picking in the fields

antebellum road into Charlotte from points north.

The people of northern Mecklenburg regarded themselves as the patricians of the county. They did not need Charlotte or necessarily care for her ways. Many of their beautiful homes remain in the northern Catawba River area, including Mount Mourne (1837), Latta Place (1800), Cedar Grove (1831), Ingleside (c. 1860), Holly Bend (1800), Beaver Dam (1829), and the Robert Potts House (1811). The gracious architecture of these homes shows a swift emergence from the early Mecklenburg "plain living" standard into a refinement of taste afforded by travel and prosperity.

On these plantations, the increased planting of cotton for ginning and distant sale required more slaves; however, slaves were never numerous on the scale found in other parts of the South. In 1790, only twenty of the seventeen hundred Mecklenburg households had more than thirteen—Tom Polk listed forty-seven slaves, John Springs fifty, and Hezekiah Alexander thirteen. The large slaveholding estates with their big two- and three-story houses were the exception rather than the rule in Mecklenburg. Many industrious families had several slaves, but Polk, Springs, and Alexander were unusual. J. B. Alexander wrote that Polk had "a goodly share of indomitable enterprise." He had a keen knowledge of property and management with "no man possessing more influence in that part of North Carolina."

Most early independent yeoman farmers

may have owned a hundred or more acres, but they began by working their small farms themselves and with the very necessary labor of their wives and numerous children. They bartered for their outside needs. By 1840, census records show a majority of Mecklenburg farmers had between two and twenty slaves. According to historian Dr. Chalmers Davidson, "A man who worked his own land . . . even though assisted by eight or ten hands, was a farmer and not a planter. The dividing line is considered to be something around twenty-five or thirty slaves, as the ownership of so large a number customarily required the services of an overseer." In 1850, seventeen Mecklenburg planters owned more than thirty slaves; in 1860, there were thirty.

The slaves were occasionally able to secure their freedom by purchase, from an owner's written will, or by an act of legislation. Consequently, there were some free blacks in antebellum Mecklenburg who worked for or alongside landless whites as farm or day laborers, as apprentices and craftsmen such as blacksmiths, stone or brick masons, cobblers, cabinetmakers, and barbers, or as well diggers, fiddlers, or peddlers.

With the increased local production of cotton after 1800, the number of slaves increased until they totaled about one-third of the county population in 1860. In nearby Guilford, Randolph, and adjacent counties, Quakers were ardent in the cause of abolition, but quietly so. In Mecklenburg, there was much antislavery sentiment, especially among the Germans in the area. Controversial Hinton Rowan Helper of Davie County wrote his antislavery book, *The Impending Crisis In the South*, which was published in New York in 1857 and widely read. Many conscientious Southerners were incensed when Helper emphatically said, "No man of genuine decency and refinement would have them [the Negroes] as property on any

terms." The threat of abolition worried the owners of large farms and plantations, for whom slaves were essential to daily life and commerce.

Latta Place, the Catawba River plantation home of merchant James Latta

Refinement and Family Tradition

James Latta was always a keen businessman. His two-story frame home stands close by the Catawba near Hopewell Church. As a traveling merchant, he brought goods from Charleston and Philadelphia and sold them to affluent upcountry settlers as well as at his store in York. Latta came to America from Northern Ireland in 1785 to settle his father's estate. After his wife died in 1792, leaving two young sons, he remarried in

North Carolina and built a handsome Federal-style home. Hessian soldiers who stayed there after the Revolution are said to have carved the elaborate mantels and fine detail on the staircase. Latta prospered and sent his three daughters by his second marriage to Salem Academy. Young ladies had to go at least as far as Salem, North Carolina, to be educated. Some parents sent them further, even as far as Philadelphia or Charleston, in order to "get the polish."

James G. Torrance built Cedar Grove, possibly the most elegant plantation home still standing in Mecklenburg. It remains as evidence that business was good in the combination family cabin and store. He was the only son of Hugh Torance, the industrious Scotch-Irish merchant-peddler who had made the original family land purchase on McDowell Creek in 1779. James G. inherited the family estate in 1816 when his parents both died, leaving over five thousand acres in Mecklenburg and Tennessee. At the time, the Cedar Grove estate included thirty-three slaves in addition to livestock, with 150 hogs. James G. Torrance altered his name's spelling to distinguish himself from another local merchant.

In 1825, he sold most of his general store merchandise to merchant Samuel McComb of Charlotte. The imposing brick home built by James G. Torrance in 1831–32 is the third Torrance residence on the site. The first, the log cabin and store a stone's throw away, is the earliest existing Mecklenburg store, restored in the 1980s as the Hugh Torance House and Store. The door knocker at Cedar Grove still bears the family name. Dick Banks, owner and Torrance descendant, has the receipt of sale from merchant James Latta, who probably brought it to his neighbor from Charleston. The large iron fire bank in the Cedar Grove fireplace says plainly, "Vesuvius Furnace, J. Graham."

Dr. J. B. Alexander, writing of Torrance and his Scotch-Irish neighbors, called them a "money-making church-loving people." And they were an intermarrying people. James G.'s first wife was Nancy Davidson, his second Mary Latta, his third Margaret Allison. When he died in 1847, he owned thirty-two hundred acres of Mecklenburg and 109 slaves. With his lands and farming, gristmills and sawmills, he was for a long period one of the wealthiest men in the county. Torrance descendants presently own and live at Cedar Grove. Even the ghosts of Capt'n Dick and Mr. John, sons of James G., remain, or so it is believed.

Like many early residents of lower Mecklenburg, John Springs leased his plantation, Springfield—about eleven hundred acres—from the Catawba Indians. A state law allowed the tribe "to grant and make leases for life or lives, as well as a term of years." In 1839, Springs and three other appointed envoys of the governor of South Carolina met with the Catawbas at Nation's Ford. The Indians had requested negotiations ceding Catawba lands to the state in exchange for land near the Cherokees in Haywood County, North Carolina, or for money if lands were unavailable.

Springs wrote in his report that the tribe had previously leased all its land to five hundred to six hundred white families. The land had been divided many times into small parcels, with few records kept. Springs and his committee requested ratification by the legislature of a proposed treaty. The Treaty of 1840 was approved, and in March 1841, Springs received title to his plantation from the state of South Carolina. (The Catawbas in recent years have persistently protested this settlement.)

Unlike most other area settlers, Springs's immediate forbears, the Springsteens, came from Holland. In Mecklenburg, Springs carried on an active town life in addition to supervising his cotton plantation. He owned

Cedar Grove, above,
and the Hugh Torance House and Store,
at right, show the progress and prosperity
of Hugh Torance and his heirs.

Springfield,
the plantation house of John Springs III

Courtesy of Katherine Wooten Springs

Springs Corner, a combination store and upstairs residence at the northeast corner of Trade and Tryon, (current site of NationsBank). When in Charlotte on business or for social affairs, he often stayed there. But wherever he was, cotton was on his mind. An early investor in one of the South's first cotton mills — the Graniteville Manufacturing Company, organized in 1844–45 — he was also a forceful proponent of the first railroad in Charlotte.

"I have come to the conclusion," Springs declared in the *Charlotte Journal,* "that, originally and naturally, the country between the Yadkin in North Carolina and the Broad River in South Carolina, an average distance of about 100 miles . . . is the most fertile, productive region that I have yet seen, and capable of the highest agricultural and manufacturing improvement, abounding with almost unlimited water power; and this opinion has been accorded by many others who have travelled through this country. . . . No one can appreciate the business it [the railroad] would likely do. . . . I believe we are entirely competent to effect it, if we only determine that we will, and this, I believe, to be all that is necessary to succeed."

John Springs III

Courtesy of Katherine Wooten Springs

Inventory of the personal property of Eli Springs, brother of John Springs, including the names and ages of slaves he held in August 1833

Courtesy of Katherine Wooten Springs

Surveyor's report for John Springs by Benjamin Withers

Courtesy of Katherine Wooten Springs

The Arrival of the Railroad

Local support rallied and assisted in raising financing for the Charlotte and South Carolina Railroad. Businessmen recognized the service was the key to possibility. Charlotte's leaders had been fighting to get a railroad since 1825. Although it did not seem logical to powers in the eastern part of the state to extend a railroad to town from that direction, practical Charlotteans knew what they wanted. The railroad brought people and goods. More important, it carried Mecklenburg produce and cotton to market. When the first passenger freight train of the Charlotte and South Carolina Railroad arrived in 1852 from Columbia, South Carolina, it was the celebrated marvel of the century. Crowds met it cheering. After Charlotteans invested to get this first line from Columbia north to Charlotte, western interests proposed to continue it to Danville,

Virginia. Eastern opponents saw a funnel draining off resources into Virginia and South Carolina. As a consequence, the North Carolina Railroad connecting Charlotte to the east became a reality in 1856.

Most of the subsequent progress in Charlotte is owed to the presence of the railroad and the aggressive personal funding and lobbying to assure its route this way. John Springs exhibited the typically farsighted business determination at work in early Mecklenburg. He and others like him rode out the sporadic national bad times and capitalized on the good with extraordinary success, as recorded by Katherine Wooten Springs from voluminous family records and letters in *The Squires of Springfield*. Springs's descendants founded and own interests in the diverse Springs Mills empire.

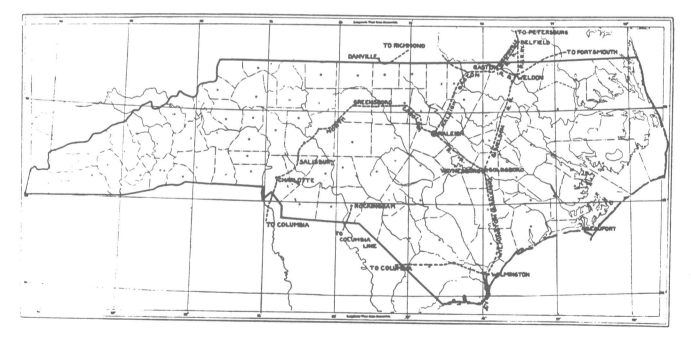

Railroad Map of North Carolina in 1856
Dotted lines mark routes of the railroads.

North Carolina Division of Archives and History

President Andrew Jackson
The first "people's president" was born near Charlotte.

Public Library of
Charlotte and Mecklenburg County

Jackson for President

He was bold, that Andy Jackson, rough-edged, and his soldiers would have dared the devil himself for Jackson.

Many people were astounded in 1829 when Americans elected him the country's seventh president. They somehow had not expected democracy to be, well, quite so democratic. Jackson was neither handsome, genteel, brilliant, nor from patrician New England or Virginia. But there was something quite singular about his presence.

A gambler, war hero, and lawyering rowdy, Jackson was born March 15, 1767, in the Waxhaw settlement near the present state line. He was captured at thirteen by British soldiers near his home, imprisoned, mistreated, and soon after orphaned. Following the war, he attended Liberty Hall in Char-

lotte and read law in Salisbury. He was licensed to practice law in Rowan County in 1787, then practiced in western North Carolina, which soon became Tennessee. Frontier Tennessee suited him. There, he rose swiftly in public life. He was elected judge and senator and appointed major general of the Tennessee militia.

His unorthodox defeat of the British at New Orleans in 1815 and his invasion of Florida endeared him to a dispirited America. In 1829, he began an equally unorthodox presidency. A controversial frontiersman who had fought hand-to-hand with Indians, British, and Spanish, he steered an independent, strong-willed presidency for two terms. He also effected mass Indian removal to western lands. His financial policy, centered on the Bank of the United States, led in part to a string of bank failures and financial panic throughout the country.

Who Is James K. Polk?

Jackson lent a significantly encouraging hand to his young fellow Piedmont Carolinian, James K. Polk. Polk, born in 1795, was twenty-eight years younger than Jackson. Most writings about Jackson and Polk amplify an ancient argument over their exact birthplaces. Both North and South Carolina claim Jackson. The Waxhaw area, where his family lived, straddled the line. His newly widowed mother went to the home of one of her two sisters, where her son was born. One sister lived in present North Carolina, the other in present South Carolina. Jackson said that he did not know his own birthplace.

The Polk family cabin stood just up the Trading Path from the Waxhaw area, near Pineville. The cabin has long since disappeared, but one thought to be similar was

James Knox Polk,
elected the eleventh United States president

reconstructed in 1967 and operates as a North Carolina State Historic Site. Polk's mother may have returned to her parents' home near Hopewell Church for her son's birth. So the question remains as to the exact birthplace of both men.

Published letters show these two very different men enjoyed a long, supportive friendship, both personal and political. Jackson may have been Polk's only good friend. Polk was as austere and serious as "Old Hickory" was colorful. Susan Barnett Smart recalled, "I have lived at home and yet I have seen two of our Presidents. I knew Andrew Jackson and many a time little Jamie Polk has passed along the road there with his breeches rolled up to his knees. He was a bashful little fellow."

When Polk was eleven, his father moved to Tennessee to farm. There, Polk met Jackson. Jackson's influence helped bring Polk to

Congress and twice to the governorship of Tennessee. Jackson was the first people's president. Polk, however, remained a lackluster politician who understood the political process and used it effectively but without imagination.

As eleventh president (1844–48), Polk negotiated the acquisition of new territories including Texas, New Mexico, Oregon, California, and Washington.

Small-Town Living

In 1830, Charlotte was a very small town with taverns and saloons and a newspaper. In the entire county, there were twenty thousand whites and about five thousand blacks. Stagecoach mail delivery now boasted four-horse coaches. The driver sounded his four- to six-foot-long tin bugle, blowing a long blast as he pulled into town. Those who received mail sometimes failed to pick it up, since the recipient of a letter had to pay. Consequently, in one issue the *Charlotte Journal* listed 127 letters waiting to be claimed. But as historian D. A. Tompkins noted, "Mail was not of much importance, as few expected to get any."

In addition to mail, the stage carried passengers. They had to have been uncomfortable, crowded, and hot. Lady travelers fainted often. After 1840, out-of-town guests stayed in the Mansion House hotel on the southeast corner of Trade and Tryon streets. The Mansion House was four stories high and covered half a block. Its front rooms were popular, since guests could sit on the wrought-iron balconies and watch the passersby. Small shops occupied part of the first floor. When the railroads brought overnight hotel guests, they were met by a coachman sent especially from the hotel.

Charlotte must have been a confusing place to get legal services. "For many years the

Village scene shows travelers by stagecoach and farm wagon.

Sheriff and Clerks of the Superior and County Courts, and Register of Deeds, kept their offices at their houses in the country," according to a description of the 1825 era in an 1875 city directory. "The Sheriff was James Wilson who lived about six miles from town on the lawyer's road, the road lawyers travelled to argue their cases at scattered courts. The Superior Court Clerk was Gen. George Graham, who lived two miles and a half west from town. . . . The County Clerk was Isaac Alexander, four miles southeast. . . . The Register of Deeds was Wm B. Alexander, nine miles north. . . . All these offices were kept in the country until the Legislature passed an act requiring them to be kept at the Court House. Then it was that the upper story of the Court House was cut up into offices, and thereby spoiling the only good ballroom in town."

Some town families who were churchgoers rode to Sugaw Creek Presbyterian Church for services. They sent their children to the several classical male or female academies, which were often connected with the thriving outlying churches. These community schools were soon followed by the Charlotte Female Academy, the Charlotte Male Academy, and the Charlotte Female Institute (1857), at the corner of College and Ninth streets. This school for women, headed by Reverend and Mrs. Robert Burwell, was later named Presbyterian College, then moved to its present location in Myers Park in 1914 with a new name, Queens College.

During the early 1800s in North Carolina, a rising social and educational awareness led the predominant religious groups to establish colleges for young men. Davidson College opened in 1837 as a liberal-arts college for men, "an infant Presbyterian seminary" that initially taught students agricultural and mechanical trades and required work on the school farm. The college boasted a modest architectural kinship to the University of Virginia. The Old Quadrangle, completed in 1850, contained small Federal-style brick dorms (Elm Row and Oak Row, completed in

Ornate silver wine filler used in church communion

Davidson College's Philanthropic Hall

Davidson College

1837, still stand) and two elegant brick literary-society halls similar to the Virginia pavilions. These two classical debating halls, Eumenean Hall (1849) and Philanthropic Hall (1850), remain in limited use. The college lay on the east side of the "Great Road between Statesville and Charlotte." Across the road was the Brick Store House (c. 1848), which still stands. It subsequently served as the Helper Hotel. According to Dr. Chalmers Davidson, students traversing the muddy red-clay road to the store in bad weather referred to their journey as crossing "the Red Sea."

Public schools finally came to Charlotte through state money in 1839. Typically, frugal local citizens chose to build their own wood schoolhouses rather than pay a building tax. Teachers in these first public schools earned only fifteen to thirty dollars per month for teaching reading and writing. This era of broadened education had long been sought by the people.

Although there was still no organized town church in the early 1800s, there was preaching from time to time. Ministers of any denomination passing through town preached in the lower-story courtroom of the courthouse. In 1818, a church building for all denominations was begun by the town commissioners with funds borrowed from the Charlotte branch of the Bank of New Bern. When it was finished in 1823, it was truly the town's church, located on one block of the original tract of Charlotte. Known as "the Brick

Church" and "the Presbyterian Church," it was bought in 1835 by John Irwin, a trustee for the active congregation that had been organized into a church in 1832. He was reimbursed in 1841. Dr. Robert Hall Morrison, who later became the first president of Davidson College, was their part-time pastor.

The church's bell, which in 1826 began calling townspeople to worship or to public meetings, was the Civil War's only clarion survivor, as every other bell in town was melted down for metal. This old bell is a treasured relic on display at First Presbyterian Church, on the original site at Trade and Church. Behind the church is Old Settlers Cemetery, where Thomas Polk and other early settlers and their servants are buried. The cemetery was and continues to be town property.

As education expanded in this era, so did religion, for the Great Awakening of the 1800s was gathering momentum in America. Farmers, merchants, and tradesmen who were Presbyterians watched the growth of Baptist, Methodist, Lutheran, Catholic, and Associate Reformed Presbyterian churches.

The liveliest annual religious events for any denomination were revivals, especially the summertime camp meetings like those at Rock Creek Camp Grounds. Families usually stayed in rude, wooden shelters. Rock Springs Campground, near Denver in Lincoln County, still comes to life each summer and has hardly missed an annual August meeting since its founding in 1830. Methodists began it on forty acres near the Catawba River, but the participants come from all denominations.

A *Charlotte Observer* article in August 1929 described a camp meeting held a century earlier at Pleasant Grove near Waxhaw, not far from Andrew Jackson's boyhood cabin. That year, a permanent campground was built and lit at night by mounds of stone "75

feet from the four corners of the arbor enclosure upon which pine knots were nightly burned." Fresh straw was piled under the arbor (the main preaching shelter) and underneath the heavy, hand-wrought seats. The rows of "tents" were simple log huts, and paths led to nearby springs.

Reverend James Hall gave a separate report of another camp meeting in 1802 in William Henry Foote's *Sketches of North Carolina*. The meeting was held in lower Mecklenburg County near the state line. He estimated there were about six thousand persons attending:

> Twelve Presbyterian ministers, one Baptist and one Methodist, attended. Worship began, as usual on Friday, and continued until near noon on Tuesday. Never did I see a set of men labor with more assiduity than the ministers labored from Friday noon until Sabbath night at 9 o'clock, during which time, among the vast multitude which attended, not more than ten persons were visibly affected with religious exercises.
>
> When night came, the people assembled at five different places in the encampment, at which the ministers attended. Near the above hour, religious exercises began in all the assemblies. . . . Exercises, prayers and exhortations continued during the whole night. . . . No two of the several assemblies knew how each other was affected until a considerable later period of the night. At break of day, public instructions ceased until nine in the morning. At that time a sermon was preached at the public stand in the centre of the encampment. Few, if any, were exercised until after the sermon, when six ministers continued worship by prayer in rotation. This exhibited a scene to which I never saw anything similar. Many more than a hundred sunk down in less than half an hour; and what was remarkable in such a scene, there was scarcely a cry to

be heard. This I perfectly recollect, that the speakers were distinctly heard during the concert of prayer: But fervent supplications and cries for mercy soon began. Shortly afterwards, one of the ministers rose to read, and make a few observations on the vision of the dry bones (Ezekiel, Chapter 37) but such were the cries, and the astonished state of the audience, that I suppose he could not call the attention of 20 persons: he read a few verses and sat down. Those in distress were generally taken to their respective tents, where many followed. Some of the ministers continued at the public stand, others went to their tents, where crowds attended. The work went on all that day, and a great part of the following night; so that I believe, could the aggregate have been ascertained, although the work began at so late a period, as great a proportion was affected as had been at any former meeting.

Gold in a Goose Quill

Twenty-five miles east of Charlotte in Cabarrus County's Little Meadow Creek, young Conrad Reed waded in a farm stream one bright morning in 1799. Possibly, the sun dappled the water, so at first he thought the bright dazzle was only a reflection. He didn't know what made the rock shine, but he toted it home. A local silversmith said it was nothing to get excited about (he couldn't identify it), so the family used it as a doorstop. It was about the size of a shoe. Three years later, they discovered this seventeen-pound gold-colored doorstop was worth considerably more than the $3.50 for which Conrad Reed's father naively sold it. A jeweler in Fayetteville fluxed it into a bar of gold about eight inches long worth $3,600. The Reed gold nugget was the earliest authenti-

cated discovery of gold in the United States.

Other nuggets (not so large, perhaps) were being found close by, and some closer to Charlotte, long before anyone ever heard of gold in California. As early as 1802, Dunn's Mine near Rozzelle's Ferry and others supplied gunsmiths with yellow ore for lining powder holes of rifles. By 1821, placer, or stream-bed gold, was being mined in Mecklenburg.

Denison Olmsted, North Carolina's first state geologist, told of gold dust and nuggets (branch gold) in common local exchange: "I saw a pint of whysky paid for by weighing off three and a half grains of gold." Miners carried their gold in a goose quill and kept a small pair of scales in a box the size of a spectacles case.

Mecklenburg farmers moonlighted for gold. When their crops were harvested, they and their slaves mined the hillsides and farm streams with picks, hoes, and shovels. Samuel McComb was an enterprising Mecklenburg farmer who in 1825 made the first successful attempt to follow a vein of gold on his farm east of Irwin Creek, at what is now near the junction of West Morehead and Graham streets. After that day, farming became sec-

Finding Gold
The first American gold nugget was found by young Conrad Reed in 1799.

North Carolina Collection, UNC Library, Chapel Hill

This sketch from Harper's *in 1857 shows miners underground working Carolina gold.*

North Carolina Collection, UNC Library, Chapel Hill

ondary, and before long, Sam was a rich man. Not surprisingly, McComb's Mine was quickly followed by the Capps Hill Mine, and a year later gold was found a half-mile from McComb's on Rudisill's Hill. It was enough to make any sensible Presbyterian leave his plow and dig at the slightest shimmer in dirt or broken rock. In summer after the crops were laid by, farmers and hired laborers scoured parched creek beds for good fortune.

The first mines were surface mines and hardly efficient. As much gold was lost in the crude processes or kept in pockets as was turned in to the owners. But the names of the mines were romantic—the Black Cat, the Queen of Sheba, and King Solomon's Mine—

and belied the hard work. By 1830, Charlotte had a weekly newspaper to report gold-mine and other local news, the *Miners' and Farmers' Journal*. A quote from Dr. Samuel Johnson ran with the dateline: "I will teach you to pierce the bowels of the earth and bring out from the caverns of the mountains, metals which will give strength to our hands and subject all nature to our use and pleasure."

But news of gold had its own superior grapevine, and soon Humphrey Bissell arrived from New York. He bought an interest in McComb's and Capps Hill mines and applied some European mining techniques to the gold he knew was there.

Bissell was a Yale man and an associate of

Descending the Ladder Shaft

Carolina gold drew national fascination. In 1857, *Harpers' New Monthly Magazine* sent its "heroic traveler," artist Porte Crayon, to view the mines from the inside. Crayon sketched and wrote of his experience:

"'Every twenty feet or thereabout the ladders terminated on the platforms of the same width, and barely long enough to enable one to turn about to set foot on the next ladder. In addition, the rounds and platforms were slippery with mud and water. As they reached the bottom of the third or fourth ladder, Crayon made a misstep which threw him slightly off his balance, when he felt the iron grasp of the foreman on his arm:

"'Steady, man, steady!'

"'Thank you, Sir. But, my friend, how much of this road have we to travel?'

"'Four hundred and twenty-five feet, Sir, to the bottom of the shaft.'

"'And those faint blue specks that I see below, so deep deep down that they look like stars reflected in the bosom of a calm lake, what are they?'

"'Lights in the miner's hats, who are working below, Sir.'

"Porte Crayon felt a numbness seize upon his limbs.

"'And are we, then, crawling like flies down the sides of this open shaft, with no foothold but these narrow slippery ladders, and nothing between us and the bottom but four hundred feet of unsubstantial darkness?'

"'This is the road we miners travel daily,' replied the foreman: 'you, gentlemen, wished to see all we had to show, and so I chose this route. There is a safer and an easier way if you prefer it.'

"Crayon looked in the Yankee's face, but there was no flinching there.

"'Not at all,' replied he; 'I was only asking questions to satisfy my curiosity. Lead on until you reach China; we'll follow.'"

Samuel F. B. Morse of telegraph fame. His stamp mill, a heavy machine that crushed ore-filled rock by stamping it, was the first used in the country. He also sank a deep shaft and quickly made Charlotte mining highly profitable. More mines produced demand for rope, lumber, and iron, stimulating local business during the 1830s, the very years the rest of the country was experiencing financial disaster.

Bissell was interesting enough. But when Italian nobleman Count Chevalier Vincent de Rivafinoli stepped off the stagecoach in Charlotte with his baggage, his servants, and his gold-headed cane, townspeople knew instantly something extraordinary was forthcoming.

He could have turned out to be a scoundrel. Other gold-mining towns died from high-flying charlatans and their stock swindles, but Rivafinoli brought style and mining expertise. The count was experienced in South American mining and represented a London mining firm. In 1830, he leased and managed the Rudisill and Saint Catherine mines and others that were consolidated into the Mecklenburg Gold Mining Company. *Miners' and Farmers' Journal* reported in 1831 that with him came a group of "most learned and practical miners" from France, England, Germany, Italy, Wales, Ireland, Scotland, and Switzerland, along with 70 or 80 workers. Adding the workmen he hired locally, Rivafinoli's mining force at one point num-

Two Charlotte miners from the Rudisill Gold Mine, J. Wadsworth and R. M. Miller,
posed for this photograph in 1882. Miller was a founder of the Union National Bank of Charlotte.

Mining stock certificate from Charlotte's Rudisill Gold Mine

bered 130 men. To house them, he built several buildings.

Daily, the count sallied forth after his mulatto barber shaved him and dressed his hair. According to D. W. Chavis's *Southern Gold*, every morning the front door of Rivafinoli's elegant house at the southwest corner of West Morehead and Tryon swung open, and the resplendent count flicked his gold-headed cane, "carefully stepping across mud puddles along the unpaved street on the way to inspect his mines." He imported whatever he needed and lived as nearly as possible in the grand manner to which somewhere he was accustomed. Rivafinoli's singular name appears in James Torrance's record books at Cedar Grove. It involved a matter of bricks, probably for the construction of the large plantation house. Possibly, one of Rivafinoli's skilled masons was subcontracted

in a slack period at the mines to do a little bricklaying on the side in northern Mecklenburg. Like much regarding the count, including his avowed friendship with Napoleon, it is speculation.

Under Rivafinoli, the Rudisill yielded approximately thirty-eight hundred ounces of gold during a three-month period. This was so extraordinary that a congressional committee came to visit the mines. To be made into coin, the gold had to travel to the Philadelphia Mint by stagecoach, a hazardous four-month trip at best, given the irregularities of tortuous roads. It could also be sent by another rural journey to Christopher Bechtler's private mint in Rutherford County. Bechtler and his brother were German immigrants and were the first to mint gold dollars in North Carolina.

A Mint for the Mines

Charlotte wanted a mint of her own. Congress's hesitancy to award such a federal jewel to a small, unknown town was understandable. Charlotte had only two thousand citizens when North and South Carolina interests petitioned Congress for a branch mint. The town was close to the center of the gold-producing region, and area receipts of gold were impressive, but they must certainly have laughed at first in Philadelphia and Washington at the idea. To award a plum such as the first branch mint in the nation to Charlotte seemed absurd to the United States senators who debated and hotly fought the proposal. It took at least five years of active agitation by miners, politicians, and business interests to convince Congress. In March 1835, mint branches were approved for Charlotte, New Orleans, and Dahlonega, Georgia. At the time, Andrew Jackson was president and James K. Polk was chairman of the Committee for Ways and Means. Both had strong ties to Mecklenburg, which no doubt helped the process along.

Gold coin minted at Charlotte

North Carolina Division of Archives and History

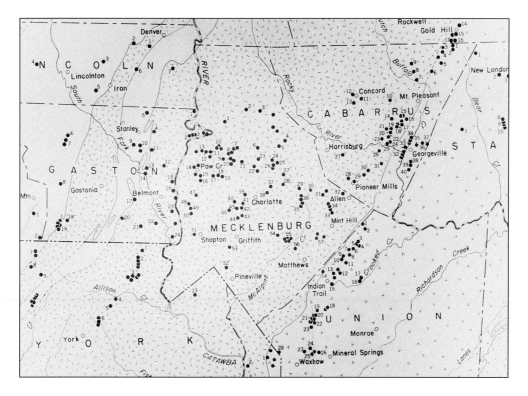

Map of Charlotte-area gold

Department of the Interior

As agent for the government, Sam McComb advertised for construction bids in the *Charlotte Journal*. It was no ordinary building going up on West Trade, that familiar road to Lincolnton. No less a talent than William Strickland, a noted Philadelphia architect and engineer, drew the plans for the branch mint at Charlotte. He had been an apprentice to the illustrious Benjamin Latrobe. Latrobe and students Strickland and Robert Mills were the nation's first generation of professional architects. Strickland's prominent designs included public buildings, homes, churches, lighthouses, and hotels. Many, like Strickland's branch mints at Charlotte and New Orleans, were in the fashionable Greek Revival style.

But the year the mint opened—1837—a national depression hit. Rivafinoli's mines had difficulties, and he left town. Coins from the mint began to appear with a *C* for Charlotte over the date on half-eagles ($5) and quarter-eagles ($2.50). The first coinage began in April 1838, and bullion received that year exceeded $100,000. In 1837, there were over fifty active gold mines within North Carolina. At that time, Mecklenburg listed more mines than any other North Carolina county. As one traveler declared in Bruce Roberts's *Carolina Gold Rush*, "You could hardly get across this county without falling into a gold mine!"

John Penman, who purchased the Rudisill and Saint Catherine mines, was nearly as colorful as his predecessor Rivafinoli. This large, ruddy Englishman commanded a manservant named Goodluck, who followed his every step. The deep shafts yielded handsomely for the new owner and his lively partners until Penman gave up riotous living and mining and chose the Methodist ministry. "In the latter part of his life he behaved very civilly and did not need so much waiting on," wrote John B. Alexander. In the North

Charlotte branch of the United States Mint on West Trade Street in 1850

Courtesy of Henrietta Wilkinson

Gold coins minted at Charlotte

Mint Museum of Charlotte

Carolina State Archives, there is the old, yellowed slip of paper on which John Penman relinquished his worldly goods—mines, interests, everything. Whether he was under duress from God or earthly creditors remains a mystery.

Despite the bustle and profits from gold mining, the hopeful itinerant prospectors, and the many taverns, Mecklenburg did not grow between 1830 and 1850. The county lost about five thousand people in 1842 in the division into Union County. Also, many small farmers whose lands were exhausted from cotton production packed up and moved west even as the miners were wandering into town.

The gold mines continued, although production tapered off. The account of the Charlotte gold story written by Dr. Henry Brown in *Gold Mining On the Rudisill Lode and The Development of Charlotte, North Carolina* traced the Charlotte mines as they were sold and resold. Costs soared as veins below the water table called for extensive pumping and ventilation. Then something else happened to

cool the fever. It was 1849 and in California someone else discovered gold.

Gold and the mint made Charlotte an important place. They brought families who became significant in the life of the town. John Hill Wheeler, the first superintendent of the mint, wrote a *History of North Carolina* and *Reminiscences and Memoirs of North Carolina and Eminent North Carolinians*. Stuart Cramer and James Osborne were two later superintendents who also figured significantly in the life of Charlotte. In addition, gold brought thousands of foreigners—Welsh, Cornish, German, Austrian, Polish, and Italian—into Piedmont Carolina.

The coinage value of the Charlotte Mint's production from 1837 until 1861 totaled $10,163,660. In Henrietta Wilkinson's *Mint Museum of Art at Charlotte*, she reported that during this early era the mint on West Trade Street did business with twenty-one states, territories, and foreign countries.

Confederate Mecklenburg

H arriet Beecher Stowe, a Cincinnati professor-clergyman's wife, wrote a series of articles for a Washington paper about her experiences with slavery in Kentucky. She described what she had seen and read about fugitive slaves' perilous flight to freedom. Her articles became the immediately popular Uncle Tom's Cabin, *loved in the North, hated in the South.* Three thousand copies of the book sold the first day it went on sale. Fueled by her book, the antislavery ethic, which was already a lively issue, spread like rampant brush fire through the North in 1852. By 1861, the rift between the North and the South widened into civil war.

General Pierre G. T. Beauregard, who made his Charlotte headquarters in 1865 at the William Phifer house, 722 North Tryon Street

National Archives

A City of Soldiers

With the electrifying news of the bombardment of Fort Sumter in April, Mecklenburg troops stood ready, and Charlotte companies hastened to war. The entire faculty and 150 cadets of the North Carolina Military Institute left Charlotte to lead in training recruits. Colonel D. H. Hill headed the parade to the railroad station; and in early June at Big Bethel on the Virginia peninsula, Hill's North Carolina regiment participated in an early victory, and also suffered an initial casualty—Private Henry I. Wyatt. The military victory and the loss of Wyatt led the North Carolinians to a rally cry, "First at Bethel!" At Davidson College, almost all of the senior class enlisted and left before commencement. Colorful patriotic music celebrated the troops' departure as the ladies of Charlotte presented each company with a battle flag.

The Charlotte Mint was immediately taken over by the Confederacy as local headquarters. Throughout the war, cannonballs and iron products from Mecklenburg Iron Works supplied Confederate armies. Cloth for uniforms was spun on the spindles and woven on the looms of the Rock Island Woolen Mill on the Catawba. When news of the first battle of Manassas reached Charlotte in July, a group of Charlotte physicians traveled to Richmond to assist the wounded. Women's societies organized and scurried to gather provisions, soliciting bedding and bandages along with wines, cordials, brandies, and other delicacies, together with half-worn garments such as shirts and drawers. A few local women left to tend the sick in military hospitals. But soon the wounded came to Charlotte.

Janette Greenwood, in her work, *On the Homefront: Charlotte During the Civil War*, quoted a Texas soldier in Charlotte in 1864:

The entire faculty and 150 cadets of the austere North Carolina Military Institute left Charlotte at the opening of the Civil War. The building, near the corner of East Morehead and South Boulevard, later served as a Confederate military hospital and into the 1900s as a public school.

Public Library of Charlotte and Mecklenburg County

"Ruthless war has not fallen so heavily upon this place," yet war was clearly evident in "the many representatives of the 'crutch and cane order,' the habiliments of mourning, and the vacant seats in the home circle." In 1862, Charlotte's location on three rail lines resulted in Wayside Hospital, for the care of sick and wounded soldiers going home and returning to the army. By 1863, extensive hospital buildings for several hundred patients were built by the Confederate government on the fairgrounds, a mile from town. By 1865, wounded soldiers in Raleigh and other cities threatened by Sherman were moved to Charlotte, overflowing crowded, ill-ventilated commercial warehouses and no doubt the churches as well. Charlotte families donated clean rags, butter, eggs, fowl, dried fruit, vegetables, and milk for the hospitals.

The large school building vacated by the North Carolina Military Institute troops was used by Confederate officials as a medical laboratory and a place for medical-supply storage. Late in the war, it also became a hospital, with Miss Maggie Graham as head nurse.

D. A. Tompkins recorded that during the Civil War, Mecklenburg furnished over 2,700 soldiers (from a county of 17,372 adult inhabitants which included 2,500 to 3,000 slaves). Drained of their manpower, Mecklenburg people at home, far from gunfire, fought an economic battle for survival. Women spun thread again on spinning wheels. They cut soldiers' shirts from woolen dresses. Improvising and making do became a way of life. Charlotte's newspaper, the *Western Democrat*, reported one patriotic woman's challenge: "No lady should be satisfied with herself if she does not devote one half her time toward assisting in the manufacture of the necessary amount of clothing for our soldiers." The *Democrat* extolled "the noble women who have taken the plow and hoe in hand." In other columns, it published war lists of the killed

Miss Maggie Graham,
head nurse at the Confederate hospital at North
Carolina Military Institute

Courtesy of Henrietta Wilkinson

and wounded as well as reports of "Yankee atrocities" and designs by "Black Republicans" to destroy the South. Serious food scarcities and notices of runaway slaves were commonplace news items. Due to the Federal blockade of ports, coffee was impossible to buy.

As war moved southward, Charlotte housed the Confederate Navy Yard in 1862 when it beached on dry (but safe) ground fleeing Norfolk, which had become hazardously close to enemy lines. The new site near the Trade Street rail underpass was far from Yankee troops and had new and excellent rail connections. The Charlotte Navy Yard never built ships but turned out forged propeller shafting, marine torpedoes, locomotive crank axles, wrought-iron rifle shot, and gun carriages to arm ships and iron weapons. About three hundred men came from Norfolk to work in the navy yard. So many of them lived

The Confederate Navy Yard moved from Norfolk to Charlotte and operated in the two-hundred block of East Trade Street from 1862 to 1865.

Courtesy of Aaron Boggs

in Charlotte's First Ward district that locals dubbed it "Mechanicsville."

A Confederate States Acid Works was located in Charlotte to produce the volatile acids needed for munitions. The technology was similar to that of gold-mining processes already operating in the area. On the Catawba at Tuckaseegee Ford-Moore's Chapel, the North Carolina Powder Manufacturing Company operated a powder mill. It exploded and burned twice before the war ended.

In a frenzy of Confederate zeal, hundreds of Charlotteans bought Confederate bonds, sold at 4½ percent interest. The Methodist, Episcopal, Baptist, and Lutheran churches were so eager to donate their church bells to the Confederate cause that only one original church bell remains. Confederate war songs became popular and Charlotteans no doubt sang "Richmond Is a Hard Road to Travel,"

"The Stonewall Quickstep," or "Just Before the Battle, Mother." The most popular novel of the era in the South was Victor Hugo's *Les Misérables*.

The Soldier and the Farmer

Although Charlotte was overrun with refugees fleeing Sherman's March, Confederate General Pierre G. T. Beauregard and his staff found gracious housing in the city in March 1865. But first he attended to the crucial matter of fortifying the all-important railroad bridge at Nation's Ford, which spanned the Catawba near the state line.

Beauregard was an extraordinary man. "Old Bory," his men called him. His curved mustache, sad, bloodhound eyes, and elegant, impeccable manners signaled his Louisiana Creole background. Some called this serious student of Napoleonic battles one of the

General Pierre G. T. Beauregard

National Archives

The William Phifer house at 722 North Tryon Street
was General Beauregard's Confederate headquarters in Charlotte.

South's most brilliant generals. However, he hardly saw eye to eye with the tense and talented Jefferson Davis, president of the Confederacy. Beauregard's coal-black hair turned white as the war progressed. His detractors swore it was not because of the hardships of command but because his French hair dye became unavailable.

The gate of the William F. Phifer home at North Tryon and Eleventh streets stayed mud-spattered from the constant arrival of mounted couriers. Beauregard headquartered there and received a constant stream of message-bearing soldiers on horseback. The elegant home and its generous family welcomed him and adjusted as best they could to constant interruptions and visitors. Military sentinels stood at the front door as messengers and officials paraded through its Corinthian-pillared vestibule.

The Phifer home occupied an entire block with five square miles of acreage, and included an elaborate front-yard garden, a sixty-foot well, springhouse, carriage house, garden house, and smokehouse. It was only part of William Phifer's four-thousand-acre estate. Phifer had come to Charlotte from Cabarrus County in 1852. A wealthy planter and gentleman farmer who inherited his land and money, he was a descendant of early Swiss settler and Assemblyman Martin Phifer of Rocky River. His household was a small

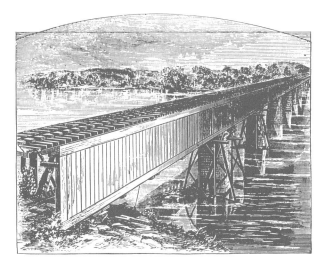

Strategic railway bridge over the Catawba River, burned by Union troops at the war's end

village in itself, housing in slave quarters the butlers, coachmen, and maids who served the family. Phifer stabled his horses in a barn nearby and had a corral of mules. He predicted a great future for Charlotte. To that end, he sold part of his land behind his home on College Street for the Presbyterian College for Women. College Street gets its name from this institution.

Phifer was also known to abhor irregular lines, so he gave land to make nearby streets exactly perpendicular. He loved trees and Shakespeare's *King Lear*. His daughter Cordelia, "Miss Codie," wrote about life in the Phifer home—her mother's elegant food preparations, the carefully trained servants, the home designed by a prestigious Philadelphia architect, the carved rosewood furniture, also from Philadelphia. The parlor held a floor-to-ceiling bookcase. "The lower part had solid closed doors and was used by the master of the house for his own private place to keep papers and letters and business books, no one ever dared to invade the place."

When Beauregard left the Phifers, he gave Willie Phifer a well-bred black mare he himself rode and gave George Martin Phifer a pistol "upon the condition that it be used with his mother's consent," according to Miss Codie.

Wars and Rumors of War

Beauregard's flamboyant presence may have lent romance and excitement to the war, but the incoming news was dire indeed. What Sherman's March did not destroy in fact, news of the destruction demoralized by rumor. At Springfield Plantation south of town, the Springs family waited warily, knowing Sherman often followed the railroad. As news came of his approach through North Carolina, they buried their silver, drove livestock deep into the woods, and set out large tubs of water to try to save the house if necessary. But the precautions, fortunately, were not needed. Sherman passed east.

In early April 1865, Mrs. Jefferson Davis fled from Richmond to Charlotte with her children and stayed in a small house on the corner of North Brevard and East Fifth streets. Mrs. John Wilkes described how neighbors collected furniture for her. Mrs. Wilkes, a prominent humanitarian and wife of the owner of the Mecklenburg Iron Works, wrote, "I sent her bread and milk and other pantry supplies as did many housekeepers. She was only in the house about a week when the news of the fall of Richmond arrived, that Pres. Davis and others were making their way South. . . . Mrs. Davis became frantic with alarm, said her husband had given her special injunctions on no account to let his children be taken." Varina Davis and her children quickly departed with troops who carried Confederate treasury funds further south.

Jefferson Davis

Charlotte's closest brush with war came toward the end when smoke billowed high over the Catawba. A Union troop detachment of Stoneman's Raiders burned the long, wooden railroad bridge at Nation's Ford. Charlotte's people shuddered. They feared they might share the fate of Columbia and would soon smell fire in their streets and be forced to flee with their children. Hurriedly, the directors of the branch of the Bank of North Carolina, locally called the Dewey Bank, gathered in the boardroom at 122 South Tryon Street. They knew a quarter million in gold and coin (as well as other assets of the town) lay in their vault. It was inconceivable that it should fall into enemy hands. T. W. Dewey, J. H. Carson, and the other officials asked help from a stockholder, A. A. Kenney, who happened to own a sturdy wagon and strong mules. Carson recorded

that by night they loaded the wagon and set out on Lawyer's Road, riding far into the countryside.

After midnight, they found a stream in a wooded glen, which they dubbed "Grasshopper Springs." They sank the kegs of silver into stump holes where trees had once burned. For the larger boxes of gold, they dug holes, buried them carefully, and covered everything. Like pirate patriots, they drew a meticulous map and returned to town. In their absence, the Federal troops passed Charlotte by. The gold remained safely buried.

In that same bank building on South Tryon (torn down in 1973), Jefferson Davis met several days later with the Confederate cabinet. General Robert E. Lee had already surrendered his Army of Northern Virginia at Appomattox when Davis arrived in Charlotte on horseback for the meeting on April 19, 1865, the same day Federals destroyed the Catawba bridge. Davis and his contingent of a thousand cavalrymen were met by a highly enthusiastic crowd. Lawyer and railroad financier Colonel William Johnston welcomed him. Standing on the southwest corner of South Tryon and Fourth streets, Davis made a moving speech of gratitude to the crowd, holding in his hand a telegram thrust at him by the telegraph operator. Davis finished talking to the gathering, then read the dispatch and exclaimed, "It is horrible! Can it really be true?" The terse message told of Abraham Lincoln's assassination.

Because General Stoneman had threatened to burn any house that offered Davis shelter, accommodations were hard to find. While in town, Davis no doubt visited the mint, where the commandant of the navy yard lived. The mint had also housed the Confederate treasury briefly in 1865.

Bad news had arrived from Hillsborough, a village about a hundred miles east of Charlotte, describing the final position of the

Jefferson Davis says good-bye to his escort two days before capture.

North Carolina Collection, UNC Library, Chapel Hill

Confederate army under General Joseph E. Johnston. Despite Davis's pleas to Johnston to continue resistance, Johnston had surrendered on April 18 with thirty-seven thousand men. In the Bennett farmhouse near Hillsborough (now a state historic site), Sherman and Johnston agreed on April 26 on final terms for surrender.

Davis and his officials met at the bank, then held the final meeting of his whole cabinet the next day at the Phifer home. Since Secretary of the Treasury George A. Trenholm was ill and a guest of the Phifers', the cabinet met in his bedroom. At that last sad meeting, sturdy Judah P. Benjamin, Davis's many-talented secretary of state, sat on—and severely strained—one of Mrs.

Phifer's graceful apple-wood chairs. The Confederacy, the cabinet, the Phifer hosts, and their house have long since vanished from Charlotte, but Benjamin's chair and other furnishings are said to remain in a Phifer descendant's home in lower Providence.

Jefferson Davis and several of his cabinet quickly took their carriage and baggage on the road south. Charlotte's last picture of the Confederate president was his crossing the Catawba at Nation's Ford, site of the great Indian battle, the place where the Catawbas offered Thomas Spratt of South Carolina an ocean of land and where they later signed their last treaty. Nation's Ford's exact site is unmarked, now lost in riverbank underbrush.

Subsequent cabinet meetings were held in South Carolina, where the few remaining Confederate officials consulted hastily. The canny lawyer and secretary of state, Judah P. Benjamin, escaped to England, where he was admitted to the bar and enjoyed his greatest professional success. Jefferson Davis was not so lucky.

William Phifer's fortunes also vanished with the Confederacy, since his vast interests lay in worthless Confederate bonds. Charlotteans said he was in affluence until after the surrender. The United States Government sued him for twenty-five thousand dollars, which Phifer as bondsman had guaranteed as surety for the branch United States Mint in Charlotte. Powerful friends put a special bill through Congress and saved what remained of his estate.

In 1875, the Phifer home was the scene of a

Judah P. Benjamin,
the Confederacy's secretary of state under Jefferson Davis

ball during a celebration of the Mecklenburg Declaration of Independence. Later, it became the Holt home, where that family's small son accidentally killed himself with a pistol around 1915. The vacant Phifer-Holt home was torn down in the late 1940s and replaced by a large Sears store, which has since moved to the suburbs.

Pluck and Perseverance

There was no name more beloved than that of Zebulon B. Vance, Charlotte lawyer, leader, and North Carolina governor both during and after the Civil War. His oratory was so dramatic that stores along Trade and Tryon often closed down so townspeople could hear him when he was arguing a case in the courthouse.

After the surrender at Appomattox, Federal troops swiftly occupied the state. Samuel Wittkowsky—a friend of Vance's—heard Vance was to be arrested and taken to prison in Washington. Wittkowsky was a Prussian Jew who had come to America in 1853 with three gold dollars and some clothes. Through relatives, he had made his way south to clerk for a Charlotte merchant. In 1856, Wittkowsky and a fellow clerk formed a partnership, Rintels and Company, which operated in several towns. Wittkowsky manufactured hats in Statesville for a time, but later returned to Charlotte and to the firm of Wittkowsky and Rintels. When he first came to town, the only lawyer who would take him as a client was a black attorney, J. T. Sanders.

More important than Wittkowsky's industry was what this immigrant merchant did for Governor Vance. The story is told that Wittkowsky, hearing of Vance's impending arrest, rode to Vance's house in Statesville and interceded with the Federal officers in

Right:
Zebulon B. Vance, wartime governor of North Carolina

North Carolina Collection, UNC Library, Chapel Hill

McManaway House (Oak Terrace) was built by merchants Samuel Wittkowsky and Jacob Rintels in 1874 at 406 West Trade Street. It is now located at 1700 Queens Road.

Courtesy of Jim Neinast

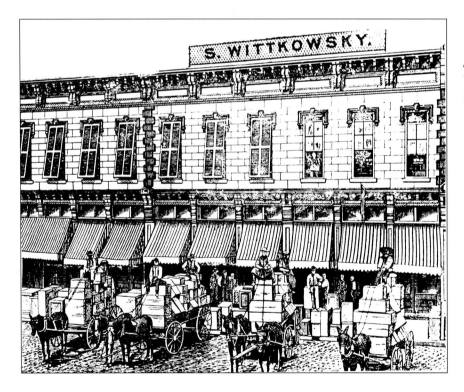

The wholesale mercantile business of Samuel Wittkowsky

Public Library of Charlotte and Mecklenburg County

Vance's behalf. He assured them that Vance was an honorable gentleman who did not need to ride horseback the thirty-five miles to the Salisbury train station. Wittkowsky offered to drive Vance in his own carriage with the two hundred Union cavalry in front and behind. In such a way, Wittkowsky hoped to spare him the indignity and discomfort of such arrest and public display.

Persuasive Sam Wittkowsky was a man of his word. Vance was delivered to Salisbury, taken to Washington, and imprisoned three months, after which he returned as a hero to practice law in Charlotte. He was elected a United States senator and again served as governor.

In Charlotte, Wittkowsky became an alderman and served in 1879 as first president of the Charlotte Chamber of Commerce. His motto was "Push, Pluck and Perseverance." He is said to have been one of a group that organized the Charlotte Country Club. Wittkowsky was also president of the building-and-loan association that became Home Federal Savings and Loan.

The beautiful house built in 1874 that Wittkowsky and Rintels owned on West Trade was bought by Dr. C. G. McManaway in 1901 and moved in 1916 to 1700 Queens Road in the fledgling suburb of Myers Park. Other properties of Wittkowsky's included the site for the Charlotte Hotel and part of Camp Greene. When Wittkowsky died of apoplexy, McManaway was the attending physician.

Quieting the Town

For several weeks after the Confederacy's surrender, Charlotteans witnessed lawless burning and looting. Not until Federal troops arrived to stay was there order again in town. With headquarters at the mint, between four and five thousand troops camped at the corner of North McDowell and East Trade streets. The mint remained headquarters until 1867. Other troops stayed on until 1872.

Soon after the surrender, bank directors asked the Federal troop commander to provide a guard to accompany them to retrieve the buried bank money. He readily agreed. J. H. Carson recorded in his diary that the ungainly wagon with a quarter million in gold and coin clattered back down the bumpy road to town and deposited its load safely into the bank vault, where it belonged.

Captain Morris Runyan commanded the first body of Federal troops in Charlotte, the Ninth New Jersey Volunteers. "I found the town filled with Rebel soldiers," he wrote on May 6. "Raids were made by mobs on stores that had been left by the Rebels. Drunkenness and disorder generally had been the order of the day. I immediately issued an order assuming command of the post; also another prohibiting the sale of all kinds of spiritous liquors. After my arrival good order prevailed.

"The following is a list of stores taken possession of and guarded by my command: Medical purveyor's Establishment, the Rebel Navy Yard, a number of boxes said to contain the records of the Rebel War Department and all the archives of the so-called Southern Confederacy, boxes said to contain all the colors and battle flags captured from the national forces since the beginnings of the war, a quantity of naval stores and a quantity of commissary stores."

Runyan telegraphed his commanding officer in Salisbury on May 9, "All is quiet. I apprehend no difficulty. I assumed command yesterday and have my force well in hand. The people are well disposed." Major General Thomas Ruger, who assumed active command of the Union forces occupying Charlotte, reported on May 16 to his superiors, "I find the citizens generally disposed to accept the new situation without complaint, and apparently desirous of resuming a condition of peace and observance of law. This region of the country is strongly rebel, however."

The following winter of 1866, the Bureau of Refugees, Freedmen and Abandoned Lands advertised the Confederate Navy Yard for sale.

Boom-Town Beginnings

For the black man, life was different soon after emancipation, but not much. His legal status changed, most certainly. At last he could vote, but old attitudes lingered in Piedmont Carolina.

Life was hard for black and white alike in that topsy-turvy decade following 1865. Both races shared misfortune, loss, injustice, and often bitterness. Anger was common though not always expressed or wisely directed. At dining-room tables, firesides, churchyards, and country stores, veterans regaled listeners with stories of gory battles, heroism and cruelty, long marches and hunger. Reflecting this, the sparse literature of the period sang a song of tragic loss, eulogizing generals and their families and holding high the antique agrarian love of the land.

The land itself was skeletal, picked clean of crops, livestock, and young men. Those who lived through the war wondered if they would survive the aftermath. Since farmers had no money to pay farmworkers' wages, many left their hard-won acreage. Credit was unavailable. These farmers, along with homeless laborers and freedmen, wandered into town.

West Trade Street, 1902

Courtesy of Bruce Julian

Planting a City

By 1869, *Branson's North Carolina Business Directory* claimed that the population of Charlotte had doubled since 1860, from three thousand to six thousand. By 1876, there were eight thousand adults and 1,730 buildings. "During that last thirty-five years of slavery," said D. A. Tompkins, "the county and city made no appreciable advance in wealth and population. During the decade after emancipation, both wealth and population doubled in the county and trebled in the city."

But it took more than additional people to account for what happened. The Civil War was as important to Charlotte economically as the gold mines had been earlier. Most of the newcomers brought by the navy yard and the munitions and ordnance supply depot simply stayed after the war. Their skills and energy infused the small town. The businesses they generated needed workers and customers. Some Charlotte families may have had safe investments elsewhere, since local recovery was swifter than frugality might normally allow. Northerners' investments here surely made a large difference. They invested in business and reopened the gold mines. If Charlotteans lacked money at first, they maintained an aura of purpose and effort gleaned from the war. Also from the war, they kept their military titles. First citizens of the era were three Confederate generals — D. H. Hill, Rufus Barringer, R. D. Johnson — plus former Governor Zebulon Vance, numerous colonels, majors, and other officers. The widow of Stonewall Jackson, Mrs. Mary Anna Morrison Jackson, reigned long as the revered first lady of Charlotte.

What followed in late-nineteenth-century Charlotte was a persistent tension between the Old South — a graceful Jeffersonian gentility tied to the land — and a New South

Mary Anna Morrison Jackson
Mrs. Stonewall Jackson returned to live on West Trade Street following her husband's death at Chancellorsville. She and two of her sisters married Confederate generals.

Public Library of Charlotte and Mecklenburg County

changed by the harsh war and different values borne by a wave of aggressive newcomers. This tension could not be hidden by courtesy or erased by prayer.

Captain John Wilkes and his wife, Jane — both New Yorkers — were in Charlotte when the war began. A United States Naval Academy graduate, Wilkes first bought Leroy Springs's Mecklenburg Flour Mills and supplied flour to the Confederate armies in Virginia. He then worked to connect a rail line for Southern supplies between Danville, Virginia, and Greensboro. His Mecklenburg Iron Works had been a strategic naval ordnance depot for the Confederacy. He was also a founder of the First National Bank and treasurer of the Rock Island Woolen Mills, which made and sold wholesale their "Cassimeres, Flannels, Jeans and other Woolen Goods."

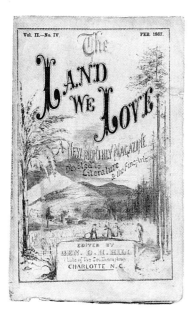

Poems, drawings, serialized novels, and accounts of Civil War battles or Charles Dickens in America filled the magazine The Land We Love. Edited by professor-soldier D. H. Hill from 1866 to 1869, it had twelve thousand far-flung subscribers.

Public Library of Charlotte and Mecklenburg County

Jane Smedburg Wilkes, daughter of a wealthy Swedish family in New York, had spearheaded turning D. H. Hill's North Carolina Military Institute into a military hospital during the latter part of the war. There, she regularly nursed the Confederate wounded. Later, she and other prominent Episcopal Charlotte women took a leading role in the opening of Saint Peter's Home and Hospital, the first civilian hospital in North Carolina, in 1878. Traveling frequently to New York, she raised money for equipment, buildings, and subsequent additions, including one of the state's earliest x-ray machines. Even J. Pierpont Morgan invested in Jane's idea to the tune of two hundred dollars. Starting in rented rooms, the original Saint Peter's Home and Hospital expanded until a separate hospital was built. Because of the carnage of the Civil War, what minimal hospitals there were in the region were gener-

Jane Wilkes,
hospital "godmother" and humanitarian who assisted Mrs. Jefferson Davis in Charlotte

Courtesy of Mrs. Stanley Black

St. Peter's Home and Hospital in 1909, located at the corner of North Poplar and West Sixth streets

ally regarded as death houses; consequently, convincing the public that hospitals were a good thing took considerable effort and time. One of the Episcopal women who helped found Saint Peter's recalled, "The first few patients were brought [in] under resistance so fierce one of the two or three policemen of which the town boasted had always to walk beside the patient, and at times to hang around the premises to intimidate the rioters who threatened to shoot into the building." The building that housed Saint Peter's Home and Hospital stands at the southwest corner of West Sixth and Poplar streets. Many current Charlotteans were born at Saint Peter's, which merged in 1940 with Charlotte Memorial Hospital, now Carolinas Medical Center.

In 1888, the indomitable Jane Wilkes solicited more Northern money to start Good Samaritan Hospital, the nation's first hospital for blacks, which operated for almost a century on Mint Street. The Wilkeses lived forty years at 508 West Trade Street and had nine children, four of whom died, two as infants. Jane was called the "Godmother of Charlotte Hospitals."

A College for the Freedmen

Other citizens besides Jane Wilkes were aware of the special needs of former slaves immediately after the Civil War.

The more fortunate freedmen had skills. Many were blacksmiths, cooks, carpenters, cobblers. But most were not equipped to earn a decent living and had little hope of education.

With freedom, the blacks not surprisingly vacated the white church balcony and gathered wherever they could, listening to black preachers and joining in their own forms of music.

Mrs. Kathleen Hayes summoned the black members of Charlotte's First Presbyterian Church "to come down out of the gallery and worship God on the main floor." She and a few others began to worship at a site on the corner of Third and Davidson streets, which Reverend Samuel C. Alexander, a white Presbyterian pastor at Steele Creek, had helped them purchase. These rousing meetings may have alarmed some, but several white Presbyterian ministers looked for a way to prepare the freedmen for becoming educated leaders and teachers of their people.

It undoubtedly was a prickly, complicated path through the presbytery meetings in 1866 discussing what must have been a radical idea—a black college in Piedmont Carolina. Nevertheless, the plan was cautiously approved by creating a new presbytery named Catawba. In 1867, the first school session met in a Union soldiers' hospital in a poor part of Charlotte called Log Town (later known as Brooklyn). Since a better location was needed, the freedmen's spokesman tried to buy 8 acres of land for the school from Confederate Colonel William R. Myers. Myers wanted three thousand dollars for the entire 130-acre plot north of town. This was far beyond their reach. But one day, as Colonel Myers walked by the old Confederate Navy Yard, he saw several white men loading wagons with old timbers from a demolished building. They told him they were taking them to Log Town for a college for blacks. They described it to him. He suggested another location for the lumber and gave the freedmen the very same 8 acres they wanted earlier, provided they place their school on a wooded promontory on Beatties Ford Road. The choice property was theirs. And with the gift of nineteen hundred dollars from Mrs. Henry Biddle of Philadelphia, Biddle Institute (later Biddle University and now Johnson C. Smith University) was begun, not to

Biddle Hall (1884) is the oldest surviving structure on the Johnson C. Smith University campus.

This 1892 photograph shows members of the Biddle graduating class and faculty:
Dr. H. L. McCrorey (front, center left) was a future president; Dr. D. J. Sanders (front, center right) was president in 1892;
and Dr. R. L. Douglass (rear, center left) was a professor. Gifts from wealthy Northerners enabled freedmen and white
Presbyterian leaders to organize the school in 1865–66.

Johnson C. Smith University Library Archives

teach agriculture or manual arts, but to become "the colored Princeton of the South," with undergraduate and theological training for young men. "So many white professors had been to Yale and Princeton, they shaped it according to what they were accustomed," explained Inez Moore Parker, archivist at Johnson C. Smith University. Parker's book on the origin of Johnson C. Smith quoted Mrs. S. C. Alexander's account of Biddle's beginning:

Rev. Willis L. Miller came to visit us in the winter of 1865–66, soon after the commission had been received, and he had conceived the idea of immediately founding the collegiate and theological school. It seemed an unreasonable thing to do when scarcely a dozen colored people in the County could read and fewer still could write, when they all were in abject poverty and the whole South was prostrated by war. But Mr. Miller urged that funds would be more easily secured then than later because the Freedmen's Bureau would aid and the Northern people were greatly interested and would give freely.

Early Biddle presidents were white Presbyterian ministers. Reverend Stephen Matoon was the first, a former missionary to Siam. His wife, Mary, taught both at Biddle and at Presbyterian College for Women on North College Street. Their grandson, Norman Thomas, grew up on the Biddle campus and later ran for president of the United States six times as an independent. Dr. D. J. Sanders became the first black president of the school, soon followed by black faculty. People said it was too soon. The first Biddle alumnus named president was Reverend Henry L.

*Dr. D. J. Sanders,
first black president of Biddle Institute*

Public Library of Charlotte and Mecklenburg County

McCrorey, who had taught Greek and Hebrew in the theological school of Biddle. McCrorey YMCA was named for him. Jane Berry (Mrs. Johnson C.) Smith, a wealthy white Pennsylvania widow, met Reverend McCrorey at a time when she was searching for an extraordinary memorial for her husband. Smith, a druggist, had extensive interests in steel. Mrs. Smith donated over seven hundred thousand dollars between 1921 and 1929 for buildings and endowment. In honor of this gift, Biddle became Johnson C. Smith University.

Duke Goes to Market

Yankee troops took something other than victory with them when they left the South for their Northern homes at the war's close in 1865. They carried their taste for "smokes" made from Carolina tobacco. Soon, they wrote back eagerly asking where to buy more.

Young "Buck" Duke and his tobacco-farming father outside Durham, North Carolina, knew an opportunity when they saw one. Tobacco required less labor than cotton. Almost as soon as he could drive a wagon, young Duke delivered tobacco to market. His father agreed to make him (at age eighteen) manager of the farm's tobacco "factory." Buck Duke was a born trader, attended Eastman Business College in Poughkeepsie, New York, and was the first to advertise widely or produce paper-boxed cigarettes in quantity. "I don't talk. I work," said Duke. He was also a pioneering whiz at promotional gimmicks. Many a Southern country store had a folding wooden chair with bold letters heralding "Duke's Cameo," a popular early cigarette product in the 1880s. Duke was among the first to use such innovative advertising for his father's company, W. Duke and Sons.

Duke's competitive talents were only exceeded by his judgment of men. "The best men come from backwoods churches," he believed. In New York in a fierce corporate contest among the nation's tobacco giants, he wound up on top of the consolidated companies of the American Tobacco Company in 1890. He was perhaps the only one who was not surprised. Duke and his less flamboyant brother Ben were also to leave their mark indelibly on Piedmont Carolina.

Duke's appointment with a New York doctor named Wylie led to a widely circulated tale of one of the happiest events to affect the Piedmont's economy in this century. One of Duke's feet felt awful and looked worse. A specialist, Dr. W. Gill Wylie, diagnosed erysipelas, which required rest and frequent treatment. In the course of bandaging and conversation, Dr. Wylie told the captive Duke of his own interest in water power. A young engineer had dammed a river on Wylie's South Carolina plantation and installed a small hydroelectric plant that gave light, heat, and power to the neighborhood. Wylie speculated that the many tumbling rivers of the Piedmont could supply power to support towns and cotton mills and supply other benefits such as electric lights and streetcars, which had recently come into use in Charlotte.

Duke knew the possibilities already. In fact, he owned sites along the Catawba and was fascinated by Wylie's working example. Eager to develop long-distance transmission of electric power, he wanted to meet that young engineer, William S. Lee. Lee presented his proposal to link the Great Falls and Mountain Island plants on the Catawba which would provide a continuity of service. Lee told Duke the endeavor "would cost $8,000,000. I thought it was about the biggest amount I had ever heard of, but it seemed to attract him."

And so began the creation in 1904 of the

View of Great Falls on the Catawba River

North Carolina Collection, UNC Library, Chapel Hill

Southern Power Company, later Duke Power, with subsequent plants on the Catawba and other rivers. The first dam at Great Falls, South Carolina, below Charlotte, was finished in eighteen months. The location was singular and had been described by historian-artist Benson Lossing in 1860: "At this place in the midst of fine cotton growing country, almost inexhaustible water power invites capital and enterprise to seek good investment, and confer substantial benefit upon the state. The place is wild and romantic. Almost the whole volume of the river is here compressed by a rugged island into a narrow channel, between steep, rocky shores. . . . There are no perpendicular falls; but down a rocky bed the river tumbles in mingled rapids and cascades, roaring and foaming and then subsides."

An advertisement for the Southern Power Company appeared in 1904: "The company begs to announce that they will be ready to supply electricity for any and all purposes on or before August 15, 1904."

By 1920, water power resulted in the establishment of over three hundred area cotton mills, among them the mills of Charlotte's neighbor, James W. Cannon, a Concord cotton broker. He was among the

J. B. "Buck" Duke

North Carolina Collection,
UNC Library, Chapel Hill

*Great Falls hydroelectricity station dedication,
with J. B. Duke, William S. Lee,
and Dr. Gil Wylie, 1907*

Duke Power Archives

Group of linemen perched atop a tower, c. 1910

Duke Power Archives

Moving transformers with oxen

Duke Power Archives

*The elegant Trust Building (center)
housed the Southern Power Company on
South Tryon Street in the early 1900s.*

Public Library of Charlotte and Mecklenburg County

first in this section to bring large-scale cotton manufacturing near the cotton fields, instead of shipping local cotton north to be made into cloth. Cannon's enterprises in Kannapolis, thirty miles northeast of Charlotte, made him "towelmaker to the world." With harnessed power, Cannon and other mills ringing Charlotte and neighboring Gaston County quickly evolved into a growing textile center. Charlotte's transportation advantages made her once more a highly viable trading path. Years later, Charles A. Cannon, son of James W., affirmed that the Cannon enterprises never would have occurred without the Southern Power Company.

Duke's story is part of Charlotte's life because of his fascination with water. He also maintained a Charlotte mansion, a handsome home built in 1915 for Z. V. Taylor in the elegant new neighborhood of Myers Park. By the time Duke finished tripling the house's original size, it thoroughly befitted a tycoon. For an international figure with homes in New York and Newport, the completed forty-five rooms and twelve baths were perhaps modest in comparison—a millionaire's "country house." But Duke's home (now known as White Oaks) was a local wonder. Charlotteans called it, in Duke's time, "the Big House."

The eleven-acre landscape extending down Edgehill Road bloomed with a profusion of flame azalea and dogwood. Duke asked Earl Draper, the full-time Massachusetts landscaper for Myers Park, to make a landscaping plan for him. He paid Draper $150 to $200, which, Draper recalled, was "plenty at the time." The earliest homes on Hermitage and Ardsley roads and on Harvard Place were those of Duke Power executives and were also landscaped by Draper.

Duke set the pattern for entertainment in Charlotte. After he gave his first dinners, social life in the town was never again the same. He loved good food. One woman

Duke mansion

North Carolina Division of Archives and History

remembered, "His dinners were always elegant with champagne. He ate his food fast and if you didn't eat yours fast too, they took it away."

Two unique features of the Big House were the fountains, one at the entry and the other a spectacular focal point downhill from the home. Duke had told Draper he wanted an enormous fountain. "I said it was a little out of scale for a private place. But he said, 'My wife wants a big display of water down there.' I remember her talking about some of the fountains in Italy." Draper recalled. "He followed my plan in part and in part departed from it. He was very original in his ideas."

Duke had built fountains on his other estates, but here he laid pipes twelve miles to the Catawba River. Pumping mechanisms supplied a lofty fountain. It threw columns of

water 150 feet into the air below his great, rambling white home. People drove long distances to park and gaze at such grandeur. Fountain View, the street above Carolinas Medical Center, got its name because of the excellent view of the spectacular fountain.

Duke amassed a vast fortune from tobacco and hydroelectricity. In 1924, a year before his death, he announced the Duke Endowment at a meeting that took place in the sunroom of the Big House's west wing. In addition to transforming Trinity College into Duke University, the gifts set forth at this meeting handsomely endowed Furman University, Johnson C. Smith University, and Davidson College. Since that date, the endowment has given over one billion dollars to Carolinas' institutions. Approximately five hundred million of this was distributed for education. Endowment funds built hundreds of Methodist churches in rural North Carolina and equipped or built child-care homes and more than two hundred Carolinas' hospitals. The original forty-million-dollar bequest to seed the endowment has been described as one of the outstanding philanthropies of all time.

Irving Harding was a Davidson girl who later married *Charlotte Observer* publisher Curtis B. Johnson. She was a frequent guest at the Duke home and at a later date recalled a particular conversation:

> One day Duke said, "I want you to go to Davidson with me. Will you?" I said, "I would love it." So I took him up to Davidson to see the college. He was then making his will and decisions about where and how he would leave his money. We went early in the morning with his chauffeur and picked up my father (a professor of Greek) and my father took him all around the buildings. A swift look was all Mr. Duke needed to comprehend a situation. I think his mind

was made up really before he went up there. He just wanted to make sure he hadn't made a mistake. He said, "This is a remarkable institution. It lives on a shoestring." He was the saviour of the college.

Davidson's endowment had disappeared into Confederate bonds. Duke's timely gift made a vast difference.

It is difficult to imagine Charlotte's economy and educational institutions without the far-reaching benefits brought by the red-headed Buck Duke.

Judge William R. Perkins wrote that Duke created the Duke Endowment because he recognized that "education when conducted along sane and practical, as opposed to dogmatic and theological lines, is, next to religion, the greatest civilizing influence."

"I have succeeded in business not because I have more natural ability than those who have not succeeded, but because I have applied myself harder and stuck to it longer," Duke said.

Street-window advertisements for electricity's newfangled benefits

Duke Power Archives

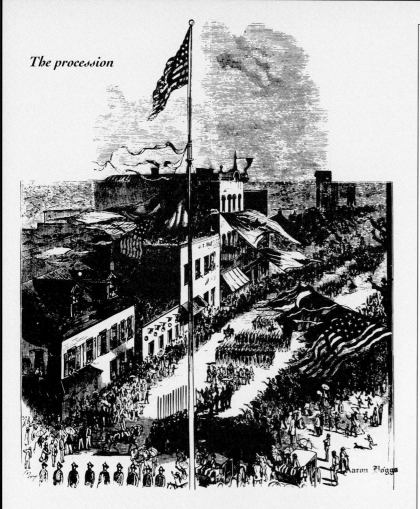

The procession

Visitors from the country

Cornwallis's headquarters, 1780

The ceremonies of the Centennial anniversary of the Mecklenburg Declaration of Independence opened at noon, May 19, [1875] at Charlotte, North Carolina. The controversy respecting the true date of this Declaration has already been discussed at length in the Weekly, and we do not propose going into the vexed question now. Whatever the historian's verdict may be, the people of North Carolina have settled the point for themselves, and held a grand and enthusiastic celebration of an event of which they are justly proud. . . .

To celebrate, great crowds of people from all parts of North Carolina and the adjoining States assembled at Charlotte on the 19th. The town was gayly decorated with flags, flowers, and evergreens. At noon the Stars and Stripes were hoisted on the Centennial flag-staff, 115 feet high, amidst enthusiastic cheering and the firing of cannon. The speeches on the occasion were eloquently patriotic. . . . In the evening many dwellings were illuminated, and the flag-staff was hung with lanterns on lines stretching to the four corners of the square on which it stood.

The next morning the town was thronged with visitors, the number present being estimated at over 40,000. The fair grounds, where the Declaration was read and the speeches were made, are about a mile from Independence Square, which is the centre of the town. . . . After the speeches, a banquet was served, and the people then returned to the town. The

Ceremonies at the fairgrounds — reading the declaration

Sketches and text from *Harper's Weekly,* June 12, 1875

evening was occupied with patriotic speeches and displays of fire-works. Among the side diversions of the day were races and a grand cock-fight between North Carolina and South Carolina birds, which might better have been omitted from the programme.

Our illustrations of this celebration, from sketches made on the spot, tell their own story. We may mention, however, that the sketch of Cornwallis's headquarters represents the rear of the building occupied by the British general in 1780, the front having been modernized. It is said to be the only relic standing of the old town of a hundred years ago. At present Charlotte has between 5000 and 6000 inhabitants. It is pleasantly situated on Sugar Creek, about twenty miles from the South Carolina line, and has fine railroad facilities. Its water-power is utilized by several cotton factories, and the people are exhibiting an enterprise that will in time make Charlotte a centre of considerable trade and manufacture. The town is embowered in green trees, shrubbery, and flowers, and the residences are neat, and some very handsome, with pretty churches, etc. There are several institutions of learning. Queen's College or Museum was established here long before the Revolution, but the museum building and the courthouse are both gone, and the site of the original Declaration is now commemorated by Independence Square.

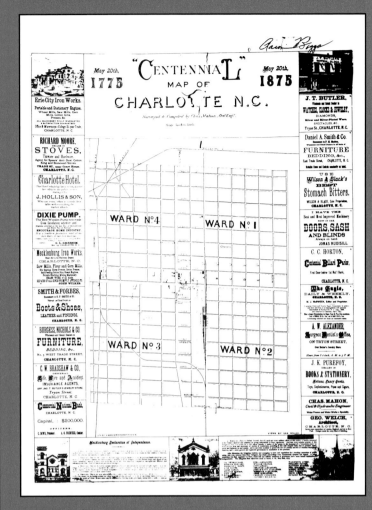

Centennial map of Charlotte, 1875

Courtesy of Aaron Boggs

Invitation to the Centennial Ball

Courtesy of Katherine Wooten Springs

INDEPENDENCE SQUARE, Charlotte, N.C.
A Souvenir of the Centenial 1875.

AARON BOGGS

Two artists' views of late-nineteenth-century Independence Square

Courtesy of Aaron Boggs

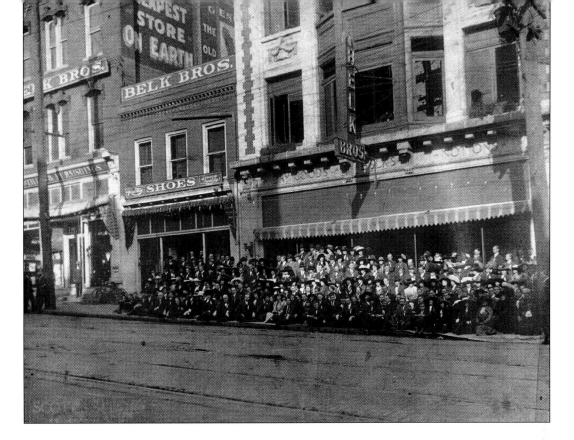

Employees gathered outside Belk Brothers' East Trade Street store, c. 1915

Public Library of Charlotte and Mecklenburg County

Tinkers and Traders

William Henry Belk, Sr., founder of Belk stores

Belk Archives

I nto the same post–Civil War town came peddlers or "drummers," itinerant traders, and some farm-boy merchants with a penchant for long hours and honest profit.

Young J. B. Ivey remembered riding to Charlotte in 1879 and stopping at Rozelle's Ferry. He loudly hallo'd Rozelle, who lived on the eastern bank, and asked him to come ferry him across. Ivey planned to be a carpenter near Shelby, but he was to remember Charlotte later as he managed and bought goods for a small store in Caroleen. When he had saved enough, he chose Charlotte to set up a store of his own, two blocks from the Square.

When Ivey came in 1900, William Henry Belk's Charlotte store had been open five years. It was Belk's fourth store, part of a unique experiment that led to four hundred stores throughout the Southeast. It insisted on cash-only sales and made promising young men part-owners in new stores. "The cheapest store on earth," he advertised. Not surprisingly, many of Belk's earliest stores lay on or very near the vigorous Trading Path route from Salisbury south.

Belk, a Presbyterian, was a bachelor until he was fifty-two. Married to his store in Charlotte, he slept upstairs and ate nearby at the Central Hotel (formerly the Mansion House). Ivey, a Methodist, had a family and also the acumen to hire an affable, outspoken Canadian, David Ovens, to help run his stores. Ovens once made the acerbic remark that the number of churches in Charlotte was matched only by the hypocrisy of some of their members. Among so many serious local sons, Ovens was a witty and welcome addition. A cultural and civic leader, it is for him Ovens Auditorium is named.

David Ovens enjoyed telling about two young men who scouted Charlotte as a place to locate a business. They saw a fellow drive his buggy up to the Buford Hotel with a large rooster beside him in the seat. The man got down from the buggy, put a feed bag on the horse, and placed the rooster under the horse's head to catch any stray grain that fell. The young visitors had been watching from the sidewalk. One said to the other, "Let's get out of here. We've got the wrong town. Nobody can make a living in a place as thrifty as this!"

Ivey was long known in Charlotte for his home's elegant tulips, which in springtime attracted hundreds of Sunday-afternoon admirers. Belk married and moved into a house on Hawthorne Lane at Elizabeth Avenue, adjacent to the financially troubled Elizabeth College. It had been a college for young women that particularly emphasized music. Belk helped the Presbyterians buy the college and half of its tract of land for Presby-

terian Hospital. He then moved the old house. For his growing family of six children, he built a large, elegant home beside the hospital. The house remains. The last hospital-surrounded remnant of the old college was torn down in 1980. The Belks gave funds to help construct buildings at Queens and Davidson colleges and other institutions. Presbyterian children in Mecklenburg for many years were given a Bible from Belk when they recited their catechism.

For many Charlotteans, it seems not so long ago when town shoppers at Ivey's and Belk's would not dream of carrying packages home. Folks said, "If you buy just a handkerchief, they'll deliver." Efird's, home of Charlotte's first escalator, was a strong uptown competitor. Belk, Ivey, and Efird were a formidable uptown merchant trio—the Presbyterian, the Methodist, the Baptist. The three stores, within one block of each other near the Square, drew shoppers daily from local neighborhoods and many nearby towns whose only shops were one-room corner groceries.

A Leader for the Black Community

J.T. Williams was a black man, educator, and alderman for the city in 1889. He had come seven years earlier to teach in Charlotte's first public school for blacks, the Myers Street School (grades one through eight). Fortunately for the town, he stayed.

Except for short interruptions, he lived in Charlotte until his death in 1928. One departure was to earn a medical degree at Leonard Medical School in Raleigh. On returning, he set up practice as one of the first black physicians licensed in North Carolina. His other major adventure was an appointment from

Elizabeth College, above, pictured in 1896, stood at the east end of Elizabeth Avenue before Presbyterian Hospital occupied the building and site. Below is Presbyterian Hospital's earlier quarters in 1911 on West Trade Street at the southeast corner of Mint Street.

Public Library of Charlotte and Mecklenburg County

President William McKinley to serve as American envoy to what is now Sierra Leone. He was one of the first blacks to serve in the diplomatic corps.

The neighborhood where Williams lived housed many prestigious black community leaders—preachers, doctors, teachers, realtors, and dentists. Williams and others founded the Grace African Methodist Episcopal Zion Church. Williams, who lived in a two-story house beside the church (203 South Brevard, near East Fourth Street), became a trustee of the very successful AME Zion Publishing House nearby.

Williams's father was a freedman who ran a successful lumber business in Cumberland County. To educate his twelve children, he hired a white widow as a teacher. J. T. Williams, born in 1859, trained as a teacher at Fayetteville State University before coming to Charlotte. J. T. Williams Junior High School on Carmine Street is named for him.

The formal name was Myers Street School, but children called it the Jacob's Ladder School. Opened in 1882, it was the first public school for blacks in Charlotte.

Courtesy of D. G. Burke

Faculty at Myers Street School

Charlotte Observer

Jewish Influence

Some of Charlotte's earliest Jewish families may have come from the North, but many traveled from Charleston, one of America's oldest Jewish communities, or from settlements in coastal Georgia. Author Harry Golden wrote that in 1850 Mecklenburg County was the home of nine Jewish families—Sieber, Drucker, Rintels, Rosenheim, Springer, Adler, Witcoff, and Baruch.

Jewish women in Charlotte put on a Purim Ball to raise money for the Confederacy. Jewish men served in the First North Carolina Regiment. They were merchants, said Golden, because that was the only enterprise open to them at the time. From 1850, numerous businesses operated by Jewish owners advertised their shops on Trade and Tryon streets. The *Western Democrat* ran this notice in 1863: "The Jewish New Year festival will come off on the 14th and 15th inst. All business will be abstained from and the services at the place of worship properly conducted between the hours of 5 A.M. and 1 P.M. Leviticus XXIII, v. 24 and 25."

Many immigrants streaming in from eastern Europe at the turn of the century found their way to Charlotte, among them Harris H. Miller and Benjamin Silverstein, wrote Morris Speizman in *The Jews of Charlotte.* Max Kahn and his brother Aaron from Dresden, Germany, settled in Charlotte because their savings for travel to Birmingham ran out and they could go no farther. They rented a room from a Mrs. Ostrowsky and stored their merchandise until they could hire a horse and wagon to peddle their wares. Not long afterwards, they opened a store on North Tryon, but Aaron was brutally beaten on a Charlotte street and died. Max mourned and left town but subsequently returned to serve on the city council and county welfare board. Charlotte teacher and actress Gladys Kahn Lavitan is his daughter.

Like other groups of kindred immigrants in town, they took solace in their religion. The first Orthodox congregation met in 1895 on East Trade Street and several subsequent locations near the Square. Soon, twenty-five member families began raising money for a new synagogue at 413 West Seventh Street. When M. B. Smith approached the superintendent of the new post-office construction on West Trade in 1915, he asked for the wood paneling and other items discarded from the demolished post-office building. The superintendent's men moved the materials and worked on the balcony, the bimah (pulpit), and stairs at no charge to the congregation.

Fits and Conjure Bags

Superstitions carried from other countries and cultures continued to thrive in the South and in Charlotte. In the late 1800s, around the corner of College and East Seventh streets was the log cabin of Aunt Judy, the village laundress, as recalled by Mrs. Sam Presson in a Charlotte Observer interview: "When she heard the weird screech of the owl, she would immediately throw salt in the fire to ward off hoodoos. . . . She found a 'conjure bag' under the rock used as a front door step to her cabin. This little bag contained a piece of hair, a chicken feather, a bone and a root. . . . She firmly believed it to be the cause of her daughter's 'fits.' . . . She was willing to pay any price for the left hind foot of a rabbit caught in the graveyard in the dark of the moon. She thought it would break the 'conjure spell.' She succeeded in getting the rabbit foot. Her daughter was cured. Aunt Judy declared she had coughed up a lizard."

Courtesy of Mary Ann Troutman

Charlotteans came to town by cart and carriage.

Opposite and opposite inset:
Charlotte City Hall, built in 1891 on the
southeast corner of North Tryon
and Fifth streets

Courtesy of Mildred Morse McEwen

Courtesy of Aaron Boggs

Charlotte
Landmarks
Commission

Mecklenburg Declaration of Independence celebration and parade, early 1900s

*The photograph above shows crowds on North Tryon looking south toward Independence Square.
The bottom photograph on the facing page was taken from South Tryon Street
looking north to the Square. In that same photograph, the Buford and the Central hotels,
Springs Corner, and city hall with its tall weather vane are visible on the right.*

Cottonseeds and Skyscrapers

Although no park, road, or building bears his name, D. A. Tompkins was more than memorable. History books have overlooked him, and Charlotte has almost erased this amazing giant from tribute, perhaps because he never married and left no complicated line of progeny. Nevertheless, he almost single-handedly forged and promoted Charlotte's early industrialization in the late 1800s. He personally took up the torch of economic transformation urged by Henry Grady, editor of the *Atlanta Constitution*, and F. W. Dawson, editor of the *Charleston News and Courier*. The call was for a New South to rise with a vision "to bring the factories to the fields." The great Cotton Mill Campaign began in earnest in the South around 1880; for the cause, Tompkins was both trench fighter and trumpeter.

A South Carolinian born in 1851, this physician's son was a relative of John C. Calhoun. Tompkins was a one-eyed, one-man whirlwind with a fervent cause—diversify the South, forsake reliance on a single crop, create industry, educate, promote. In 1882, he believed the South could manufacture anything as well as any other part of the nation. He set out to prove it.

A black man known as Peter drove the sturdy, energetic Tompkins everywhere in a one-horse carriage—to his business, the D. A. Tompkins Company; to his mill, the Atherton Mill at Tremont and South Boulevard; to his newspaper, the *Charlotte Observer;* or to the railroad for one of his many trips to meet with the likes of President McKinley and Theodore Roosevelt's United States Industrial Commission. Columnist-character "Red Buck" Bryant dubbed Tompkins a man who did not stop for obstacles.

D. A. Tompkins

Public Library of Charlotte and Mecklenburg County

At the University of South Carolina, a professor who had been chief engineer on General Robert E. Lee's staff persuaded Tompkins to enter Rensselaer Polytechnic Institute at Troy, New York. There, Tompkins studied mechanical engineering and worked afternoons and weekends in the Troy mills and shops. He then worked as an apprentice for Bethlehem Iron in Pennsylvania and went to Germany to introduce American machinery to Europeans. With important connections in the industry, he came in 1882 to Charlotte selling engines, boilers, and cotton gins for Westinghouse. Cotton and machinery married in this area, thanks largely to Tompkins's dominant force.

He envisioned Charlotte as the best of the South, having all the resources necessary for industrial possibility. One of the first things he noted was the cottonseeds left to rot. This residue pulled from the fluffy white bolls of

Southern Cotton Oil Company at South Tryon Street and Worthington Avenue, spring of 1910

Carolina cotton rotted and stank, lying piled in fields and ditches. Tompkins knew the cottonseed's oil had many uses, so with Fred Oliver he built an oil mill in Charlotte, an enterprise that later became Southern Cotton Oil Company. They built oil mills all over the South and experimented with cotton hulls for fertilizer and cattle feed.

Tompkins is said to have helped E. D. Latta's fledgling Dilworth development by buying an entire block for twenty millhouses in 1893. The mill was Atherton. Tompkins started housing factory workers in small frame homes, which workers from rural Southern backgrounds preferred. "The ideal arrangement," said Tompkins, "is to preserve the general conditions of rural life." Many workers were unused to any semblance of urban ways. Some tore out and put the new

bathtubs in their yards and set up cots in those small bathrooms, or even started fires with books from the mill library. Tompkins nevertheless believed in progress and education. Overall, however, Atherton Mill workers were proud of their village and mill, always calling their community Atherton rather than Dilworth.

Tompkins was not content to figure it out and do it—he wanted to tell about it also. He was a rousing speechmaker, a pamphleteer, and author of whatever ideas or projects interested him—roads, the cotton-gin lawsuits. He published a long list of booklets, many of which were his own speeches given up and down the eastern seaboard. He published and distributed these when he got home. He noticed there was no written history of Mecklenburg County, and he rectified that with a detailed two-volume work in 1903. Not until fifty years passed did a dusty box in the Charlotte library reveal the notes of Tompkins's ghost writer. A letter from Tompkins to Charles Coon reads, "The book is to be mine. All the work is to be done under my direction. The title of the book is to be determined by me. December 3, 1888."

Coon's literary effort did not survive his interpretation of the Revolution in 1775, because he and Tompkins disagreed vehemently about the Mecklenburg Declaration of Independence. Tompkins fired Coon and hired a Presbyterian minister-writer to complete the work more to his opinion.

Men respected Tompkins for his technical expertise, financial acumen, and power. He not only sold textile machinery; he designed and equipped textile mills and power plants. He attracted distant money to Charlotte for industrial investments. His successful finan-

cial plans showed many small communities how to start a cotton mill and pay in installments. The scheme was impressive. It worked. People came to him often to make their ideas work also.

One day in 1905, a group of prominent businessmen appeared in Tompkins's office. They thought Charlotte needed a skyscraper, and they believed Tompkins was the one to approach the owners of Osborne's Corner, the northwest corner of the Square. Tompkins agreed, and so rose the Independence Building (Realty Building), built by an energetic young builder, J. A. Jones. Floor by floor it climbed, as newspapermen reported that Charlotteans craned their necks to see "every morning whether or not it had climbed during the night, and every night, how high it had climbed since morning." It was the tallest in the state, and Charlotte could hardly contain her pride. It was a

Construction of streetcar tracks and the Independence Building on the Square, 1908

Courtesy of Frank Thies, Jr.

*North Carolina's first steel-frame skyscraper, the Independence Building (1908),
on the northwest corner of Independence Square*

Courtesy of Mrs. William Hargett

marvel to all, with office space above and the Woodall and Shepherd Drug sharing the street floor with Charlotte National Bank. The bank thoughtfully offered "a concealed corner of the bank for the use of lady customers, thus enabling them to enter from the Tryon Street door and transact their business without shoving into the general crowd."

Another group of men came to Tompkins—Colonel William Johnston, Major Clement Dowd, and Hamilton C. Jones. They felt Charlotte needed a new newspaper. Since 1824, the city had weeklies and various papers, but they were not what the group wanted. They pressed Tompkins to invest in the purchase of stock and to become a director of the *Charlotte Chronicle*, subsequently named the *Charlotte Observer*. Tompkins did not have time to direct, he said, but he bought five hundred dollars' worth of stock.

The paper fared badly, and they came back to ask him to take charge. "I told them if they would get up all the stock, I would buy it and upon that condition alone would I undertake to run the paper," Tompkins said. In 1892, Tompkins immediately found the best newspaperman around—J. P. Caldwell, editor of the *Statesville Landmark*—organized the financial structure, and returned to his textile machine company office while Caldwell edited the paper for twenty years. It was not an entirely public-spirited act, however. Tompkins wrote, "The only thing that I wanted the paper for was to preach the doctrines of industrial development. There was the need for the South to get away from one single crop as income."

One of Tompkins's most successful promotions was the Southern Manufacturers' Club, begun in 1894 (forerunner of the Charlotte City Club). More than a private men's social and dining place, it was a regional businessmen's mecca. The building at 300 West Trade was quite imposing and ornately furnished, with dormitory rooms on the third floor for bachelors.

As president, Tompkins described it as a commercial exchange where members could agree to sell cloth and yarn or make contracts for an oil or cotton mill. He believed it provided "a perfect atmosphere and all the surroundings necessary for any man to get a hearing from each individual of the best element in Charlotte. In this way any man can quietly try his hand at getting up a new factory."

Columnist "Red Buck" Bryant observed, "There was no indication in Tompkins of money first." It seems he pushed, persisted, and enjoyed the doing of what he felt important. He gave extensive textile machinery to North Carolina technical institutions and Clemson University for the purpose of educating both blacks and whites. Howard B. Clay noted that Tompkins's dealings on the United States Industrial Commission "reveal he was not opposed to arbitrary and high handed methods as such. He merely doubted their wisdom at times."

Weave and Spin

Except for household spinning wheels, early Southern cotton consistently traveled north for factory spinning and weaving into yarn and cloth. Then it returned south—priced considerably higher—for sale.

Inventive individuals began experiments to keep cotton at home. Often, they were astute merchants who saw the constant demand for yarn and yard goods. The first continuing mill in North Carolina (and perhaps in the South) was built by Michael Schenck just over the line in Lincoln County about 1814. He ordered spinning machinery from Rhode Island and operated it with Absalom Warlick on a fork of the Catawba until the 1860s. The

Picking cotton

Public Library of Charlotte and Mecklenburg County

Cotton on its way to market

Courtesy of Aaron Boggs

Rock Island Woolen Mill made wool cloth during the Civil War and later made cotton cloth as the Rock Island Manufacturing Company. It was the only known mill in the immediate area at that time other than General Neal's small Steele Creek yarn factory, located in an old flour mill near what is now Withers Cove.

In Mecklenburg, David Alexander moved his wool-carding mill to Mallard Creek in 1833, and Wilson Parks ran a wool-carding machine on McAlpine Creek in 1842; but the Glenroy Cotton Mill between Matthews and Providence, which opened in 1874, is called the county's first cotton-spinning mill. It ran for only eighteen months, spinning bale yarn for twenty-two cents a pound. The Glenroy operated 350 spindles and two frames, but cotton and yarn prices fell. The mill lost money and sold its equipment to a South Carolina mill.

Colonel R. M. Oates walked through the Glenroy Cotton Mill before he and his brothers decided to open Charlotte's first cotton mill in 1881. They took the plunge at 508 West Fifth Street, at the corner of Graham Street. A textile knitting-machine sales firm, Speizman Industries, still operates in this same building.

It is puzzling to read of the thriving early mills in Fayetteville, Greensboro, and Rocky Mount forty years prior to Charlotte's venture. In 1873, there were thirty-three cotton factories in North Carolina, nine within thirty-five miles of Charlotte, but few, if any, in Charlotte until Oates's venture in 1881.

Three Gaston County mills—the Woodlawn (or Pinhook), the Mountain Island, and the Stowe mills—had manufactured cotton prior to Reconstruction. Great wagons pulled by double and triple teams carried their cloth and yarn to markets in Charleston, Virginia, and North Carolina.

Charlotte had railroads as well as local and other capital after 1870, but it apparently took time to convince people that factory management was a respectable way to make a living. It may have seemed an alien desertion

Rock Island Manufacturing Company stock certificate

Courtesy of Louise Smith Thompson

Farmers unload cotton at rural cotton gin.

Public Library of Charlotte and Mecklenburg County

Right:
Laborers loaded down with sacks of cotton

Courtesy of Mildred Morse McEwen

of the land. Merchandising never seemed so, but manufacturing was somehow riskier and different. However, prospects for greater profit tantalized local businessmen, and Tompkins's presence was difficult to ignore. A major consciousness-raising effort was undertaken by newspapers and leaders. Then once the gate opened in 1881, the flood tide began—two cotton-oil mills in 1882 and five cotton mills in 1896. These included the well-known Ada, the Alpha, and the Victor mills. The Alpha (East Twelfth and Brevard) and part of the Ada (West Eleventh under the Brookshire Freeway) still stand. The Atherton, which Tompkins built next to Dilworth in 1893, was adapted for other usage and stands at 2136 South Boulevard. A few adjacent millhouses remain. Typically, each mill was surrounded by small, frame, mill-owned villages, where mill workers (called operatives) lived with their families.

Charlotte was again in the right place at the right time. The city had railroads for bringing in raw cotton and dispatching finished products. Charlotte had cheap and plentiful labor, skilled leaders, and craftsmen, as well as investment capital and energy to operate the mills. By 1904, the astounding figures show seventeen mills in Charlotte, with mills in Pineville, Davidson, Huntersville, and Cornelius—and three hundred cotton mills within a hundred-mile radius. In fact, half the looms and spindles of the South lay within that radius. Also in Charlotte were companies that built, supplied, and repaired textile machinery.

This was the era of Tompkins, Duke, Stuart Cramer, John H. VanLandingham, James W. Cannon, Thomas M. Barnhardt, A. C., Caleb, and Lewis Lineberger, R. Y. McAden, R. L. and S. T. Stowe, and C. W. Johnston. According to Mildred Andrews's history of Southern textiles, *The Men and the Mills*, the Charlotte area was "a loose collection of unincorporated mill villages joined by

John H. Van Landingham,
cotton investor

University of North Carolina at Charlotte,
Atkins Library, Special Collections Unit

central business districts."

One of these villages was North Charlotte, where C. W. Johnston's Highland Park Mill had a town life of its own. Johnston operated two plants in Charlotte and one in Rock Hill, South Carolina. As a boy, Johnston clerked at Sloan's Country Store in Davidson. Rising to Charlotte's "high cotton," he owned the Highland Park Mill (known as the "Gingham Mill") and poured mill profits into the ornate Johnston Building at 212 South Tryon, which became headquarters for his companies. The building housed dealers in cotton and textile industries. On the tenth floor, a cotton exchange operated. Surrounding this building were many other offices housing cotton brokers, whose male cotton classers worked under skylights that pointed north.

Cotton-mill operatives
Entire families worked in the mills. Many came from mountain or Piedmont Carolina farms.

Courtesy of Aaron Boggs

True northern light, not direct sunlight, was deemed optimal to judge accurately the fine gradations of cotton quality. The remaining roofs of these buildings retain these northerly directed skylights.

Johnston is said to have been so pleased with his fine Johnston Building that he stood across the street admiring and said, "Not bad for Goose Creek!" Johnston grew up in the Coddle Creek vicinity of Cabarrus and Iredell counties.

Thomas M. Barnhardt's cotton manufacturing company began in Charlotte in 1909, producing layered batting from unbleached cotton fibers. The one-room plant and office cottage created made-to-order batting and sold it through Baltimore. In 1911, it received an order from the Packard Company. Soon,

Barnhardt cotton replaced the curled-hair upholstery in car seats. "If it needs padding," so the slogan went, "Barnhardt can supply it."

During this era, mill towns arose from the fields and beside the rivers, lakes, and spur-line railroads—Cramerton, Belmont, Pacolet, China Grove, Kannapolis, Gastonia, Kings Mountain, McAdenville, Mountain Island, Mooresville, Fort Mill, and Rock Hill. McAdenville and Kannapolis remain two original and unusually attractive mill-centered communities. Cramerton was another model village with a careful, innovative design and function. Linking these Carolina textile towns with Charlotte was the Piedmont and Northern (the P&N, as it was called), a rail line with excellent passenger service. Many Christmas and Easter shoppers in uptown

Lewis Hine photograph of a ten-year-old spinner in a North Carolina cotton mill, 1909

International Museum of Photography at George Eastman House

Charlotte were mill workers and families from these towns who came by rail to spend the day. They often brought empty suitcases to carry their collected purchases; they then opened the suitcases to admire their new store-bought goods on the short train journey home.

In Charlotte, millions of miles of cloth emerged as fine and coarse sheeting, shirting, gingham, plaids, duck, and drills from mills with the names of Chadwick, Elizabeth, Hoskins, Crowley, Mecklenburg, Johnston, Savona, and Magnolia.

Duke's power plants fed cheap electricity to the plants, whose workers in turn needed clothes, houses, schools, and cars. In such a cotton-driven whirlwind of success, the need arose for suburbs, parks, roads, financing, and entertainment. Mill wages attracted a steady stream of families and young people from Piedmont and mountain farms. Entire families worked in the mills, and numerous interviews describe the early workplace as one of leisurely pace and family-like camaraderie. A fifty-five-hour workweek was not unusual.

Statistics from Mecklenburg mills are scarce, but in Lincoln and Gaston counties, mill workers in 1889 raised their voices for shorter workdays of ten hours, as recorded by the North Carolina Bureau of Labor Statistics. A Lincoln County worker protested, "Twelve hours per day is too long to keep operatives at work, especially women and children." Not until 1913 did North Carolina have laws prohibiting the employment of children under twelve. The widely published photographs of Lewis Hine glimpsed the youthful mill workers and culminated in a most effective national propaganda campaign to protect child workers.

Cotton-mill operatives, Long Island Mill at Buffalo Shoals

Courtesy of W. G. Frye

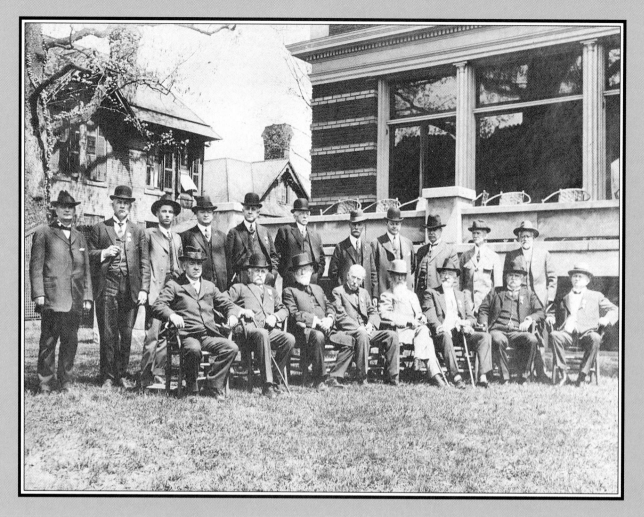

Members of the Society of the Cincinnati at Charlotte's Southern Manufacturers' Club, 1916

Public Library of Charlotte and Mecklenburg County

Charlotte Gun Club, 1880

Public Library of Charlotte
and Mecklenburg County

Luncheon at the Southern Manufacturers' Club, 1916

Courtesy of W. G. Frye

Steel's Foundry workers in Statesville, c. 1890

Courtesy of W. G. Frye

Portrait of the Charlotte Police Department, c. 1910

Public Library of Charlotte and Mecklenburg County

Corner store at East Trade and Brevard streets

Public Library of Charlotte and Mecklenburg County

Northwest corner of Independence Square at the turn of the century

Public Library of Charlotte and Mecklenburg County

The 1896 courthouse stood in the three-hundred block of South Tryon Street on the site of Queens College for young men (subsequently Queens Museum and Liberty Hall), the first tax-supported college in North Carolina, 1771.

Courtesy of Jo Hackney Huntington

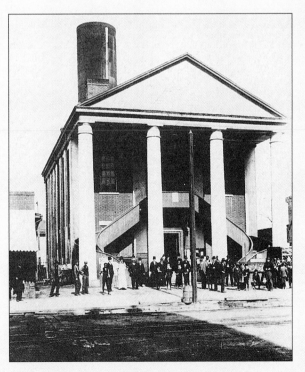

Courthouse scene c. 1890 at the corner of West Trade and North Church streets

Courtesy of W. G. Frye

Streetcar conductor for the Charlotte Electrical Railway

Charlotte Landmarks Commission

Mill Towns and Streetcar Suburbs

James Latta of early Mecklenburg would have been pleased with his great-grandson. Adventurous merchandising ran in the family, but Edward Dilworth Latta did not sell clothes very long in New York or at E. D. Latta and Brother Company in Charlotte. In 1881, he began manufacturing clothing at his own factory at Fourth and Tryon. Then he had a better idea.

The horse-drawn streetcar was new to Charlotte in 1887. Latta soon bought the business, then built a power house and laid tracks for his electric streetcar system, which took eager Charlotteans wherever the tracks led. In 1890, Latta formed the 4C's Company (Charlotte Consolidated Construction Company), buying a thousand acres of rural land for a hundred dollars an acre and calling it Dilworth. It became Charlotte's first streetcar suburb, with its own reservoir, electric plant, and gas works. For seventeen years, it remained a separate community, loudly fighting annexation. A trolley ride at about twelve miles per hour to Dilworth was supreme entertainment and ended near the large lake where Latta Park now is. There were ball games, gazebos for picnics or rendezvous, boating, swimming, and a wide variety of

Charlotte trolley to North Myers Street

Charlotte Landmarks Commission

Laying trolley tracks on North Tryon

Courtesy of G. B. Warren

other amusements. Many Mecklenburg children, now grown, recall attending the circus in Dilworth.

Charlotte had never seen anything quite like Latta's promotion of Dilworth. He began advertising its wonders, whetting the town's appetite for luxury, the good life, fun, and an amazing future. "Buy a house with the rent money," he coaxed. Over a month before the land sale, an advertisement beat the drum: "If we all follow unitedly in the wake of the 4C's, we will build a city where we now have a town."

Everyone knew from the ads and the rumors that Dilworth was to have a pavilion designed by a Swedish architect, fourteen pin alleys, billiards, a ballroom, and an auditorium. A contest open to anyone asked for suggestions for the pavilion's interior decor. The botanical garden turned a steep ravine into a graceful lake bordered with serpentine walks and variegated flower beds.

Opening day of the land auction for lots was the historically significant May 20. The year was 1891. Latta capitalized on Charlotte's festive spirit, and more than two thousand people crowded to attend. Prospective buyers could choose a house of their own design, or the 4C's would build or rent them a

Lake Forsythe in the Dilworth neighborhood, which was later drained to become Latta Park

Charlotte Observer

home of Queen Anne, Colonial, or Modern American design. But after the first spurt of success, sales lagged; seventy-eight lots sold in the first year, four lots in the second.

Consequently, Latta modified some of his grand designs for the pavilion and was undoubtedly grateful his project was not a purely residential venture. Dilworth's location

Residence of E. D. Latta at 600 East Boulevard

on the Charlotte, Columbia, and Augusta Railroad made it a convenient industrial park. Atherton Mills and its accompanying housing, Charlotte Trouser Company, Charlotte Pipe and Foundry, and other developing industry comprised a very diverse community. At the time of Dilworth's opening, Charlotte's black citizens visited the park and events. They occasionally held a camp meeting there. Mrs. Sam Presson recalled in the *Charlotte Observer* how their songs echoed and re-echoed through the neighborhood. In 1900, 4C's constructed a separate park for blacks outside Dilworth.

Lots in Dilworth sold for $350 to $500, with choice sites along Park Avenue. Latta himself moved into the elegant Neoclassical mansion on East Boulevard in 1906. It was later owned by worldwide builder J. A. Jones. Demolished in the 1960s, the home was replaced by the Greek Orthodox Cathedral, but its elegant mantels, woodwork, light fixtures, and hardware are scattered in restaurants and homes throughout the city.

Latta's vision extended beyond Dilworth. He was described as the first man to see Charlotte's possibilities. His faith in its future never wavered. Latta grew up in Pendleton, South Carolina, graduated from Princeton, and was known widely as a contentious man and a real autocrat, but one who gave elaborate Christmas dinners for his employees. Now, he is known as a man far ahead of his time.

The geometric skylights so evident in today's architecture were the focal point of the 4C's offices in the sophisticated Latta Arcade, designed by William Peeps in 1914.

They pleased Latta as he mounted the wide marble stairs to his office of Philippine mahogany and leaded glass. From his desk, he could gaze at the courthouse, then at South Tryon and Third streets. Most Charlotteans considered the Latta Arcade strange and ugly, but office space there was in such demand that he was asked to extend it. He declined. Miss Julia Alexander, Charlotte's first woman lawyer, had her office there. Brevard Court (behind the arcade) is a quaint individual extension of early offices. To find Latta Arcade, the searcher must be on foot and know where to enter at 320 South Tryon. In Latta's day, everyone knew.

Latta also had plans for the future of South Tryon Street. In 1910, he and J. B. Duke built the Mercantile Building, and Latta began buying large tracts along the street. He influenced the members of the Masonic Temple to venture onto South Tryon with their stalwart Egyptian Revival building designed by C. C. Hook. Latta and a group of Charlotte businessmen pooled their resources to build one of Latta's dreams—a large hotel. Latta wanted it on South Tryon, but the other investors chose West Trade instead. They built the Hotel Charlotte across from First Presbyterian Church. Incensed, Latta withdrew his funds, and a lawsuit ensued. Soon afterwards, Latta moved to Asheville.

Newspaper notices of Latta's death in 1925 on Sunset Drive in Asheville said he came there "in search of health." Latta was a diabetic and died of a stroke. He was one of the wealthiest men in the state. Before he died, Latta had announced plans for a theater, office building, and skyscraper in Asheville.

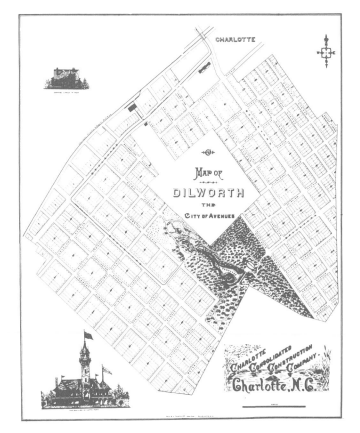

Map of Dilworth

Dilworth Community Development Association

Liddell-McNinch House
One of the original grand dames of old Fourth Ward, built c. 1892 at 511 North Church Street, it remains in its original
location. Built by industrialist Vinton Liddell, it was later owned by Mayor S. S. McNinch.

Public Library of Charlotte and Mecklenburg County

Fourth Ward homes, c. 1900

Courtesy of Mildred Morse McEwen

Charles M. Tillett residence, 801 North Tryon Street

Public Library of Charlotte and Mecklenburg County

Residence of Dr. Simmons Jones (1896) on block bordered by South Tryon, Morehead, and Vance streets and the railroad

Public Library of Charlotte and Mecklenburg County

"Victoria,"
pictured above at right and on the opposite page,
was built in 1890–91 at 400 North Tryon. In 1915, it was moved to the suburbs
at 1600 The Plaza. It is the only remaining unaltered example of the grand
nineteenth-century homes of Trade and Tryon.

This panoramic view is of Presbyterian College for Women and the neighborhood of 600 North College Street. In 1912, college trustees voted to vacate this imposing new building, built in 1896. The college moved to a new campus in the suburb of Myers Park. There, its name was changed to Queens College.

Queens College

View of Grange Hall School near Hoods Cross Roads in 1898, with teachers Turner Hooks and L. H. Yandle

Public Library of Charlotte and Mecklenburg and County

Railroads and Reclaimed Women

In 1888, a book of *Sketches of Charlotte* described Charlotte as a "thrifty" and "bustling city" free of debt and having telephones, electric lights, fire alarms, a fire department, waterworks, sewage disposal, free postal delivery, streetcars, brick and stone sidewalks, and macadam streets for her twelve thousand citizens. She was quite proud of her three banks—First National, Commercial National, and Merchant and Farmers National.

She boasted of her advanced schools—Biddle Institute, Saint Mary's Seminary, Charlotte Female Institute, nearby Barber-Scotia College in Concord, Davidson College in Davidson, and Belmont Abbey College in Belmont. In the heart of town were the Central and Buford hotels, the opera house for lively entertainment, and separate grade schools for black and white students. "It appears the school facilities are indeed almost

Expense account from Charlotte Female Institute, the forerunner of Presbyterian College for Women and Queens College

Queens College

Railway stock certificate

perfect," *Sketches of Charlotte* said. The town had an orphanage, a Carnegie Library, day nurseries, a House of Refuge for reclaimed women, rows of fine homes along Trade and Tryon, and parklike Elmwood Cemetery behind the elegant homes in Fourth Ward. At the time, there was no saloon in the county outside the Charlotte city limits.

Despite such progress, First Presbyterian Church still had a few problems with wayward members. *The Doings of the Session* in February 1888 recorded, "Elders having oversight of Wards 1 and 3 were instructed to visit members in these Wards who had lately engaged in dancing."

Four railway depots served the city for freight, and twenty passenger trains arrived and departed daily. The Carolina Central Railroad and the Richmond and Danville Railroad each had two depots for passengers and freight. Since Charlotte lay on the main line between New York and New Orleans, frequent news of travelers and train schedules appeared in the local news. The Atlantic, Tennessee, and Ohio Railroad served Statesville, Richmond, Washington, and West Point. While the Seaboard AirLine took passengers to Norfolk and Wilmington, the Carolina Central and the Atlanta and Charlotte AirLine served points south. These local railroads came together in 1894 under the Southern Railway System. Charlotte's rail connections transported products of home companies such as Liddell Company Foundry, Mecklenburg Iron Works, Carson Brothers' Carolina Spoke and Handle Works, and Elliot and Marsh Furniture. City fathers acknowledged, "Some of our largest property owners and manufacturers are Northerners."

Turn-of-the-century fashion
for women and children

University of North Carolina at Charlotte,
Atkins Library, Special Collections Unit

A Sure-Enough City

The morning of the first day of 1900 was like any other day. The early sun rose quietly and glistened on finger coves of the Catawba. Wind-up clocks rang in bedrooms, and neighborhood dogs sniffed their usual rounds. And the other events of motion—of politics, finance, and industry—pulled Charlotte citizens forward toward noon and evening, toward weeks and years of a new century. The story overlaps the decades as lives do, for history circles and shows no respect for straight lines.

Ready to be "up and coming," neighbors display their motto, "Watch Charlotte Grow," c. 1900.

Courtesy of Mary Ann Troutman

Looking west from the first block of East Trade Street,
c. 1920s

*Northward view (c. 1900) of Fourth Ward from Tompkins Tower,
which was located in the 100 block of South Church Street*

Earmarks of a City

One man snapped a verbal photograph of what it was like on such a day. "The Charlotte citizen who has not been on top of the Tompkins tower does not know Charlotte at all," wrote Isaac Erwin Avery, city editor of the *Charlotte Observer* around 1900. In a collection called *Idle Comments,* he described looking down on Charlotte from a fourteen-story observatory platform above the factory, surveying the domes and steeples of the city. The extraordinary view covered "every street and house in Charlotte, and the suburban towns are as plain as pictures on canvas. . . . One building near Davidson College is clearly indicated, as are also farmhouses about Sharon Church. The view of the mountains is surprisingly fine. . . . The bang and rattle of a loaded truck passing in the street below seems tenfold greater at this height. . . . The clatter of horses' hoofs and the exhaust of steam engines come up with piercing keenness . . . the living current of people and vehicles, the smoke from factories and the exhaust of the railroad engines on the four sides of town." Avery described the afternoon train coming from Atlanta and crossing the Dowd farm and the trestle west of the city under a "sinuous cloud of smoke. He noted that "a beautiful picture of a busy and thrifty city is framed in the white and black of the steam and smoke of industry." Clearly, industry in many ways became beauty to the people of Charlotte.

Tompkins Building and Tower
Public Library of Charlotte and Mecklenburg County

Eastward view from Tompkins Tower

The town changed visibly. Avery noted the signs that

Charlotte has passed through the transition stage and become a sure-enough city. A strange woman wearing a Parisian gown, her body at a forward incline of forty-five degrees, and a poodle in evening dress, may parade the streets without causing a block in traffic or bringing all the shopkeepers to their windows. Recently a revival and a ball were in progress on the same night, and the city officials do not drop their work and follow a brass band. Residents who travel abroad and return are no longer surrounded at the square and eagerly questioned about the private life of the King or the Pope. A whole week instead of a day may be required to carry a choice bit of scandal into every part of the town. And the preachers no longer attend courts, plenty of people stay away from funerals; you may dodge a creditor for days without remaining in hiding, the country mules do not shy at automobiles or silk hats walking around on weekdays; and no one thinks about fainting when a Charlotte woman goes off to get a Ph.D. vocal degree and comes home singing in a high Dutch or broken Eye-talian. In fine, Charlotte has all the earmarks of a city.

Even so, Charlotte in 1900 was so small it had a single water supply, a small lake just across the old town limits to the east, filling a basin that later became Independence Park. A Charlottean recalled, "One dark night the watchman in charge discovered two grown men out in the lake up to their hips in water, enjoying a little fishing. Officers were summoned and under the bright lights at the police station, they discovered they had bagged two city aldermen, two who had passed the ordinance against swimming and fishing in the reservoir. The event created quite a sensation when the story appeared in the papers the following day."

But by 1905, when President Teddy Roosevelt arrived, the signs of the New South were well in place. Commerce. Factories. Schools and colleges. A concert hall. A library. In his speech, Roosevelt sang a welcome melody: "I rejoice in the symptoms of your abounding prosperity . . . here in a great center of cotton manufacture." Within a hundred miles of Charlotte, there were three million spindles and eighty-five thousand looms representing $100 million in capital. The outlying cotton mills immediately surrounding the town employed six thousand mill workers, with an average raw-cotton trade of $1.2 million each year, according to Mildred Gwin Andrews in *The Men and the Mills*. Important also were the many textile-equipment suppliers and manufacturers. Charlotteans were producing iron, tobacco, wagons, carriages, doors, spokes and handles, harnesses, and marble works. Alongside the commerce on uptown streets were numerous saloons. Charlotte was known as "a bustling, prosperous city," wrote Andrews, "a good example of the New South — the manufacture of cotton was the lifeblood of the Piedmont."

A prime example was engineer and textile designer Stuart Cramer's design of Highland Park Mill No. 3 and its mill village for William E. Holt, J. S. Spencer, and C. W. Johnston in 1904. The large mill lay along the Southern Railway tracks just north of town. Historian Dr. Dan Morrill wrote, "Cramer oversaw every detail, choosing a design for his mill cottages that would make them look like the farm houses many workers had known before moving to town. He left enough room for vegetable gardens, pig pens,

and chicken coops. Cramer regarded the mill with its tall gray tower as his masterpiece. It was the largest cotton mill built in Charlotte, creating a whole community — north Charlotte — with more than 100 homes and its own business district."

Edna Hargett described life in a Charlotte mill. She was born in a mill village near Rock Hill in 1907 and worked in Charlotte's Chadwick-Hoskins Mill. In the book *Like a Family: The Making of a Southern Cotton Mill World*, Hargett recalled that "the mill child had to go in the mill and the others didn't. We knew that was the way of life we was brought up to, and that would be the way of life we had to expect." Mill workers were a close, loving community, she recalled. Work at the mill for her meant days in "a loud, noisy place, and awful dusty and linty." Work was often quite leisurely before the stretch-outs, when employers tightened up and often doubled work loads. Young men in mill villages didn't like town boys dating mill girls. If they saw an intruder, they chased him out.

In the early 1900s in Mecklenburg County, cotton was still the chief crop and the basis of the local economy.

Courtesy of Mildred Morse McEwen

Traveling by automobile at the turn of the century was sometimes difficult, but Charlotteans braved the mud and toured often to the mountains, where the roads were merely trails. Auto sales in the state soared from 2,400 in 1910 to 150,000 in 1921.

Courtesy of Spencer Folger

The Auto Invades

When the first automobile chugged around a Charlotte corner in 1900, Osmond Barringer drove it. Barringer was the city's first car dealer. One of the two steam Locomobiles he received, it was described as having "a small boiler under the seat with a two cylinder steam engine in the rear driving the axle through an oversize bicycle chain." He sold the second car to Dr. C. G. McManaway to use in his practice. Next, he purchased an Oldsmobile Runabout.

Barringer loved to be first. He experimented with x-rays in a Davidson College lab before x-ray photographs were made elsewhere. Later, the use of x-ray by Dr. H. L.

Smith of Davidson College led to saving a little girl's life. A lodged thimble was located and cut from her throat by Dr. C. A. Misenheimer, assisted by Dr. John R. Erwin and Dr. Robert L. Gibbon. This is said to have been the first operation performed in the South with the use of x-rays.

Barringer rode a bike from Canada to Charlotte, drove a Hudson Speedster up the steps of the Southern Manufacturers' Club, and took his White Steamer from Charlotte to Blowing Rock (a popular new resort in North Carolina) in 1908. People said it could not be done. So Barringer did it with three intrepid Charlotte friends, rope, block and tackle, chains, shovel, and six five-gallon cans of extra gas. They drove rugged macadam roads, crossed the Catawba on a ferry, drove mountain trails that had never seen an auto before. When he drove his car right out onto Blowing Rock, he said he felt like Hannibal crossing the Alps. He looked it, too, and the photograph of the feat was Blowing Rock's most popular postcard. He inspired other well-to-do Charlotteans to seek the cool summer relief of forest breezes in daring excursions to

Charlotte motorists on a mountain holiday

University of North Carolina at Charlotte, Atkins Library, Special Collections Unit the mountains. They fled to Little Switzerland, Chimney Rock, Linville, Black Mountain, Asheville's Grove Park Inn, and Blowing Rock's Mayview Manor and Green Park Inn. Like Barringer, they were undeterred by frequent flat tires and hazardous roads that were little more than trails.

Barringer operated the Charlotte Speedway on Old Pineville Road and drove a Packard roadster until the Depression. When he lost his investments, he bred parakeets, minnows, and worms and chauffeured four visiting presidents in Charlotte. He gave away General Rufus Barringer's land for Revolution Park and Barringer School, as well as his own grape jelly and dandelion wine. Columnist "Red Buck" Bryant described Barringer's love affair with the automobile: "He delighted in its speed, novelty, and the fear it gave the population."

Automobiles were cautiously received by more conservative Charlotteans. People who had for generations trusted their travel needs to horses, trains, bicycles, and those unpredictable mules became fascinated by the auto. Those who could afford them bought them almost as a toy at first. Once their advantage was realized, the push for better roads began. By 1925, Cramerton Mill's brochure noted, "Henry Ford is certainly emancipating the average small town worker. Even the most casual observer has noticed the amazing number of automobiles of all vintages in mill communities. The mills generally close down on Saturday forenoons and by early afternoon, large numbers of workers are out for the weekends even as their former envied society neighbors."

Initially, the Ford Motor Company underestimated the Southerner's yen for motorcars. When Ford built its Charlotte service branch in 1914, there were only forty employees. These furnished service parts to Carolina Ford dealers; but the enthusiastic market altered the plan. In 1915, workers assembled 6,850 Ford automobiles. In 1916, the plant met a payroll of approximately sixty thousand dollars, and in 1918, it turned out 85 cars daily. In the mid-twenties, after expansion to a new plant on the large Hutchison farm at Statesville and Derita roads, 300 cars a day rolled off the assembly line. The plant closed in the early thirties, leaving a large, empty plant for local realtors to peddle.

Some have suggested that the only reason General Sherman avoided Charlotte was that he heard about the mud. Surely there were other reasons, but Mecklenburg mud was so formidable that it has been referred to in accounts of Charlotte history ever since the first wagon wore away the undergrowth, making ruts in the compact clay. The Plank Road from Lincolnton around 1850 was a travel miracle. Subsequent macadamized roads stretched through town in the 1880s. Railroads through Charlotte tied her to trade and tourists, but the daintily slippered, sophisticated foot had to walk at some point. Goods had to journey from field or factory to the loading platform.

One of the favorite street games along the town's unpaved sidewalks was to drop Mother's sewing pins down the deep cracks in the dried summer clay hoping they would find their way to China. And if streets were not muddy, there was all that dust. In 1915, Earl Draper noted teams of horses pulling water wagons to spray West Trade Street.

Captain Sydenham "Syd" Alexander saw the need for better roads. He owned Enderly, a large farm two miles west of Charlotte. Soil and its consistency and growing capacities were his main interests. He had orchards, sheep, turkeys, dairy cows, and vineyards—which meant he had products he badly needed to get to market.

When he was elected to the state senate in 1878, he introduced a bill allowing municipalities to use tax money to build and keep up public roads. That in itself was a radical

Ford Motor Company's assembly plant, 1920s
Charlotte opened a Ford assembly plant in 1915 and in 1918 turned out eighty-five cars daily.

departure from common practice then. The law also required every able-bodied man ages eighteen to forty-five to work one day each year on public-road upkeep. Captain Alexander was not a popular man after that. It became state law only by exempting all counties except Mecklenburg. He lost the next election, and his strange law was repealed. But meanwhile, people noticed that the roads built because of the brief law spurred commerce and were also convenient. Alexander was back in favor. So was his law. His idea was the early basis for Charlotte Mayor T. L. Kirkpatrick's (1915–17) successful road-promotion program. This was largely implemented statewide by Cameron Morrison of Charlotte, the "Good Roads Governor," in 1921–25.

Above:
Gas station owned by
W. A. "Bill" Frye

Left:
Many cars needing
repairs found their
way to W. A. Frye and
Dock Crowell's
Ford garage at
221 North College Street.

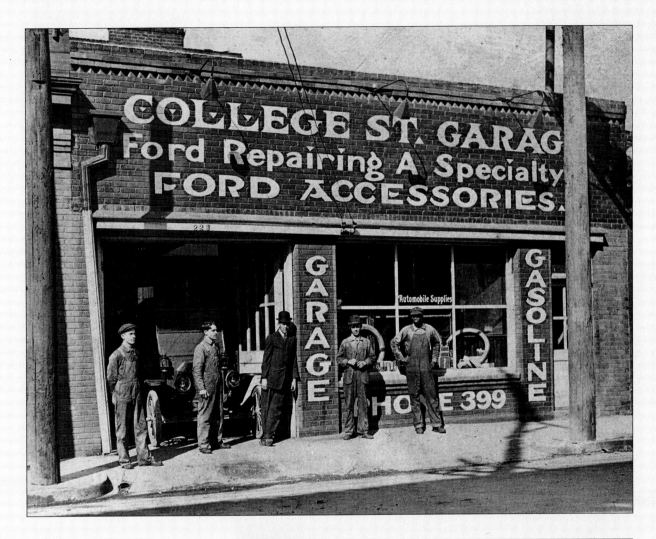

Above:
Frye and Crowell's
establishment
was the first Ford
garage in Charlotte.

Right:
This 1917
Pepsi Cola truck
fell through the bridge
on Rocky River Road
at Newell.

Army tents arranged in perfect rows at Camp Greene

National Archives

This is the Army

Syd's farm and his firsthand acquaintance with mud are part of the Camp Greene story in 1917. Camp Greene introduced the sons of America to Mecklenburg mud. On Syd's farm and an adjacent farm, thousands of United States troops camped in tents and barracks during World War I. The record-breaking rains turned the training fields into a dark morass of remarkable adhesive quality. Appropriately, the camp newspaper was named the *Mud Turtle*.

Camp Greene appeared almost by magic when the United States entered World War I in Europe. At war's end in 1919, the teeming camp vanished, marking one of the most heartwarming stories in Charlotte history. Miriam Mitchell and Ed Perzel described in

The Echo of the Bugle Call how Camp Greene transformed an energetic town into a thriving, gracious city.

America's entry into the war required immediate training of troops for military action in Europe. Like modern "industry hunts," Charlotte actively sought the government's interest in placing a major base in the city. Officials courted the scouting General Leonard Wood at the home that was later to become the Duke mansion. Then they wined and dined Wood at the Southern Manufacturers' Club. They showed him three sites, including one in the new neighborhood of Myers Park. Approximately eight thousand people waited to hear General Wood speak under the trees at First Presbyterian's churchyard.

It must have been a dry day, because the general liked the looks of the soil at the southwestern site. He liked the creeks and rolling hillsides. He also noted its rail connections and the two high elevations—the old James C. Dowd farmhouse and acreage on Sloan's Ferry Road, and Syd Alexander's farm on Tuckaseegee near Lakewood Park. Lakewood Park offered swimming, boating, a merry-go-round, rides, a dance pavilion, and a zoo. One Charlottean recalled riding the popular streetcar to Lakewood: "You could smell the bear cage for a mile before you got there."

The whole town waited eagerly as Z. V. Taylor, Cameron Morrison, Mayor Frank McNinch, and David Ovens blitzed Washington. Competing cities were equally active, but Charlotte won. The good news came on July 13. On July 23, whirlwind construction began. On August 28, the basic units—a thousand buildings—were completed. Camp Greene took its name from George Washington's most able general, Nathanael Greene, who matched wits with Cornwallis around Charlotte and came to know the Catawba River like a Carolina farm boy.

Lakewood Park

Members of the French Army Band were guests of the United Services Club in Charlotte in January 1919.

University of North Carolina at Charlotte, Atkins Library, Special Collections Unit

Covering twenty-six hundred acres, Camp Greene housed thirty thousand to sixty thousand men during its brief lifetime. Consequently, it was always larger than the town. Payroll for construction workers and demand for materials quickened the town's economy. Business proved excellent for banks, restaurants, saloons, amusement parks, churches, stores, and prostitutes. Uniformed soldiers were everywhere. The enthusiastic patriotic spirit within the town made it commonplace for Charlotteans to approach soldiers on street corners or in stores and invite them home for a meal or overnight. The townspeople put their names on a standing list offering hospitality posted at the camp. The hosts never knew beforehand who their guests were or where they were from.

Edwin Clarkson remembered approaching soldiers on a streetcar and taking them home to supper with his family on Clement Avenue. "Everybody did it. We hardly ever brought home anybody higher than a sergeant. It was an entirely different time." Families visiting their soldier sons or husbands were courted by local hostels, especially the Red Circle Inn at the corner of West Trade and Mint, which offered "proper chaperonage under the management of an experienced woman, for the wives, sisters, and mothers, sweethearts of soldiers. Soldiers with week-end pass privilege may take lodging at the Inn, where there are comfortable beds, and a limited number of cots and bath privileges."

Wounded soldiers returning from Europe came by rail to the Charlotte depot and were relayed to Camp Greene's base hospital, which housed a thousand patients. One army doctor entertained three Charlotte lady visitors to the camp and gave his definition of good coffee, which they reported back in town: "Sweet as love, black as sin, and hot as hell." Charlie Chaplin and Mary Pickford also visited Camp Greene and Charlotte promoting war bonds.

Charlotte's sunny personal and business

A horse-drawn carriage travels the well-worn trail through Camp Greene.

National Archives

During World War I, soldiers trained for European duty at Camp Greene.

Public Library of Charlotte and Mecklenburg County

climate was not matched by mild weather or good health in camp. A severe influenza epidemic left coffins of soldiers stacked at the railroad station awaiting shipment home. The winter of 1918 was the worst in Charlotte's memory. Weeks of rain, mud, and snow battered soldiers sleeping in tents with only small stoves and wool blankets to protect them.

When the war ended, "the Square was bedlam," said one resident. "Paperboys crying 'Extra' ran through the streets all over town the day of armistice. Mobs of people congregated, hollering, autos could hardly get through." People swarmed into churches to give thanks.

With the war's end, Camp Greene was gone in ninety days, several hundred buildings dismantled as quickly as they had been built. In one day, hundreds of army horses, mules, and saddles were auctioned to the highest bidders. Left behind were telltale foundation markings and a mountain of

manure at the Remount Station, where soldiers changed horses and remounted for continued duty near present Remount Road. Now, granite markers remain, and the original Dowd farmhouse (built in 1879), which was briefly Camp Greene's headquarters, is a historic site at 2216 Monument Avenue.

Camp Greene gave Charlotte an even greater economic boost than the gold-mine boom almost a hundred years earlier. The city sadly said good-bye to Camp Greene. It had planned all along for the camp to stay. The soldiers were the tangible, immediate answer to the chamber of commerce's 1905 cry to "Watch Charlotte Grow." After the war, many soldiers returned to Charlotte to visit, to marry, or to live out their lives in such a warmly generous town.

Despite the mud, war, winter, and influenza, it was somehow one of the best of times because of the singular spirit called forth among the people.

Catawba River took the trestle. At one crossing, officials parked a train engine in the middle of the river bridge hoping its weight would hold it, but all was swept away. A five-thousand-spindle mill at Monbo, near Rock Hill, was never seen again. After three days of rain, not a bridge or trestle was left crossing the Catawba. The flood crested fifty-five feet above the river's normal height.

Newspapers reported on July 20 that "the body of J. N. Gordon of Charlotte, a Southern railway car inspector, was found lodged on Rock Island, seven miles below Belmont in the Catawba river. This now leaves two white men and six negroes unaccounted for as the result of the washing away of Southern's Belmont bridge Sunday afternoon. All now are given up for dead." The receding Catawba revealed 350 bales of ruined long-staple cotton valued at thirty thousand dollars piled

in a ravine near the Monbo Mills, north of Charlotte. An additional 50 bales were missing entirely.

"Buck" Duke and engineer William S. Lee stood in the rain at Great Falls watching helplessly as the brown water covered the huge generators. Only after several days did the plant dry out enough to begin working again.

When she was a girl in Davidson, Irving Harding Johnson saw the effects of the flood at close range. She went out to where the Buster Boyd Bridge had been the day before. "There were bureau dressers, tables, beds rushing down," she remembered. "It was a fearsome sight." One Charlotte resident recalled not seeing his father for three weeks after the flood. "We were in Little Switzerland and all the bridges along the Catawba were out. Finally he came up on horseback to

After the flood, only the rails and ties were left suspended high above the trees for several hundred feet on the Southern Railway near Old Fort.

Duke Power Archives

us from Marion." Another remembered, "I didn't see the flood but we felt its effects. We had a houseguest who stayed forever because she couldn't get home."

Henrietta Wilkinson, author of *The Mint Museum of Art in Charlotte,* was in the last train to cross the trestle before it collapsed. "Luck-ily we children didn't know it." And Ralph E. Hood, growing up at the foot of Crowders Mountain, remembered hearing about the river and the danger: "My brother and I were dying to go over and see, but Pa wouldn't let us."

The Armon Cotton Mills on the Catawba at Mount Holly
The upper view shows the mill before the flood. The lower view shows the site swept clean by the floodwaters, leaving only twisted machinery and piles of sand. Seven-hundred bales of cotton were lost with the cotton warehouse.

Duke Power Archives

Too Many Words

T. L. Kirkpatrick put on his best suit one spring morning in 1916. After all, it was going to be quite a day. As mayor, his was the task of introducing the speaker, President Woodrow Wilson, to the people of Charlotte on May 20, that first day of celebrative honor. Lawyer Kirkpatrick was a small man, long on words and short on humility. Folks said he could strut sitting down. Thousands had come from outlying towns to see Wilson, a former student at Davidson College. Kirkpatrick began his introduction. In her book, *My Memoir*, Mrs. Wilson wrote:

> In May, 1916, we went to Charlotte, North Carolina for the celebration of the anniversary of the Mecklenburg Declaration of Independence. It was a boiling hot day; one of those sudden descents of summer that cause unexpected discomfort. The ceremonies were in the open to accommodate the thousands of people from all over the State who had poured into the town. A large wooden platform or stage had been put up, with no cover, not even an awning; and rows of chairs placed to seat the official party, all facing a blazing afternoon sun. The hapless Marine Band had been summoned from Washington, and they wore the thick, red uniform coats of winter weight. It was terrible for them. Fortunately for me, I was wearing a thin white dress and a large straw hat—which did afford a little shelter.
>
> The front of the platform was draped in bunting, and a table, with ice water and glasses, placed before the Mayor of Charlotte who was to make the address of welcome and introduce the President.
>
> This dignitary arose—and I can see him now as though it were yesterday! He was about five feet high and wore a frock coat which must have belonged originally to an ancestor who was a giant; for the tails of the coat just escaped the ground, and the sleeves were of proportionate length. Nothing daunted by this handicap, the little man began, and as he warmed to his subject the sleeves were pulled above his elbows, the coattails would be lifted nearly as high as his head, and after holding them there a few minutes the hands would release them only to come down with forensic force on the table where the pitcher and glasses would jangle their contribution to the uproar. On and on he went—thirty, forty, fifty minutes—when suddenly the members of the Marine Band began to succumb. They dropped like flies, and the valiant little Boy Scouts tried to lift and carry them to some blessed shade.
>
> The speaker would look at the prostrate forms, but, with a debonair flirt of his coattails, attack another paragraph of the pages of typed matter before him. Hardly had the band received first aid when women all around me began to faint, and the Scouts, with perspiration pouring down their boyish faces, came to tender their services.
>
> Up to this time it had been funny, but I suddenly found myself as hot from anger as I had been from the sun; for the man had no right to punish other people so. At last he stopped, for lack of breath, I think, and sat down, looking more like a vanquished prize fighter than anything I can think of, for both cuffs had slipped their moorings, and one was open. His hair was standing on end, and the necktie had sought sanctuary under his left ear.
>
> My husband's address was calm and mercifully short.

Other reporters said Kirkpatrick had been asked to spare the president, who was not feeling well, and to fill up some of his time. In

Woodrow Wilson in Charlotte, May 20, 1916

Public Library of Charlotte and Mecklenburg County

either case, he amply performed his duty.

Kirkpatrick will long be remembered for his introduction that day. What has been forgotten is his push as alderman for building permanent streets, sidewalks, and school-houses for Charlotte. This effort—plus his statewide campaign for connecting roads between counties and adjoining states—won him the chairmanship of the North Carolina Bureau of Highways in 1918. Governor Thomas Bickett was not much interested in roads, so Kirkpatrick organized a car caravan without Bickett's endorsement. As a result, Kirkpatrick became the father of the fifty-million-dollar bond issue. He was not alone. Syd Alexander, J. S. Myers, George Stephens, and later Cameron Morrison (all of Charlotte) joined the people of North Carolina in supporting road improvement. The impassable roads throughout the region precipitated such concentrated action.

Politics and Poetry

Cameron Morrison carried his ivory-tipped walking stick with him to the governor's mansion in 1921. He was the third Charlottean who had made it east as governor, following Nathanael Alexander in 1805 and Zebulon B. Vance in 1862, reelected in 1864 and again in 1876. Nothing equalled the bitter battle to get Morrison elected. Charlotte Judge Heriot Clarkson was campaign manager, and was later appointed by Morrison to the North Carolina Supreme Court. "Cam" was tough and determined. The *Observer* noted, "Few Carolinians have been so extravagantly praised or so bitterly assaulted in their lifetimes."

Morrison staked his campaign on better roads and schools for the people. "I promised them the roads would come to them especially in places where they had no railroads. I think they believed me," he said. He also opposed women's suffrage.

Morrison was born in Richmond County in 1869. He practiced law in Rockingham during the volatile period when white supremacists and the Red Shirts kept the upper hand with threats and intimidation. Although elected mayor of Rockingham, he decided to move to Charlotte in 1907 to practice law.

After much persuasion, Morrison finally agreed to run for governor in 1920. His winning slogan—"From the ploughshare to the mansion"—capitalized on the fact that North Carolina was a predominantly rural state. Once in office, he fought wide opposition to accomplish his enormous road appropriations—amounting to sixty-five million dollars—in two sessions of the general assembly. North Carolina got its roads, as well as expansion of the University of North Carolina at Chapel Hill, the University of North Carolina at Greensboro, and North Carolina College for Negroes at Durham.

Cameron Morrison

North Carolina Collection, UNC Library, Chapel Hill

Morrison returned to Charlotte to practice more law and politics. His speeches often rang with the poetry of Robert (he called him "Bobby") Burns. Once, Morrison exhorted, "May I appeal for men and women from every class to study Burns' poetry and Jefferson's politics, and come together for a determined defense of representative, democratic government against every group flying a hostile banner." He served in both the United States House of Representatives and the Senate. In his eighties, he described his long career: "The Lord has just used a knotty-headed old Scotsman who uses his fists, instead of a standard kind of statesman." His large, working farm and mansion, Morrocroft (built in 1926 on Sharon Road), covered the present Foxcroft, Barclay Downs, Southpark, and more. A group of 25 tenant families tended his 750 head of cattle, 300 pigs, 4,000 turkeys, and 50,000 fryers to produce $250,000 in meat, eggs, butter, and milk each season. Today in that area, silos and remains of greenhouses coexist with suburban houses and are startling reminders of vast pastures, barns, and herds that many Charlotteans still remember.

CHARLOTTE ELECTRIC RAILWAY TIME TABLE

JNO. S. BLAKE DRUG CO FILL PRESCRIPTIONS DAY OR NIGHT
PHONE 41 AND GET IT QUICK

Published as information and not guaranteed. Subject to change without notice. It will
be found a great convenience to patrons. Keep copy in your pocket, in your office and at
home. Ask conductor for one if none in car. R. L. WOMMACK, Supt. Transportation,
Phones 90, 155, 1074-J

FIRST CAR LEAVES	LAST CAR LEAVES
Latta Park Fourth Ward....6.23 a. m.	Latta Park to Square and 1st Ward..11.59 p.m.
Hoskins............7.00 a. m.	Hoskins to Belmont............11.20 p.m.
Belmont............6.27 a. m.	Lakewood Park to Belmont............11.23 p.m.
North Charlotte............6.37 a. m.	Belmont to Square and Barn............11.59 p.m.
Chatham (Elizabeth)............6.30 a. m.	North Charlotte to Square and Barn 12.07 a.m.
Seversville............5.30 a. m.	Chatham Elizabeth............11.30 p.m.
Barn to Square............6.00 a. m.	Seversville to Square and Barn......11.42 p.m.
Square to Hoskins............6.40 a. m.	Square to Latta Park............11.50 p.m.
Square to Belmont............6.05 a. m.	S. A. L. Depot to Square and Barn..12.15 a.m.
Square to North Charlotte......6.10 a. m.	Square to Barn............12.25 a.m.

STARTING AT INDEPENDENCE SQUARE

FOURTH WARD—First car goes North
6:20 a. m. and every fifteen minutes until 12:05
a. m. First car goes South at 6:35 a. m. and
every fifteen minutes until 12:20 a. m.

FIRST WARD—First car goes East at 6:25
a. m. and every fifteen minutes until 12:10 a. m.
First car goes South at 6:40 a. m. and every
fifteen minutes until 12:25 a. m., except at
11:40 p. m. Last car South goes to barn only.

NORTH MYERS—First car goes North
6:30 a. m. and every fifteen minutes until
11:15 p. m. First car goes South 6:45 a. m.
and every fifteen minutes until 11:30 p. m.
Last car to barn only.

NORTH CHARLOTTE—First car leaves
6:10 a. m.; next car 6:40 a. m.; next car 7:02
a. m. and every fifteen minutes until 11:47 p.m.

HOSKINS—First car goes West 6:40 a. m.
and every twenty minutes until 11:20 p. m.
Saturday nights until 11:40 p. m.

BELMONT—First car goes East 6:05 a. m.,
second car 6:40 and every twenty minutes until
11:40 p. m.

ELIZABETH—First car goes East 6:15
a. m.; second car 6:35 a. m., and every twenty
minutes until 11:15 p. m. Saturday nights
11:35 p. m.

SEVERSVILLE—First car goes West 6:15
a. m.; second car 6:45 a. m. and every twenty
minutes until 11:35 p. m. Saturday nights
11:45 p. m.

SUMMARY—North Myers cars leave Square
on the hour, quarters and halves.

FOURTH WARD—5, 20, 35 and 50 minutes after the hour.

FIRST WARD—10, 25, 40 and 55 minutes
after the hour.

HOSKINS-BELMONT—On the hour 20
and 40.

NORTH CHARLOTTE—2, 17, 32 and 47
minutes after the hour.

ELIZABETH—15, 35 and 55 after the hour.

SEVERSVILLE—5, 25 and 45 after the
hour.

Above:
Looking west on West Trade Street, with Hotel Charlotte on the left and Presbyterian churchyard on the right

Charlotte Landmarks Commission

Left:
Streetcar schedule

Queens College

Right:
Looking south on North Tryon Street around the turn of the century

Courtesy of Louis Asbury, Jr.

Above:
Not everyone had a car.
Mail delivery was slow but gave personal attention.

Left:
North Tryon Street looking south,
with Independence Building in the
background, c. 1920s

—

Charlotte Landmarks Commission

Auto excursion in the mountains

—

University of North Carolina at Charlotte,
Atkins Library, Special Collections Unit

First Ward students, 1912

———

Courtesy of Fred Hasty

First Ward School classroom, 1920

———

Courtesy of Louis Asbury, Jr.

Charlotte Open Air School, 1920s
Cold air was believed to be good for students.

Public Library of Charlotte and Mecklenburg County

Graduating class of Charlotte University School in 1911

Public Library of Charlotte and Mecklenburg County

Four views of Charlotte's May 20 celebration, c. 1900

The view below shows a crowd gathered before the courthouse on South Tryon Street, while the view at upper right shows young ladies of Charlotte dressed to represent the states.

Courtesy of Mildred Morse McEwen

Is There A Doctor?

Annie Lowrie Alexander of Charlotte was a doctor—the first woman doctor licensed to practice medicine south of the Potomac. If Mecklenburg was ever without a Dr. Alexander, it was for so brief a time no one noticed. But everyone noticed Dr. Annie. She was a historic first, which certainly would not have surprised her ancestor, fiery Alexander Craighead.

She returned to Charlotte after medical education in Philadelphia and New York. In 1885, Dr. Annie and ninety-nine men listened as their scores were read out from the Maryland Board of Medical Examiners. Hers were the highest. Later in North Carolina at a meeting, the chairman of the state medical society asked all men who wished to join to come forward and sign the book. Her father, Dr. John B. Alexander, promptly escorted Annie to the front to sign. She practiced a year in Charlotte before she received her first income from her practice—two dollars.

She served on the staffs of Saint Peter's and Presbyterian hospitals, was physician for Presbyterian (later Queens) College, and was appointed acting assistant surgeon at Camp Greene during World War I. She practiced in Charlotte until 1929 and assumed the responsibility for educating nine nieces and nephews. Thanks to her gentle manner, ability, and community roots, she succeeded in an era when most women found lofty goals beyond their reach. Her career began just as the first black physicians came to practice in Charlotte in the late 1880s.

Few women of the period in the South achieved any professional status. Even the prospects for women teachers were bleak. "The injustice of man has so ordered matters that work and labor when performed by women is much more poorly paid than that of men, even though equally well performed

Dr. Annie Alexander

Public Library of Charlotte and Mecklenburg County

both in quantity and quality," reported *Hale's Weekly*. "Of course, this is wrong, radically wrong, and of course ought not to be so."

In the mid-1880s, no white medical school existed in North Carolina when Dr. Paul Barringer, physician at Davidson College, established a private one in that town. It was not connected with the college, but the next college physician, Dr. John P. Munroe, bought the medical school and moved the entire medical student body to Charlotte. The new quarters of North Carolina Medical College at 229 North Church Street allowed for clinical teaching allied with town hospitals. They contained a dispensary, separate waiting rooms for black and white patients, laboratories, classrooms, a dissecting room, and a large lecture hall.

The Carnegie Foundation, in evaluating the college in 1910, reported a lack of adequate facilities. Local legend says the evaluators came on a day when the college was closed, with key equipment put away in closets. The college packed up in 1913 and transferred to the Medical College of Virginia in Richmond. The college graduated 340 doctors in twenty-one years.

One of Charlotte's best-known turn-of-the-century physicians was Dr. F. O. Hawley, a native Scot and graduate of the University of Edinburgh. A striking, patriarchal figure with a long, flowing beard, he drove a carriage pulled by two Shetland ponies and unceasingly attended the poor, even getting out of a sick bed to answer calls. If necessary, he could send patients to one of several hospitals. Behind Saint Peter's Catholic Church on South Tryon, the Sisters of Mercy from Belmont, North Carolina, organized in 1906 a twenty-five-bed hospital, which later moved to East Fifth and became Mercy Hospital. The nearby early Presbyterian Hospital at · West Trade and Mint streets formed, in conjunction with the college and with Saint Peter's Hospital, what might be called Charlotte's first medical center.

Another prominent uptown physician was Dr. Charles E. Walker, a native of the Steel Creek community and a Davidson graduate. Walker graduated from medical school at the University of Maryland in 1891. He and his family lived at 308 North Brevard Street. He had his office over Tryon Drug at 200 North Tryon, close to uptown physicians' offices.

Meanwhile, the country doctor, like the minister with his small, scattered churches, spent the greater part of his time in the saddle or carriage. He was often summoned twenty or thirty miles to see a patient. Since country doctors were usually able to attend a patient only once or twice, they gave instructions on how to manage in their absence. Several prominent rural doctors traveled perimeters that were well-known. One example was Dr. Lester Walker Hunter, an alumnus of Bellevue Medical College, who continued at the age of seventy-six to practice in the Sardis community.

Dr. L. B. Newell from Newell taught seven years at North Carolina Medical College. He practiced medicine in the county for sixty-three years and was chief of general practice when Memorial Hospital opened in 1940. The village of Newell bears the name of his uncle, old "Squire" Newell, who bred mules and ran a "jay-pee" court in the office of his barn, where he played a little politics on the side. Newell was like many rural outposts circling Charlotte. Connected to Charlotte by a well-traveled farm road and the railroad, it consisted of a post office, a general store, some houses, a depot, and a neighborhood doctor.

Similar but larger depot communities were Matthews, Pineville, Huntersville, and Davidson, villages that usually had a physician and housed an all-important cotton mill or cotton gin or sawmill. Carts and wagons piled with cotton circled the town of Matthews waiting to have their precious loads ginned, then sold to be shipped at the depot. Just up West John Street from Matthews's cotton gin was the 1890s Queen Anne–style house of Dr. Thomas Neely Reid, who practiced medicine for fifty-seven years from his home. His practice served not only neighbors, but people in other remote farmhouses and villages of Mecklenburg, Union, and Cabarrus counties, as well as upper South Carolina. In their rural travels, Reid and other country doctors saw that despite the hifalutin' progress going on in Charlotte, these outlying cotton farms fed the backbone economy and rural character of the region as late as the 1940s.

Myers Park — An Extravagant Idea

Two sign painters could be kept busy a week noting and posting all the Charlotte places on which George Stephens left his mark. He began business in 1896 with Walter Brem and Brem's father in insurance. Next, Stephens, banker and boyhood friend Word Wood, and F. C. Abbott organized Southern States Trust Company. This soon became American Trust Company, with Stephens as president in 1901. American Trust Company was a forerunner of North Carolina National Bank, now NationsBank.

In 1910, Stephens fleshed out a longtime dream for his father-in-law, John Springs Myers. Myers was a legislator who pushed

for early macadam roads in Charlotte. He was the first to give school and park sites in Cherry, a residential community of blacks. Cherry was located between uptown Charlotte and the Myers family's farmhouse in what was to become Myers Park. Many households in Cherry supplied servants to the big houses uptown and those to come in Myers Park, where "a man and a cook" were considered bare essentials.

The idea for Myers Park took shape on Myers's eleven-hundred-acre plantation. Under the direction of Stephens Company, well-known city planner John Nolen and landscape designer Earl Draper—both of Cambridge, Massachusetts—laid out parks, wide, treeless lots on gracefully curving streets with 100-foot rights of way. The main boulevards were 110 feet wide, with a street-car median. At the time, it was called the best

Houses were springing up on the former cotton fields by 1915.

Public Library of Charlotte and Mecklenburg County

Crew moving trees into Myers Park

Public Library of Charlotte and Mecklenburg County

development south of Baltimore.

Along the streets and within the homesites, Stephens transplanted in regular rows large willow oak trees retrieved from fields around the county. Stephens's men would knock on the door of a farmhouse and ask to buy particular trees. Folks were happy to sell, but thought the whole idea mighty peculiar. "Buck" Duke felt small saplings would take

too long to develop on the broad, bare pasture turned into a prestigious neighborhood. He sent the foreman from his New Jersey estate to show the local people how to move large trees successfully. Such efforts naturally focused attention on the new Myers Park. But many people contended that nobody wanted to live that far out of town.

Stephens also urged relocating Queens

College (then called Presbyterian College for Women) from College Street out to Myers Park. Other neighborhoods wanted Queens, but Stephens and several benefactors donated land for the campus, and Myers Park residents subscribed eight thousand dollars toward early construction in 1912. Stephens's idea was to have a boys' school also, so he convinced the well-known Horner Military School to move from Oxford, North Carolina. Another savvy relocation into Myers Park was the McManaway-Wittkowsky House, which Dr. McManaway moved from the declining glory of West Trade Street.

The streetcar came directly to Myers Park through the stone entrance at Fourth Street and Hawthorne. Every thirty minutes, it carried businessmen and servants to and from uptown past Queens College to the end of the line at the Horner Military School, current site of the Myers Park Country Club. There, the streetcar conductor reversed the seats to

Horner Military School moved to 2501 Roswell Avenue in Charlotte's Myers Park about 1920.

Public Library of Charlotte and Mecklenburg County

Queens College, formerly Charlotte's uptown Presbyterian College for Women, moved to Myers Park in 1916 on land donated by the Stephens Company.

Inset: Queens student, 1920s

Stone entrance to Myers Park at Hawthorne and Fourth streets,
showing fledgling tree plan and streetcar median at the beginning of the original Queens Road

Public Library of Charlotte and Mecklenburg County

Residence of F. M. Simmons
Planner John Nolen and Earl Draper offered custom landscaping with each Myers Park house.

Myers Park Homeowners Association

Opposite page:
Early mansion along Myers Park's Hermitage Road:
Philadelphia's "society" architect, Charles Barton Keen, designed
this home in 1927 for Charles and Laura Cannon Lambeth.

Courtesy of Tom Hanchett

face forward again, and the streetcar and passengers then returned. People visiting Charlotte took the streetcar to Myers Park for entertainment. The Stephens Company bore the expense of the streetcar, utilities, street development, and landscaping—six hundred thousand dollars on public improvements by 1921, a staggering sum in that day, according to *Legacy: The Myers Park Story*, a history of Myers Park.

Myers Park was so successful that a parallel development piggybacked on the model. Another developer opened Hermitage Court, whose stone gates proclaimed "Ye Easte Gayte" on one end and "Ye Weste Gayte" on the other. Competitive E. D. Latta, developer of Dilworth, refused to be outdone and hired the firm of Frederick Law Olmstead, Jr., to design some handsome, curving streets as a stylish, comparable addition for Dilworth. Myers Park was a separate incorporated town, but the problems of growth and government left her wishing for city advantages of police and fire protection. The suburban governing body passed an ordinance requesting to become part of Charlotte.

Stephens's influence was exerted in matters such as the Seventh Street Rose Garden, a North Carolina route for the Blue Ridge Parkway, and Kanuga, an Episcopal conference center in the North Carolina mountains. For a while, he and Word Wood owned the *Charlotte Observer* and used it widely to promote Myers Park. He also helped organize the Charlotte Country Club on W. D. Rock's farm. But Stephens was proudest of Independence Park, bounded by Seventh and Hawthorne (and later Independence Boulevard). Buying up tracts of land in the Elizabeth neighborhood for a park and garden seemed an odd and extravagant idea. For Charlotte, Myers Park itself was a wildly ambitious scheme. But most of Charlotte's favorite, best-used places, including Freedom Park and Latta Plantation Park were originally thought to be very odd and extravagant ideas.

Unfortunately, one extremely solid idea was lost in the civic chaos following World War I. In 1917, city planner John Nolen, so successful with Myers Park and other American towns and neighborhoods, was asked to draw a city plan for Charlotte. The plan he designed featured a bracelet of urban creekside parks, a belt road, school-site designations, and an urban civic center. Had it been adopted, Charlotte would have been quite a different place.

*Growing up
in Dilworth and Fourth Ward,
c. 1900*

Courtesy of
Mildred Morse McEwen

First Presbyterian Church, West Trade Street

Courtesy of Mildred Morse McEwen

Housekeeper (left) and residence of William M. Morse family at 605 North Poplar Street in Fourth Ward, c. 1900

Courtesy of Mildred Morse McEwen

Dr. and Mrs. Charles E. Walker on the steps of their home at 308 North Brevard Street, early 1900s

Courtesy of Claire Trexler

The family of W. A. and Nancy Wilhelm Frye, with Mrs. Frye's two sisters (center back)

Courtesy of W. G. Frye

Top right:
Charlotte picnickers in the mountains

University of North Carolina at Charlotte, Atkins Library, Special Collections Unit

Bottom right:
Margaret S. Bryan's wedding party, 1905

Courtesy of Kenneth Long

*Two views of the
Charlotte
Fire Department
behind city hall
in 1916*

Fire Masters and Hand Engines

Fighting a fire at a
Charlotte business

Courtesy of
Mildred Morse McEwen

The entire town mourned the death of
Fire Chief J. H. Wallace at his funeral
procession in July 1914.

Courtesy of Jo Hackney Huntington

Organized firefighters have battled Charlotte's flames since the 1840s. The engine company consisted of part-time firemen or volunteers who hurriedly left their jobs to answer a fire bell's insistent ringing. Five appointees called "Fire Masters" supervised operations that included a hook-and-ladder company beginning in 1861. The early force had three volunteer companies—the Hornet Steam Fire Engine and Hose Company, the Neptune Hand Engine Company, and the Independent Hook and Ladder Company. The Neptune was black, while the Hornet and Independent companies were white. The second fire station, which was built in 1908 to serve Dilworth and southeast areas, still stands on South Boulevard and houses a business. One of the most memorable fires in Charlotte's history was the 1922 fire that destroyed the city's most elegant office building, the six-story Trust Building at 212 South Tryon (where the Johnston Building is today). Built in 1902, it housed the Academy of Music, Charlotte's foremost entertainment hall for live shows and films, as well as other offices, including those of the eminent Southern Power Company. A big-city visitor found the 1,350-seat Academy of Music at its opening to be "a very handsome place. The interior has a metropolitan tone and bears no visible blemish." In 1954, the Charlotte Armory Auditorium burned. It had been built in four months in breakneck preparation for a Confederate reunion in 1929. The site now hosts another large hall, the Park Center, beside Central Piedmont Community College.

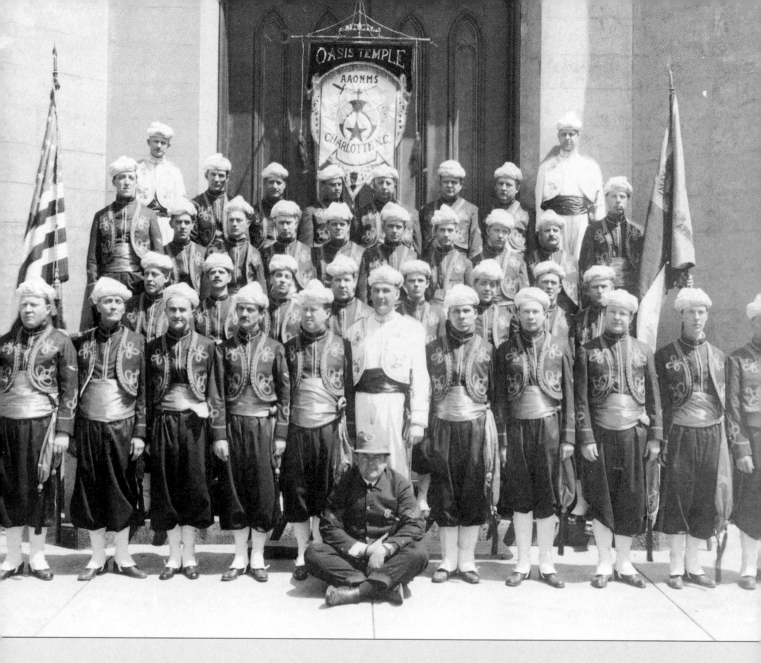

Above:
**Oasis Temple,
the Charlotte chapter of the
Ancient Arabic Order,
Nobles of the Mystic Shrine**

Left:
**Shriners Parade
on West Trade Street, 1916**

Public Library of Charlotte and
Mecklenburg County

Above:
Parade float, c. 1920

Public Library of Charlotte and
Mecklenburg County

Right:
*Hornets Nest Riflemen on
parade*

Courtesy of Mildred Morse McEwen

Growing In A Good Time

Charlotte landmarks are clearly visible in this view looking north from the courthouse on South Tryon, 1899.

Business was good as Charlotte headed into the 1920s. Big, new houses rose in Dilworth and Myers Park. The downtown buildings (Johnston Building and First National Bank) were visible signs of prosperity. WBT radio—the Carolinas' first radio station and later its first television station—broadcast the good news from offices in the Independence Building above the Square. Wherever the streetcar line stopped, a subdivision sprouted. Some were mainly residential, like Elizabeth or Chatham Estates on The Plaza, but many were close to a mill, like Piedmont Park, Hoskins, and North Charlotte. A Baltimore visitor was so impressed with Charlotte, he declared, "Change is the breath of its nostrils." Others were not so impressed. Charlotte's David Ovens had the audacity to ask Enrico Caruso to perform here in 1920. At the train, hundreds greeted Caruso, who said Charlotte was the smallest city in which he had ever sung.

For those who did not care or come to see, Clarence Kuester went to tell them about Charlotte. He was Charlotte's number-one booster. He went wherever anyone would

listen. Kuester knew healthy, growing cities did not just happen. He had watched members of the Greater Charlotte Club (later the Charlotte Chamber of Commerce) make things happen in 1905. "We brought the Norfolk and Southern Railroad in here and had lots of trouble doing it," he recalled. "We had to raise $50,000 before they would come. We got the old Horner Military School to come here from Oxford and raised $15,000 to help put up the building [currently condominiums beside the Myers Park Country Club]. We got the first permanent pavement in town, from Seventh Street to the YMCA on Tryon and one block each way on Trade. We got the Piedmont and Northern Railroad in here too. If Mr. Duke was alive he'd tell you so. He sold the people on it, and put up most of the money. . . . Why one night we had a meeting in the Selwyn ballroom with five telephones in there. They'd call up people they knew and sell them stock. . . . We got up $100,000 for the railroad right here. . . . It would take the whole *Charlotte News* to put down the names of the men who helped build this town."

Right:
This early 1900s street scene shows the dome of the former First Baptist Church, now Spirit Square Center for the Arts.

Courtesy of Frank Thies, Jr.

Things were obviously happening—the Charlotte Hotel, the Ford Motor Company plant, Central High School, a new Armory Auditorium, the Carolina Theater, a new stadium, and an airport under construction. The best evidence, however, was the opening in 1927 of the Charlotte branch of the Federal Reserve Bank of Richmond on the twentieth floor of the First National Bank Building. This was solid proof of Charlotte's stature, her success, and her future possibilities. It was the kind of evidence pragmatic Charlotteans had always understood.

Meanwhile, young Jack Wood rode the streetcar with his father on Sunday afternoons to his two favorite places, "to Myers Park and then to Lakewood, the amusement park way out Tuckaseegee. They were the farthest places you could go." His father was a carpenter from Randolph County and later a contractor. They lived on Fifth Street where Central Piedmont Community College is today. The Memorial Stadium site at that time was the city reservoir. "Then they drained it and it became a meadow," Wood noted. "We kids got rabbit tobacco there, rolled our own, dammed up the spring at the culvert under Fox Street and skinny-dipped in a swimming hole we made by damming the spring as it ran down toward Sugar Creek. My uncle kept his pigs where Park Center is now." Wood watched Charlotte grow. He planned for college, but during his senior year at Alexander Graham (then a high school), an unexpected event altered everyone's plans.

Charlotte Drum Corps, with the rallying slogan "Watch Charlotte Grow" visible on the bass drum to the left

Public Library of Charlotte and Mecklenburg County

Depression Too Well Remembered

A door-to-door photographer persuaded mothers to have their children's pictures snapped in 1928. Claire Courtney took the offer.

Courtesy of Mrs. Hugh Ashcraft

In early October 1929, a few indicators of change appeared in the Charlotte Observer. Cannon's chain of mills began to close four days each workweek due to a depressed textile market. On Wall Street, the stock market, which had been petulant for months, sank and rallied, then appeared stable. But on Black Thursday, it reeled. On October 31, the New York Stock Exchange suspended trading for two and a half days. Panic selling precipitated a tidal wave of losses. Depositors lined up outside banks to withdraw whatever money they could grasp.

Passersby saw the lines and became frightened. They also rushed to stand in line.

Richard Bigger of Charlotte was an investment banker for R. S. Dickson Company in its New York office in 1929. He had advised his customers earlier to sell their stocks. Because of the solvency of North Carolina bonds and the market conditions, some people were able to buy when others were frantically selling. Suicides were frequent. Bigger saw a man jump to his death on the street next to the Morgan Guaranty Trust in New York.

Streetcars on East Trade, soon to be replaced in 1938 by city buses

Charlotte Landmarks Commission

Depression Hits Home

Throughout the South in the spring of 1929, labor-union organizers had moved into mill towns to unionize mill workers. *Time* magazine reported, "Textile mill strikes flared up last week like fire in broom straw across the face of the industrial South."

During the days immediately following the October stock-market crash, Charlotte was temporarily diverted by a sensational murder trial that commanded national attention. A strike disturbance at Gastonia's Loray Mill had resulted in the bullet-in-the-back murder of Chief of Police D. A. Aderholt. One juror in the trial went berserk, causing a mistrial and a change of venue that put the case in Mecklenburg County Court.

Seven men (a union organizer and six labor leaders) were charged with second-degree murder. An all-white male jury (nine farmers among them) was scrutinized by a national labor group that represented labor interests in the North and South. The labor group included seven white men, two black men, two white women, and a boy. During the trial, the League of Women Voters took a vocal public stand asking for women jurors. At the time, women did not sit on juries.

In a tense courtroom drama, the solicitor fell to the floor acting out the chief's death. He prayed and sobbed and eulogized Aderholt with biblical incantations. The defendants were convicted. Several—said to be Communists—skipped bond and fled to Russia.

In Charlotte, spectators had to return to the mills and the tough business of personal financial disaster. As the ripple effect of the Depression made its way south, J. B. Efird, prominent Charlotte merchant, tried to see a hopeful side. "We should be better off down here because there ought to be more money for home enterprises," he said. But before

long, hardly anyone had money.

According to Earl Draper, land values dropped so low that a block on East Third Street right off Tryon brought a high bid of two hundred dollars at a forced sale. "The judge refused to allow the sale, as he said it was ridiculously low and they would have to wait until conditions improved," Draper noted.

Charlotte streets were like most of the nation—soup lines at the Salvation Army, people everyone knew selling apples on the corner of Trade and Tryon. Even with hamburger costing three pounds for a quarter, many people lived on potatoes and turnips. The lucky ones caught rabbits for food. The cheapest place to eat in Charlotte was the Canary Cottage—fifteen cents for a hamburger and a nickel for a Coke. Kress's sold lunch with a drink for a quarter. Charlotteans rented out rooms in their houses or moved in with relatives to share expenses. "Everybody cut his scale of living down as low as he could cut. We were all in the same boat," one resident recalled.

It was the era of Kate Smith, Boris Karloff, Adolphe Menjou. H. V. Kaltenborn barked the news. Most Americans could afford no romance in their lives; but they wanted it, so they read avidly of kings and queens and debutantes' elopements. Newspapers wrote in detail of society events and people who received five-year attendance pins.

By the time the Emergency Bank Bill was introduced in Congress in March 1933, nearly a quarter of the entire national work force was unemployed, and 5,504 banks had closed. In Charlotte, a run on deposits caused the First National Bank to close the elegant brass door of its brand-new twenty-one-story skyscraper. Those were the "most closed doors Charlotte has ever seen," said a resident. He remembered the crowd of people gathered around the door. An irate depositor got his shotgun and demanded his money.

Frank Sherrill and
Susan Frye Alexander
in 1913 at the "original S & W"
on West Trade Street

Courtesy of W. G. Frye

J. T. Hasty Groceries sold
necessities to neighbors at
Twelfth and Davidson streets.
Mill families and other workers
did most of their shopping in
similar one-room neighborhood
stores.

Courtesy of Fred Hasty

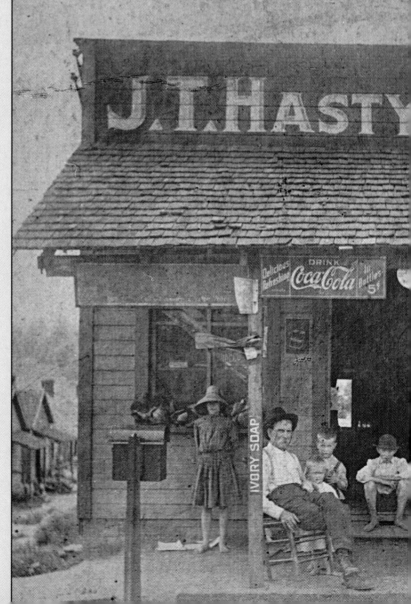

The original Brockmann
Book Store on South Tryon Street

Public Library of
Charlotte and Mecklenburg County

Neither the Mechanics and Farmers Bank nor the Independence National Bank re-opened after a bank holiday when banks closed because they couldn't meet depositors' demands. Charlotte National (now Wachovia), Commercial National (now NationsBank), Union National (now First Union), and the installment-loan banks survived.

A *Charlotte Observer* description told how H. M. Victor, stern president of Union National, impressed his skittish depositors. "The stalwart Mr. Victor wanted to make certain that [closing] didn't happen to the bank he had founded. Sitting in hat and coat at his rolltop desk just inside the bank's lobby [on the corner of Fourth and Tryon streets], he would occasionally summon one of the waiting depositors and ask what he or she needed the money for. The rest of the time he simply glared at each of them. His iron gaze and indomitable presence was enough to persuade many people they didn't need their money after all."

In those days, Jack Wood was neither a depositor nor an investor. Like most seniors in his high-school class in the spring of 1930, he looked for a job instead of a college. "I was lucky," he said. He found one with a tire company, then became a traveling clothes salesman to New England prep schools. He came back home and throughout the thirties sold made-to-measure clothes out of a satchel anywhere he could find a customer, whether it was "on the mezzanine of the Carolina Theater, the lobby of the old YMCA, in filling stations, drugstores. I showed swatches and took a $5 deposit on a $23.50 suit. Seersucker was only $8.95."

Black businessman Thad Tate was able to survive also. "When I had hair, he used to cut mine," one balding Charlotte businessman confessed. Tate was Charlotte's foremost barber downtown for over fifty years. He came from Morganton to Charlotte in the

1890s, and no large social affair was complete without him to welcome the guests. He later became a stockholder and director of a large publishing company and invested widely in real estate. At one time, his shop was in the Central Hotel, and later on East Trade next to a fruit stand run by a family from Greece. Still later, it was on East Fourth. In the narrow shop with four or five chairs, black barbers shaved and tonsured all the bankers, doctors, and lawyers in town. "An excellent barber, Tate could talk knowledgeably about anything," David Ovens wrote.

The Charlotte school system's budget diminished by half between 1931 and 1934, and the school term was reduced to eight months for the first time since 1882. Educator Harry Harding recorded, "Growth was halted and many advances wiped out."

And out in rural communities surrounding Charlotte, large farm families held on, raising their food, patching clothes, and rarely seeing hard cash money. If you lived near the road, hardly a day went by without somebody coming to the door for a handout. Jim Dumbell recalled,

The regulars talked fast and had a very sad story. The others just asked for work and were obviously embarrassed. You felt awfully sorry for them. We didn't have any work to be done, but Mother always found something in the kitchen for them. They came year round, but you felt sorriest for them on the cold days of winter. I remember a heavy cardigan Dad seldom wore. He didn't miss it for a year. When finally he asked where it was, I blurted, "Mother gave it to somebody at the door." He didn't get mad. People helped each other. The embarrassment was on both sides. You'd say, "We've got more of this than we can use," or, "These apples will go bad," or "So-and-so has outgrown this and I wondered. . . ." You'd see a family's household furniture stacked high but neatly on the sidewalk, naked for all to see. They had been evicted for not paying the rent.

On the old Harper place out Monroe Road, a Canadian company operated the Bennett Gold Mine near McAlpine Creek. But the low-grade ore yielded little profit from the rocky, red land. West of town, a heavy rainstorm broke the dam at Charlotte's favorite playground, Lakewood. There were no funds to repair it, so Lakewood closed and never reopened.

When President Franklin Roosevelt took office on March 4, 1933, he immediately declared a four-day national bank holiday and called Congress into emergency session. One of the first measures was the Emergency Banking Relief Bill. It provided for the reopening of solvent banks and the management of those that were insolvent. FDR's famous Fireside Chats and the Hundred Days programs, such as the New Deal, were soon to follow.

The Kokenes family owned the Star Lunch, a Greek restaurant at the corner of West Trade and Graham streets that also sold homemade candies, chewing tobacco, and snuff, as well as shoeshines.

Courtesy of Steve Kokenes

America, America

The gradual migration from Europe that had flowed into and settled America for 150 years became the great migration. Two million immigrants had arrived in 1905–6 alone. America needed labor for her factories and railroad lines. She sent promoters abroad saying, "Come, the land of opportunity wants you. Anything is possible." And they came by the thousands seeking freedom and a better life. Many young men from Greece scattered throughout the land, independently working, always working. Often, they started restaurants or were cooks because that was something they could learn and work at without speaking English. It was common practice for two men to work different shifts and save money by renting one bed, in which one man slept while the other worked; when the night worker came in, he slept in the same bed the day worker vacated. "It was very hard for them," recalled Steve Kokenes, whose father opened the Star Lunch on the corner of West Trade and Graham streets in Charlotte. The Star Lunch was a restaurant as well as a store selling fruit, tobacco, and homemade candy. The people from Greece did not live in a cluster in Charlotte but scattered throughout the town living and working wherever they could.

In the age-old custom of immigrants, when they succeeded, they sent boat fare for brothers and nephews to come to America, or for young girls from Greece to come and be their wives. The Karnazes brothers came to the Square early every morning to ready their fruit stand for customers. Around 1900, they became the first Greek citizens in the town.

Constantine Kokenes was fourteen, the only boy in a family of girls in Arcadia, Greece. Word came that his uncles in America were looking for help, so he came to America. He spoke not one word of English. The small tag on a string around his neck read, "Send this boy to Charlotte." When he got off the boat in New York, he was put on a train that took him to Charleston instead. A policeman found a Greek pushcart vendor, who rerouted the boy back to Charlotte. Each day, he worked for his uncles unloading fruit and helping in the small shop beside Osborne's Corner, the northwest corner of the Square.

Before World War I, about ten Greek families lived in Charlotte. Constantine Kokenes returned to Greece at twenty-two and fought in the Second Balkan War for the freedom of Macedonia and Thrace. He mar-

ried a nineteen-year-old girl named Baseleke in Greece and brought her back to Charlotte. She was the first Greek woman in the city.

Other families came. Together, they started a church, brought a priest, and organized a Greek school (first grade through high school, teaching Greek as well as a regular curriculum) in the second story of a building on East Trade near Brevard. Later, they operated a Greek school in a borrowed classroom of a high school (Old Central, which is now Central Piedmont Community College). The Greek community grew very slowly during the thirties.

New Life For An Old Eagle

The Kokenes family lived on Graham Street behind the old Charlotte Mint, at the current site of the Charles R. Jonas Federal Court Building at 401 West Trade. Behind the mint was a ramshackle toolhouse. All the neighborhood children knew what was in it—lawnmowers, junk, and "an old busted eagle," recalled Constantine Kokenes. "We used to play on it." The large, carved eagle had flown in place over the door of the mint. More graceful than any sign, it was the assayer's symbol.

After Confederate soldiers vacated the mint, the government never minted money in the city again. It operated the mint as an assay office from 1867 to 1913. The eagle suffered badly after the assay office closed, leaving its perch for casual, irreverent storage.

Local tradition insists that Thomas Alva Edison visited the mint in the late 1890s looking for a way to extract gold from ore by using electricity. Oscar J. Thies identified himself, his brother Ernst, and Edison in a

Fascinated by minerals, Thomas Alva Edison visited Piedmont and Charlotte-area mines. The figure at center is believed to be Edison at the Haile Gold Mine.

Courtesy of Frank Thies, Jr.

photograph taken at the Haile Gold Mine in South Carolina. Edison's notebooks omit this but show that he spent considerable time in Piedmont Carolina in 1890 and 1906 looking for cobalt for his experimental storage batteries. He also searched for sources of platinum for lamp filaments and was interested in all types of metals and minerals, including gold, silver, and galena. His handwritten notebook entry from January 4, 1890, is filled with descriptions of Piedmont and mountain mining locations and mentions numerous Charlotte-vicinity mines. During his 1890 visit, Edison resided at the Buford Hotel. His wife stayed an extra ten days, enjoying the mild climate. When the news got out about Edison's plans to set up an ore-milling plant in the region, he was deluged with letters from Carolinians offering to sell him land. The plant was never built, since ore tests were unsatisfactory. With Edison's interest in gold, he was undoubtedly squired down Trade Street to visit the mint during his stay in Charlotte.

Edison was recorded in the *Charlotte News* of February 24, 1890, as being entertained at the residence of E. D. Latta. The large affair was "decidedly pleasant." Less than a year after this visit, Latta's 4C's Company signed a forty-thousand-dollar contract with the Edison General Electric Company to install trolleys in Dilworth, Latta's new suburb development.

By 1917, the mint stood empty. It was used as headquarters for the Red Cross during World War I and later as a Charlotte Women's Club meeting site. The women became quite attached to the classic building and its history. People familiar with the building and its significance were horrified when the federal government began to dismantle the mint in order to build a larger post office.

Mary Myers Dwelle had always wanted Charlotte to have an art museum. Such a historic and classic structure as the mint seemed ideal. She and other articulate spokeswomen made talks around town to spur protest and action. Alternate designs for preservation were rejected.

In retrospect, it seems like a tidy rescue. But it was at best a very near thing. Except for Dwelle and others who pushed the idea forward, the Charlotte Mint would have vanished into demolition dust like many other local landmarks. Dwelle called J. E. Steere, and together they quickly invited twelve interested friends to meet. As the workmen finished removing the roof and windows and doors, then began on the walls, the committee bought the bricks, stones, and pieces for fifteen hundred dollars, pledging to store them at some other location until something could be done. Money was gathered, largely in five- and ten-dollar donations—the country was, after all, in the midst of the Great Depression.

Architect Martin E. Boyer donated his services for the building's restoration on three acres of land in Eastover given by E. C. Griffith. Boyer offered alternate designs to adapt and preserve the mint for further use on the site. Then he marked each stone as the building was dismantled and carefully supervised its re-erection. The Federal Administration for Public Works office in Mecklenburg County approved the application for federal funds to rebuild the mint as an art museum. Much-needed jobs were created by the construction effort, although payrolls were not always met.

When the Mint Museum opened in 1936, prankish Osmond Barringer stuck a red Ford taillight in the eagle's eye. Charlotte badly needed a laugh and a victory. It was the first

The Charlotte Mint moves.
When the federal government decided to rebuild its main post office (left) on West Trade Street, it began dismantling the Charlotte Mint (right). Last-ditch efforts saved the mint for relocation east of uptown. It reopened as North Carolina's first art museum in 1936.

art museum in North Carolina, and it could not have been born in a more deprived time.

Just as singular were the births of other Depression babies—the Little Theater in 1929 and the Charlotte Symphony in 1932. It was as though these stubborn citizens refused to let physical poverty envelop the city's spirit as well. The first president of Charlotte's symphony board was a young lawyer who was also the orchestra's flutist, Spencer Bell. Bell later became a distinguished federal judge. Decades later, a symphony tuba player named James G. Martin would become governor of North Carolina.

During the Depression years, several North Carolina gold mines were reopened and operated. In 1935, 1936, and 1937, Charlotte's Rudisill Gold Mine was the state's chief producer. When operations were suspended at the Rudisill in 1938, $130,000 in pure gold (at $25 an ounce) had been produced by the mine.

Cotton-mill production, the backbone of the local economy, was, however, at a disastrous low. In the early 1930s, many mills were idle, bankrupt, or operating at less than half time. Raw cotton was plentiful, and its price was incredibly low—under a nickel a pound—but there was no money to buy it, no cash flow, no credit. Profit was nonexistent. Ben Gossett had to do something. President of Chadwick-Hoskins and a chain of thirteen cotton mills (Gossett Mills), and also president of the American Cotton Manufacturers Association, Gossett closed his Charlotte office and called on President Herbert Hoover. He asked for a temporary congressional resolution to authorize the Federal Farm Board to convey to the Red Cross 500,000 bales of cotton that it possessed. The mills would use the cotton to make cloth *at no*

profit and turn over the cloth and clothing to three million needy families on relief. The plan would create needed goods and employment. In 1932–33, this plan put more than 840,000 bales of cotton into production.

During this period, a wide effort was undertaken by the Cotton Textile Institute to promote and effect voluntary adoption by mill owners of a fifty-five-hour workweek and discontinuance of night work for women and minors. It was also a landmark period of dramatic unionization efforts. President Franklin D. Roosevelt's sweeping New Deal programs are given much credit by workers and reformers for channeling the discontent of the Depression.

The Mint Museum of Art is now located in the Eastover neighborhood.
A restored golden eagle flies above the original entrance.

From Taverns To Finger Bowls

Buford Hotel, located at 139 South Tryon Street and shown here in 1916, was where Thomas Edison and his wife stayed on a visit to Charlotte. The building was later occupied by Union National Bank and the Charlotte City Club. It is now the site of Home Federal Savings and Loan.

Practically every uptown Charlotte street used to have a hotel. All the early ones have vanished—the Mecklenburg, the Clayton, the Selwyn, the Central (later Mansion House), the Alexander, and the Sanders House in Brooklyn. But the Buford was the best. D. A. Tompkins lived there. Prominent Charlotteans ate fine meals in the place named for Colonel A. S. Buford, president of the Richmond and Danville Railroad. It dominated the corner of Fourth and South Tryon streets, closed in 1915, and was occupied by the Charlotte City Club from 1945 to 1991.

The Central Hotel threads Charlotte's past. It reigned in the railroad heyday, when "drummers" sat on the balcony or leaned outside the street floor to watch the local scene. Self-conscious Charlotte matrons picked up their petticoats and crossed over or sent servants instead to do their errands near the four-story yellow-brick hotel from 1840 to the early 1900s. In its grand ballroom, all the popular dances of the town were held. The Central was Charlotte's first real hotel. Its early patrons, transported from the depot in a lumbering three-horse bus over the rough, unpaved streets, enjoyed almost as good exercise as horseback riding.

Earlier still, George Washington slept briefly and left his powder box at Cook's Inn on West Trade. Liquid revolutionary spirits were served by none other than Patrick Jack, the father of the Mecklenburg Declaration of Independence messenger, Captain James Jack. Jack's tavern in the two-hundred block of West Trade Street took in weary, thirsty travelers along the Trading Path.

Modern hotel history began in 1907, when the Selwyn Hotel opened beside the First Presbyterian Church. It remained in business until 1960. In those early days when Charlotteans went out to eat, it was usually to a hotel, since there were few restaurants in town except for hotel dining rooms and boardinghouses. An ad for the Selwyn in 1919 advertised 150 rooms, 75 with baths, polite service, bountiful table. The rates were $1.50 and up. Luncheon was served from noon until three and cost only $.75.

When the city came into her own as a financial and textile center, the Hotel Charlotte rose in 1923 on a site on West Trade that investor E. D. Latta vehemently opposed. It was built despite his objections. With its massive, marbled lobby, lemon-scented finger bowls, and silver centerpieces, the elegant dining room hosted guests such as President and Mrs. Franklin Roosevelt, Jack Dempsey, and singer Lily Pons. Visitors and conventioneers

Visiting dignitaries were guests at the old Central Hotel, built in the 1840s and located at Tryon and Trade's southeast corner until the 1930s. Its earlier name was The Mansion House.

Selwyn Hotel opened in 1907 at the corner of Trade and North Church streets. It was Charlotte's finest at the time.

Hotel Charlotte, built on West Trade Street in the 1930s, had an elaborate ballroom, a high-columned, open lobby, and an ornamental exterior facade with symbols of Charlotte.

Courtesy of Hilda Kirsner

crowded in to hear Guy Lombardo and a variety of well-known bands play in the huge, mirror-walled ballroom. The hotel site is now a park and the Carillon Building.

Charlotte's Marriott, between the West Trade churchyard and the Square, includes the site of Cook's Inn, where George Washington stayed in 1891 and left his powder box. Across Independence Square is an angular glass upstart that handsomely reflects the high-rise images of older landmarks. The Radisson claims this key hotel corner where the Central and the Belmont hotels once sat. It is named for a seventeenth-century French fur trader, Pierre Esprit Radisson, who explored the region around Minneapolis, Minnesota, in the era when the Catawba Indians were the chief citizens of Mecklenburg. The Dunhill, at 237 North Tryon Street, is the only Charlotte hotel listed as one of the Historic Hotels of America by the National Trust for Preservation. It was designed by architect Louis Asbury, Sr., and built in 1929. In Charlotte's peak of textile prosperity, regional cotton came to town by rail and was unloaded near the current site of the 1990 Omni Charlotte Hotel, at South College and East Third streets.

Motoring to the Green Park Inn in Blowing Rock or to Linville for a 1932 golf tournament were ways some Charlotteans found temporary flight from the Great Depression.

University of North Carolina at Charlotte,
Atkins Library, Special Collections Unit

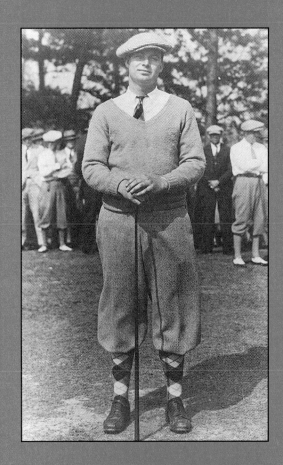

Charlotte Mayor Ben Douglas (center) visits President Franklin Roosevelt in Hyde Park, 1939. Roosevelt's programs directly aided the South.

Courtesy of Ben Douglas

Not Afraid To Fly

It was easy to get up a crowd in those days of the Depression. The town had around eighty thousand people in the 1930s. There wasn't much excitement except perhaps at the new Memorial Stadium or the Armory Auditorium next door, so when word spread that something was happening, naturally everyone went.

Gene Brown's arrival with the mail at the Charlotte airport attracted thirty thousand people in 1930. They waited into the evening, and finally, long overdue, he taxied in through the darkness with the city's first airmail delivery. More than twenty-five thousand pieces of outgoing mail had been gathered for him to airlift. From then on, it was official. Charlotte was in the air lanes, receiving mail.

Mayor Ben Douglas was determined to

keep the city aloft. "I started the airport," Douglas said. "People said, 'What's the use. We've got one.' But Cannon Airport's runway was only 3,000 feet long. Churches, schools, libraries are nice, but to build a community you have to have water and transportation. I felt we had to have it."

The airport began as a WPA project with sponsoring funds from the city. Defeated in the first try for a bond issue to buy land, proponents tried again and won the second election. W. S. Lee, Jr., headed the successful airport bond campaign. Many people still thought the airport was a harebrained idea and much too far out of town. Douglas wanted it near railroads, where early fliers could find it by following the "iron compass" of tracks. The airport—paltry and distant— opened in 1936. The terminal was little more

*World War II military brass and Mayor Ben Douglas survey airport needs
prior to the location of Morris Field in Charlotte.*

Courtesy of Ben Douglas

than a long room with a lonely row of folding seats.

Douglas admitted he was more afraid of getting in an airplane than of fighting for an airport. With an appointment in Washington, he forced himself to board the DC-3 used for early passenger service. "Like a lot of other people I was actually afraid to fly, even though I knew it meant so much to the people to have air travel here." Today's modern airport, Charlotte/Douglas International, is named for Ben Douglas.

Another controversy arose over the airport in 1940. Douglas and others sought government use of the airport for an army base during World War II. It was to be called Morris Field, after a distinguished flier of World War I, William C. Morris of Cabarrus

County. Commercial and mail planes would continue operations, with civilian flying curtailed. Civilian pilots opposed the idea. The army wasn't interested in local wrangling. Quickly, city leaders pushed the necessary action so the army could begin construction of expanded airport facilities in a cornfield and pasture plateau.

Douglas estimated about ten to fifteen thousand soldiers were at Morris Field for advance training as overseas pilots and combat crews during World War II. The Twenty-ninth Air Service Group was also trained at Morris Field to repair and service planes. Many trainees, like Hubert Smith, had no experience with planes. He ran a service station in West Virginia. They learned about each task as they went, studying each type of plane in textbooks. Smith remembered, "The people in Charlotte they told us, 'If you come and go to church, we'll feed you a Southern dinner.' I'd trade an hour in church any day for good Southern fried chicken, rice and gravy and all that stuff. They'd take us home and feed us. Then, we went to youth activity in the afternoon. Somewhere in all that process, I met Margaret." And he married her.

Another large local military installation was Camp Sutton, south of Charlotte near Monroe, a training base for United States Army engineers. At one period, it housed a thousand German prisoners of war captured in North Africa, Italy, and France.

When the war ended, the newspaper reported that "young girls, almost insane with joy, grabbed and kissed folks indiscriminately. Boys rattled cowbells. Some came with kettles and pans and any household article that would make racket. For an hour not an auto got through the square."

The bases brought business to Charlotte. In

Mass is served to an overflow crowd at Saint Peter's Catholic Church on South Tryon Street, c. 1940. Soldiers on training maneuvers attended Charlotte churches.

Courtesy of Jim Wittman

Families in homes like these along Elizabeth Avenue brought soldiers home for Sunday dinner.

Courtesy of Frank Thies, Jr.

1946, the property and improvements at Morris Field were turned over to the city, representing an investment of about six million dollars for land, barracks, hangars, mess halls, and other structures. Runways were extended for expanded airport use. A number of Charlotte homes are relocated barracks from Morris Field and are currently well camouflaged.

While Morris Field operated in town, the army also purchased the long-empty Ford Motor Company building for a Quartermaster Depot. This vast supply post for thirty-seven army stations in Virginia and the Carolinas employed twenty-five hundred civilians and an army staff of eighty. Its payroll topped three hundred thousand dollars monthly. Several interesting stories circulate about whether F. C. Abbott or Ben Douglas first brought Charlotte to federal attention as a depot site. But however it happened, it made an immense difference.

*An example of
C. C. Hook's architecture is
the Villalonga-Alexander House
at 301 East Park Avenue,
built in 1901.*

Sunbursts and Symmetry

Classical symmetrical elegance is the signature of a man named Hook, whose work is still evident throughout Charlotte. Charles Christian Hook, Charlotte's first practicing architect, moved to the city in 1891 to teach mechanical drawing at the Charlotte Graded School (now the YMCA site at the corner of East Morehead and South Boulevard). E. D. Latta's 4C's Company hired him to draw plans for some of the earliest homes in Charlotte's first streetcar subdivision, Dilworth. Charlotte's most elegant building, the Trust Building (1902) was Hook's design. Several structures remain bearing the hallmarks of his general Queen Anne design: tiny balconies, whimsical diagonal entrances, overhanging gable ends with sunburst motifs. Among them are Colonial Revival homes—the Walter Brem House (1902) at 211 East Boulevard; the Gautier-Gilchrist House (1896) at 320 East Park Avenue; the Villalonga-Alexander House (1901) at 301 East Park Avenue; and the Mallonee-Jones House (1895) at 400 East Kingston Avenue. Other significant Hook designs include the initial design of the James B. Duke (Taylor) House on Hermitage Road now called "White Oaks"; Charlotte City Hall at 600 East Trade; Charlotte Women's Club at 1001 East Morehead; and the Seaboard Passenger Depot at the corner of Twelfth and North Tryon streets at the underpass. Another of his designs, the old Commercial National Bank Building at Fourth and South Tryon, was the scene of Hook's death in 1938 by a tragic fall from the top floor.

New Faces

Following World War II, immigration opened up, and again numerous restless natives of Greece left their war-ravaged islands. Over two thousand came to settle in Charlotte.

The Greek community needed a larger church than the one on South Boulevard, so it bought the E. D. Latta–J. A. Jones mansion at 600 East Boulevard. The Greek community used the palatial home for a center and church building while constructing its new sanctuary next door. Then, in the face of disrepair and a leaking roof, it tore the old home down in the 1960s to build the present Greek community building and Greek Orthodox Cathedral. "At that time preservation efforts had not begun," Constantine Kokenes remembered. "Everybody was tearing everything down then. It did not serve our needs and would have cost a fortune to restore." The mansion's delicate tulip sconces now light the Open Kitchen restaurant. An octagonal chandelier and one of the many carved mantels from the mansion greet diners at Gus's Forty Niner Restaurant near the University of North Carolina-Charlotte.

The Jewish community was also expanding actively. "I vividly remember 700 Jewish servicemen marching into Kol Nidre service [at Temple Israel] during the war," said Sam Gittlin. "Our good friend Russell Crump recruited his entire fleet of yellow cabs in Charlotte and donated their use for transportation of the men to Jewish homes."

The Reform congregation separated from Temple Israel in 1942 to form Temple Beth El. Charlotte merchant and civic leader Sam Wittkowsky would have been distressed at the prospect of not one but two synagogues. He once said he would gladly contribute to a campaign not to build a synagogue.

Author Harry Golden taught at Temple Beth El and penned the first draft of its constitution. But Golden had an idea of his own. Support for Golden's fledgling newspaper came from within the Jewish community in 1941. Hermann E. Cohen, in *The Jews of Charlotte*, recalled his version of how the venture began:

> He [Golden] said to me: "We need a Jewish paper in this community." I asked him what we needed a Jewish paper for, because Jews around here can't even read Jewish. He said, "You are foolish as usual. It will be in English, but it will be devoted to Jewish interests—and I've got a name for it—*The Carolina Israelite*. Not only that, I already know whom I want to be associated with me in this venture besides you." "Who?" "Arthur Goodman," he replied. At that time, Arthur Goodman Sr. was a member of the North Carolina State Legislature.
>
> I spoke to Arthur Goodman, and he asked if Golden could write. I told him I really didn't know. "Tell him to write me a letter." Arthur called me up the next day and said, "Hermann, that fellow can write! I'll go into it with you. We have to furnish the money—he hasn't got any, of course."

Golden's brother contributed, too, and the *Israelite* was born.

From the Jewish brotherhood came a long list of exceptionally successful community members, including Jay Harshinger, Dannie Heineman, Leon and Al Levine, and I. D. Blumenthal. Blumenthal founded Radiator Specialty Company in 1923 in Charlotte, and later developed the North Carolina Jewish Home for the Aged, as well as Wildacres, a conference center in the North Carolina mountains. Textile industrialist Morris Speizman recalled how Ivey Stewart of

Commercial National Bank loaned him money in 1937 to purchase used equipment from a hosiery mill in Wisconsin. Speizman was the son of a Polish immigrant and new in town. The loan was the beginning of world-wide Speizman Industries.

Changing Laws and Education

World War II did not just shape Charlotte. Its spirit captured her. Although there were meat and sugar shortages and some products were entirely unavailable, spirits were high. The city had just passed a hundred thousand in population. Instead of building dams and skyscrapers, J. A. Jones Construction Company turned its efforts to government contracts and built large Liberty ships and coastal transport vessels on the Georgia coast. It also con-

structed the plant for early atomic-energy development at Oak Ridge, Tennessee. In an effort to assist the ailing economy and also decentralize defense work, the federal government targeted Southern sites and contractors.

Reminiscent of Camp Greene days, soldiers visited in Charlotte homes. A group of Charlotte doctors and nurses formed the United States Army Thirty-eighth Evacuation Hospital to support front-line aid stations during the war in North Africa and Italy.

The opening of the Barringer Hotel (now Hall House) on North Tryon Street in 1940 was a major social event and temporary diversion from military news. Just as in World War I when the army bought all the flat-weave cotton "huck" towels that Cannon Mills could produce, so Piedmont Carolina textile manufacturers supplied the World War II effort with cotton and synthetic fabrics. Barnhardt Manufacturing Company produced vast quantities of surgical bandages for battlefield wounds and developed flame-proof cotton processes. The Carolina Pied-

Black rationing board during World War II

Courtesy of D. G. Burke

*J. A. Jones Construction Company of Charlotte moved employees
to Georgia and Florida shipyards to build Liberty ships and coastal cargo vessels for the government.*

J. A. Jones Construction Company

Shipyard workers exercise.

J. A. Jones Construction Company

mont had long since firmly claimed first place, surpassing New England, as the nation's center of textile products.

Everyone knew somebody who had gone off to war, so each morning's news of Poland, France, or Berlin was personal. Hitler and Mussolini were the personal enemies of children and adults alike. To honor Charlotte's soldiers who died in battle, civic leaders raised over four thousand memorials of forty dollars each toward building a commemorative park in Charlotte. Freedom Park, they called it. Corporal Eugene Graeber, Jr.—a Charlotte soldier in General George Patton's Forty-second Mechanized Cavalry—sent his donation all the way from Germany.

United States GI's returning home from war wanted to go back to college under the GI Bill, but there was not room for them all in the state's existing colleges and universities. A move by the University of North Carolina and the Department of Public Instruction set up twelve college centers throughout the state.

School Superintendent Elmer Garinger helped set up a Charlotte center, which was to become the state's largest. In it, Bonnie Cone taught engineering math the first year and was named head of the college in 1947. Her office was the lost-and-found closet at Central High School. "We began with what we could find—a handmade table with no drawers, a used Royal typewriter and a new two-drawer file cabinet," she remembered. "We had classes from 4 P.M. on at nights. That was all the classroom time we could get."

The bootstrap operation became Charlotte College in 1949 and a four-year college in 1963. Early in the process, Dr. Bonnie saved up fifty thousand dollars toward a building. "With the help of the City School Superintendent we built a little square building on Cecil Street next to what is now CPCC [Central

Math teacher and aggressive educator Dr. Bonnie Cone's determination led to the creation of Charlotte College and its transition to UNC-Charlotte in 1965.

University of North Carolina at Charlotte, Atkins Library, Special Collections Unit

Piedmont Community College]. 'Woody' Kennedy obtained an option for us on acreage out on highway 49. In 1957, when I went to meet with the committee on accreditation, they said, 'We've never accredited any college without buildings before, but you look like you are going to do it here.' We were determined."

Carver College operated in a parallel role to Charlotte College during the postwar years. Beginning in 1949 under the Charlotte School Board, it provided a two-year college program for blacks in the Second Ward High School building in late afternoons and evenings. In 1954, Mecklenburg voted a tax to support the Charlotte Community College system, made up of Carver College and Charlotte College. In 1958, the two schools qualified for financial support under the state system and continued a dual operation.

Carver College (later Mecklenburg College) and the Industrial Education Center combined to create Central Piedmont Community College in 1963. As of 1992, CPCC, at its central campus and thirty-four satellite

Charlotte College held night classes for war veterans at Central High School (above). Subsequently, Charlotte College became UNC-Charlotte, the fourth campus of the University of North Carolina system. The Central High building now serves as part of Central Piedmont Community College.

University of North Carolina at Charlotte, Atkins Library, Special Collections Unit

Second Ward School, a black high school used for Carver College night classes

Public Library of
Charlotte and Mecklenburg County

sites, had approximately sixty thousand students. It is one of Charlotte's best success stories in concrete, economical, bootstrap help for its community's citizens.

Charlotte College became the fourth campus of the University of North Carolina in 1965, and has since been known as UNC-Charlotte. As of the fall of 1991, UNC-C enrolled approximately fifteen thousand students in its graduate and undergraduate degree programs.

Pasture and farmland became the home of the University of North Carolina at Charlotte.

University of North Carolina at Charlotte, Atkins Library, Special Collections Unit

Aerial view

University of North Carolina at Charlotte

Query's Turnout

The postal stop known as Query's Turnout was in Elam Cochrane's living room. He served as neighborhood postmaster in mid-nineteenth-century Mecklenburg, and his home and 270-acre farm are now the site of the University of North Carolina at Charlotte.

A handmade walnut desk with hinges that Cochrane likely forged himself held official postal business. Above the desk in alphabetized boxes, the letters waited to be claimed. Each day, Cochrane loaded outgoing mail into a bag, walked nearly a mile to the railroad, and hung the bag on a tall hook. The incoming train hurtled by at thirty miles an hour, caught the bag, and tossed a new sack of mail at Cochrane's feet. If neighbors failed to come by and pick up their letters from the living-room pigeonholes, on Sundays Cochrane would carry the mail to church and spread it out on a long, flat rock known as the "mail rock" at the Back Creek Associate Reformed Presbyterian Church.

Elam married Mary McGinnis in 1842, and their farmhouse stood in the trees to the left of what is now the university's main entrance. Nearby, the family kept crocks and pitchers of milk in a spring walled on three sides by moss-covered rocks. "Cool water ran continually," Mrs. Maude McLaughlin remembered, "the pitchers and crocks sitting in an orderly row in the clear flowing water. There was a brown pitcher containing milk for the day, a large crock in which the 'churning milk' was stored, fresh golden butter in a wooden bowl and a large jar of white delicious buttermilk. I particularly remember a blue flowered bowl, such as you might find today in an antique shop, containing the most delicious beet pickles ever made, and a crock that had a lid that was easy to lift containing thick fresh yellow cream for sipping and for coffee. If one was quick enough, a finger could be slipped into the cream jar while Aunt Lyde's back was turned."

Elam Cochrane's blacksmith shop and the shed where he custom-built cabinets and coffins stood near current university parking areas and the earliest classroom buildings. Gifts of 90 acres from Tom Belk and 500 acres from the county (added to 140 acres from the state) turned the Cochrane farm into a 1,000-acre spread for the new campus. In July 1965, UNC-C was designated the fourth campus of the University of North Carolina. In 1992, with numerous graduate programs long in place, UNC-C received approval for Ph.D. programs in electrical and mechanical engineering and in applied mathematics. In 1990, a new building was completed for the College of Architecture. Other notable buildings include the Applied Research Building, with space for evolving research projects, the Urban Institute, the Center for Engineering Research and Industrial Development, and the Center for Economic and Business Research. In 1986, Charlotte native and eminently successful businessman C. D. Spangler, Jr., moved to Chapel Hill to become president of the UNC system.

Briarhoppers, Banjos, and Helen Trent

Charles Crutchfield, WBT radio announcer and later president of Jefferson Standard Broadcasting Company, organized the well-known Briarhoppers group. Following the purchase of the station in 1933 by Buick dealer C. C. Coddington, the call letters reportedly stood for "Watch Buick Travel." A few of the many performers whom WBT launched were the Johnson Family singers, familiar folk announcer Grady Cole, announcer-journalist Charles Kuralt, musician-composer Loonis McGlohan, bandleader John Scott Trotter, and cowboy singer Fred Kirby.

Country-music chronicler Frye Galliard wrote, "In the 1930s WBT was a major competitor with Nashville's Grand Ole Opry—one of a handful of places where you hoped to wind up if you were an aspiring hillbilly picker, looking for a little fame and fortune or at least a steady job." Bill Monroe on the mandolin and his brother Charlie on the guitar made their first records in a local warehouse and later formed The Bluegrass Boys. Other regulars in Charlotte included Snuffy Jenkins, the Carter Family, Uncle Dave Macon, and Jimmie Davis. Arthur Smith wrote and recorded "Guitar Boogie" and "Duelin' Banjos." "Charlotte was an important center

*Members of the Charlotte Symphony and other musical groups
played popular weekly classical concerts as part of WBT's "Conservatory of the Air."
WBT was the first fifty-thousand-watt radio station in the region in the 1930s.*

Charlotte Symphony Association

for this kind of music," said musician and historian Tom Hanchett, who organized a rousing Charlotte Musical Reunion and a regional musical and social-history exhibit in 1985.

In 1935, WBT aired the first broadcasts of "The Lone Ranger" and "The Romance of Helen Trent," as well as "The Amos 'n Andy Show" and André Kostelanetz. The pioneering station also played late-night concerts of classical music in a program called "The Conservatory of the Air."

And there were also movies. Charlotte's snazziest theater was the Carolina, which carried Hollywood's best first-run movies, including *Gone With the Wind*. A boy from Hamlet came by train to see it. Tom Wicker, novelist, journalist, and associate editor of the *New York Times*, wrote, "I well remember riding with my mother and sister on a local train derisively called the Boll Weevil along the old Seaboard Air Line Railway to Charlotte, N.C., where at the Carolina Theater on Tryon Street we had mail-order tickets for the great event. Every seat was taken, though the movie had been showing for weeks. I loved it."

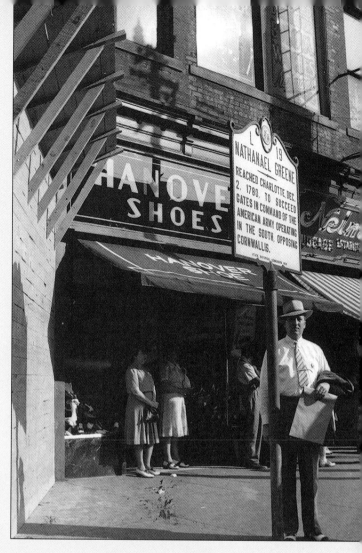

Charlotte street scenes, c. 1940

Lawyers of Merit

One Charlottean, Judge John J. Parker, went to Germany as everyone else was returning home from World War II. Long ranked as one of the top United States jurists, Parker sat as a member of the International Military Tribunal trying Nazi war criminals at Nuremberg.

Parker grew up a few miles east of Charlotte in the town of Monroe, where he worked briefly in William Henry Belk's first store. Parker carried a trunkful of medals away from his graduations at the University of North Carolina at Chapel Hill and went on to serve as presiding judge of the United States Fourth Circuit Court of Appeals in Richmond, which hears cases from Maryland, West Virginia, Virginia, and the two Carolinas. A Republican, he lost in the race for governor against Cameron Morrison. He also lost a nomination by Herbert Hoover to the United States Supreme Court. His nomination was blocked by two votes in the Senate—principally because of labor opposition to his rulings involving union contracts.

While practicing law in Charlotte, Parker began the prestigious Philosophical Club, a form of intellectual shootout between gentlemen. In 1949, Parker was a judicial adviser to the United States courts in occupied Germany. It is ironic, though not unusual, that Parker—defeated repeatedly in politics—should have been so unanimously acclaimed on his merit by the judiciary. Circuit Judge Morris A. Soper said of Parker in 1958, "In the 67 years of the court's existence he was the youngest man ever to be called to sit upon its bench and he served longer, both as a member and Chief Judge of the court, than any other man. By reason of these facts, as well as his extraordinary services to the cause of justice, he gave to this court a prestige and

Judge John J. Parker as a young man

North Carolina Collection, UNC Library, Chapel Hill

standing amongst the appellate courts of the nation which, but for him, it would never have attained."

Mecklenburg lawyers who have served on the Supreme Court of North Carolina are William Preston Bynum (1873–78), Armistead Burwell (1892–1924), Platt D. Walker (1903–23), Heriot Clarkson (1923–42), and William H. Bobbitt (1954–74). Bobbitt served as chief justice from 1969 to 1974.

Of Pigs and Property

Pat Hall once gave a friend a pig for a Christmas present, and the friend was no farmer. Hall loved jokes and deals. As a boy, Pat Hall was a messenger at the Quartermaster Depot when it was under construction. After World War II, the depot was enlarged and leased by the Douglas Aircraft Company for producing the Nike Zeus and other missiles. Pat Hall and Alex Shuford bought the property in 1967. Hall picked the bid figure of $1,820,000 out of the air—the street address of the complex at 1820 Statesville Avenue, no less.

Another Hall property venture had an equally interesting wartime genesis. Energetic efforts to attract United States Rubber's plant here in the early 1940s were quite purposeful. The Charlotte Industries Committee actively pursued a wisp of a lead that the company was looking south. The committee worked to attract it near Charlotte and was successful. United States Rubber's plant manufactured shells under the direction of navy personnel. As many as ten thousand male and female employees commuted long distances to produce ammunition for the war.

When the government in 1958 put up the shell-plant property for sale, with its internal rail service, thirty-six miles of roads, water, sewage, and gas and electric power, it was offering a regular town all by itself. Hall put together a company that raised money to bid on the property.

Pat Hall, his fellow investors, and their wives went to the Billy Graham Crusade in Charlotte the night before the checks were due in the shell-plant property bidding. Ushers passed out the collection boxes while the imposing choir sang "How Great Thou Art." Hall was sitting between investors Henderson Belk and Alex Shuford. Pulling the cashier's check for $140,000 from his pocket, he whispered, "Boys, I've seen the light, and I'm putting in this money." Hall later said, "Those two men grabbed that check like lightning. They just didn't have quite that much religion."

They bought the land and called it Arrowood, a giant industrial park. From his office in a private railway car at Arrowood, Hall put together large land packages that led

to Westinghouse Corporation's $65-million turbine plant here as well as his last fanciful concoction, the Carowinds theme park.

The combined war legacy of the navy shell plant, the Quartermaster Depot, and Morris Field made an important economic impact on postwar Charlotte. The benefits continue, even as the lingering assets of the Confederate Navy Yard and Camp Greene remained long after those two earlier war projects.

Dancers, Dinners, and Balls

Charlotte was once a town for celebrating. There were always the usual parties and dances throughout the year and open houses in Fourth Ward on New Year's Day. But the great day of the year continued to be May 20.

Clarence Kuester must have known of the festive, if not riotous, past celebrations of the Mecklenburg Declaration of Independence—

Clarence Kuester, town rallier

the one in 1825 and the nationally reported centennial event of 1875, the year before he was born. Even in off years, there was a "to-do," a parade with flags or a fancy event. In 1840, and again in 1844, Charlotteans thronged to a parade and an elaborate public dinner. In 1897, Vice President Adlai Stevenson surveyed floats and veterans and sat on the podium with the widows of Confederate generals. In 1909, Charlotte draped her buildings in flags for William Howard Taft.

As a boy, Kuester had been a town lamplighter. Later, he became a traveling salesman. Charlotte's celebration did not go as he hoped in 1920. But in his role as professional town rallier—he was a chamber-of-commerce executive from 1921 to 1947—Kuester dreamed of an extraordinary celebration. In 1925, a pageant was written and a special amphitheater was designed by Earl Draper. Then, to draw a spectacular crowd, Charlotte sent an august contingent to Washington to persuade President Calvin Coolidge to attend. But the taciturn Coolidge refused the twenty-four formidable petitioners, including T. L. Kirkpatrick, Mr. and Mrs. W. Carey Dowd, John J. Parker, E. A. Cole,

Wade Harris, J. A. Yarborough, and Dr. Luther Little.

Kuester parked his dream. Instead, he rushed efforts in 1929 to build the Armory Auditorium as a WPA project. The government built the auditorium where Park Center is now, just in time for the last large reunion of the United Confederate Veterans. Mrs. M. A. Bland noted in 1939 that the "twentieth of May balls were held at the Central Hotel," although that year there was no great, unusual celebration.

At the war's close in 1945, Kuester saw his chance. Pulitzer Prize–winning musician Lamar Stringfield and author-journalist Legette Blythe were commissioned to originate music and script for *Shout Freedom*, a historical pageant celebrating Charlotte's early history. But just after one of the last meetings before the event on May 20, 1948, Kuester collapsed with a heart attack. He died May 12, and the performance ran in his honor from May 20 to June 5. No comparable celebration, other than the 1968 bicentennial of the city's founding and the national bicentennial in 1975–76, has been held in Charlotte since.

A snowy winter keeps pedestrians indoors, as seen from South Tryon Street looking north near Masonic Temple.

Public Library of Charlotte and Mecklenburg County

The Road to Independence

South Tryon Street at night, looking north

Once again, it began with a road—not a path or a muddy track anymore, but a real road, eighty feet wide. Surely after such a world war, things in Charlotte would stay peaceable. But in 1945, the battle of the boulevard began, and it raged memorably for three years. No local war before or since has rivaled it.

Ben Douglas heard federal money was available for highways, so he put his hand in and grabbed. In 1935, the only four-lane highway in the state was Wilkinson Boulevard, stretching west of Charlotte. In 1945, it was still Charlotte's only big road. The city saw the need for thoroughfares. Engineering surveys said 89 percent of motorists wanted not a bypass but an into-town route running northeast-southeast. The new road veered sharply at Stonewall Street, so those who chose could come in but return quickly. The route crossed everything, it seemed—it disrupted property, razed churches such as Friendship Baptist, exposed to public eyes a thicket of poor housing in Brooklyn, between East Trade and East Morehead streets, and sat (too profitably, some felt) in the mayor's yard. Douglas was used to controversy. He proposed Charlotte's first slum clearance and picked up the nickname "S.O.B." when he pushed for Independence Boulevard. "I thought," said Douglas, "it stood for Sweet Old Ben, for getting 2.5 million in Federal funds to build the road."

No one loved it, but everyone knew it was needed. So Independence Boulevard was built along the engineer's route in three stages for four million dollars. It changed Charlotte inalterably, cutting through neighborhoods and eventually contributing to the redevelopment of Brooklyn and the addition of low-cost housing.

This road was evidence of a postwar energy that would change the South and Charlotte and many once-leisurely towns and cities. Urban historian David Goldfield in his book, Promised Land: The South Since 1945, described this "startling metamorphosis." New Deal legislation, with its Southern-directed federal construction contracts, paved the way for change from a cotton-based economy with a huge labor surplus and chronic low wages. Young men, both white and black, who had been isolated in rural Southern farms and villages, returned from far-flung military service and good pay with a different view of the world and its possibilities. Atlanta journalist and Southern oracle Ralph McGill foresaw in the postwar South that the symbol of progress would be "a test-tube rather than a cotton field."

Charlotte began to join a new urban hierarchy, cities that relied on railroads rather than traditional water traffic and transport. Goldfield wrote, "By the late 1940s, Charlotte had already surpassed the seaports of Charleston and Wilmington as the Carolinas' leading urban center and had expanded its railroad network, which in turn generated major highway and airport development. . . . Charlotte possessed the type of diversified, service-oriented economy that would characterize the national economic trend by the 1960s."

Congregation celebrates the anniversary of Friendship Baptist Church in 1928.

Courtesy of Mrs. Eugene Russell

dship Baptist Church
son, Pastor. Sept. 9 - 1928

Carolina Studio Charlotte N.C.

Joining a Community

Into the solidly Democratic South came a visitor. Southerners have long held an inordinate reverence for generals and colonels, and Dwight D. Eisenhower, fresh from the European triumphs of World War II, was a natural hero.

More than twelve thousand Charlotteans astounded campaign workers in the fall of 1952 by turning out at eight o'clock on a weekday morning to hear the war hero–presidential candidate at Memorial Auditorium. "Ike" wore a new business suit, a wide Midwestern grin, and the affable aura of victory. Two years later, Eisenhower came back as president, landing at the newly completed municipal airport. He spoke in Freedom Park after Norman Vincent Peale preached, after the Boys' Choir and Choral Society sang, and after Queens College girls served him Southern fried chicken and country ham. Then he was welcomed by Mayor Phillip Van Every and introduced by new Congressman Charles Raper Jonas (a Republican) and Democratic Governor William B. Umstead. It was an odd thing to Charlotteans to have a Republican in power locally and nationally. The story is told of two women sitting on a Queens Road porch in Myers Park, one of them "Miss Patsy" Harry Goodwin, a witty, well-known Charlotte figure with very firm opinions. Her friend on the porch began praising a matronly neighbor they saw walking down the shady sidewalk. "But my dear," Miss Patsy countered firmly, "she's a Republican!"

A bipartisan and segregated Charlotte audience listened to Eisenhower that afternoon in 1954. Schools were still separate and unequal, as were restaurants, hotels, and transportation facilities. When blacks came to town to shop, they could not eat at Kress's lunch counter or use the restrooms. To pay property taxes at the county courthouse, blacks had to ride a separate elevator. Drinking fountains were not to be used by blacks. Buses were the main means of transportation, with Charlotte's whites sitting up front. Blacks walked the long aisle to the back. It took the Supreme Court decision that year to begin to change the unequal status quo.

But not much really changed until 1960. Johnson C. Smith University students sat down one day at a lunch counter at Kress's dime store on Charlotte's Square. Quickly, Mayor James S. Smith created a Friendly Relations Committee, which met with the lunch-counter proprietors and the students. The result was that lunch counters in Charlotte were soon integrated.

Then on May 21, 1963, Smith students marched up Trade Street to the courthouse. Sit-ins in restaurants and department stores were happening daily in Durham, Fayetteville, and Wilmington, with marches in High Point and Chapel Hill. An economic boycott was proving effective in Birmingham.

Charlotte's wittiest stand-up book reviewer and social commentator was "Miss Patsy" Harry Goodwin.

Courtesy of Claire Trexler

President Dwight Eisenhower at Freedom Park during his 1954 visit to Charlotte

Courtesy of Grant Whitney

Statue of Dr. Martin Luther King, Jr., in Marshall Park

President John F. Kennedy is greeted at the airport during his visit to Charlotte.

Charlotte Observer

The Charlotte leaders—aware of a scheduled May 31 visit and speech by Dr. Martin Luther King, Jr., to six Charlotte black high school senior classes—saw it was late indeed.

Chamber-of-commerce leaders J. Ed Burnside and Buell Duncan, Mayor Stan Brookshire, C. A. McKnight, Dr. Warner Hall, Dr. John Cunningham, and others moved quickly with positive action. Street strife and economic boycott were closing in around Charlotte. In one tense but dramatic week, black leaders joined white leaders. They went in mixed pairs by prearrangement to local public restaurants and sat down to lunch together. Slug Claiborne had suggested it. This beginning—so simple in retrospect—propelled a community effort. Charlotte began also to integrate her hotels, motels, buses, and movies. King came, spoke, and praised the effort, which preceded the 1964 congressional act opening public accommodations to all persons.

A landmark lawsuit brought by black parents against the Charlotte-Mecklenburg schools placed the school board in federal court for court-ordered integration under United States District Court Judge James B. McMillan. The case of *Swann v. Charlotte-Mecklenburg Board of Education* will be long remembered.

McMillan began as district judge in 1968. In 1969, he issued the opinion on the *Swann* case. A Robeson County farm boy, he earned his tuition at Presbyterian Junior College, then at the University of North Carolina. He borrowed money to attend Harvard University Law School, where he earned his degree. He returned to North Carolina in 1940. The *Swann* decision made national headlines. Northern jurists looked up his credentials and found he represented "a courageous strain of Southern liberalism."

In essence, he stated the 107 Mecklenburg schools and 83,000 students (29 percent black, 70 percent white) were not sufficiently integrated to fulfill Supreme Court requirements. "You've got to do more," he wrote. He recommended elimination of predominantly black schools and a systemwide racial balance—70 to 30 percent. McMillan's opinion and order stated, "The system of assigning pupils by 'neighborhoods,' with 'freedom of choice' for both pupils and faculty, superimposed on an urban population pattern where Negro residents have become concentrated almost entirely in one quadrant of a city of 270,000, is racially discriminatory. This discrimination discourages initiative and makes quality education impossible."

The board, supported by a large, vocal part of the community, repeatedly resisted the tough measures necessary to accomplish the order. McMillan named the school-board members defendants in the case. Busing children away from neighborhood schools made citizens see red. Since North Carolina state law requires school buses to transport students who live more than a mile and a half from their school, integrating schools required vast changes in pupil assignments and, consequently, long bus rides. One group of parents pushed for an antibusing law in the legislature. Others brought suit to assign schools on a color-blind basis. McMillan rejected as inadequate the plans the board offered to effect desegregation. He ordered an outside expert to formulate a plan for Charlotte that, with modifications, was adopted by the court. The board and attorneys for the black parents appealed the case to the Fourth Circuit Court of Appeals and on to the United States Supreme Court.

The Supreme Court responded in 1971 by unanimously affirming McMillan, finding his desegregation order "reasonable, feasible, and workable." The real work then began. Under such legal duress, the community summoned its own special brand of creative grit. A workable plan had to be submitted by May 1974. The outside expert's plan did not take into account many essential personality factors and needs of the people, so vying groups joined forces to find something that would work.

Margaret Ray, chairman of the divergent Citizens Advisory Group, remembered that feelings were so high she was not sure the members could even communicate, let alone negotiate. They began by meeting for dinner, where, Ray noted, "Southerners have been taught to be polite." They worked day and night together for months and came up with a plan that the board and McMillan endorsed. It was implemented in September 1974.

Charlotte's consolidated public schools became a living laboratory long before those of Boston, Louisville, or other, angrier cities. The nation watched and is observing still. The busing of students was designed to minimize change while trying to equalize education and to approximate closely the racial balance of the community.

Busing here involved a highly complex, expensive, and volatile plan that finally was effected peaceably through wide community effort. Private schools proliferated, but white flight—though present and organized—did not prove debilitating. The number of white children in private schools more than doubled—increasing from three thousand to eighty-four hundred—but it involved only a small percentage of the nearly eighty thousand students.

Public harassment of the judge and his home occurred, but the city survived and underwent long, patient travels of black and white children to compensate for old, unbalanced housing patterns that are traceable in town history.

Reverend Coleman Kerry, a Baptist minister and local black leader, was the first black to serve on the school board (1968–70). He warned of the possibility of a lawsuit as a result of the board's continuing segregated system. Since Kerry's tenure, the elected school board has been consistently integrated and on several occasions chaired by a black member.

William Poe, school-board chairman during much of the period of desegregation, questioned the overall educational effect but remarked in 1979, "I think there are more pluses than minuses. The desegregation order was the key to most of our interracial relations here. It was the biggest single thing we have done in terms of race relations, and I think the manner in which the community has handled it says a good deal about Charlotte as a place that has diversity and makes the best of it."

The *Wall Street Journal* looked at Charlotte as a national pioneer nine years after the order, reporting in 1979, "Busing probably will be linked forever to this pleasant city in the South. Here essentially is where it all began. . . . After nine years, Charlotte has one of the most thoroughly integrated school systems in the country and the turmoil normally surrounding busing has faded into general acceptance. Blacks now share equal resources."

"When white children came to Billingsville [a formerly all-black school], that's when the books came," said one black parent interviewed by the *Journal*. At PTA meetings, there were many white housewives whose husbands were lawyers, doctors, and middle-class professionals. "Those people just know how to get what they want. They know exactly whom to see."

Judge McMillan himself said he remains "impressed by the constructive way Mecklenburg people have supported their schools through a rough period." Charlotte author and journalist Frye Galliard chronicled this fascinating struggle with social change in his book, *The Dream Long Deferred*.

Many citizens, black and white, agree no one was entirely satisfied with the solution, but an alternative remained elusive. In 1991, public pressure and school-system leadership pushed for workable and innovative amendments in the pupil-assignment plan based on current population changes and local needs. The United States Supreme Court in April 1992 sent the famous case of *Brown v. Board of Education* back to a federal appeals panel with instructions to apply a new, relaxed standard for weighing the legal duties of school districts once segregated by law. On March 31, 1992, the Charlotte-Mecklenburg School Board adopted the new student-assignment plan. Part of the new plan's objectives are to achieve integrated schools in a more equitable, acceptable way and to focus on quality education, not transportation.

Commenting on the change, C. D. Spangler, Jr., president of the University of North Carolina system and vice chairman of the Charlotte-Mecklenburg School Board from 1972 to 1976, said, "I haven't heard anyone from the Charlotte area talking about abandoning the concept of integration. I am among the people who believe integration and academic excellence can occur simultaneously. The new effort has to be in that direction."

The Printed Word

Of course, it all could have been solved much easier back in the 1950s by asking Harry Golden, Charlotte's rotund Solomon. Author Golden came up with a unique solution to the problem of segregation. He had lived in Charlotte since 1941, working for a labor newspaper and later the *Charlotte Observer*. He began writing amusing, perceptive essays and reflections for his own *Carolina Israelite*, which gathered an ever-widening circulation throughout the nation. Golden watched the growing unrest surrounding school desegregation here and elsewhere. One week, he quietly offered in print what came to be known as the Golden Vertical Rule. It was quite simple.

Golden observed a complete lack of segregation in the South as long as the black man remained standing. He shared grocery and bank lines with whites, paid his light and

Journalist and best-selling author Harry Golden, editor of the Carolina Israelite, *enjoyed having his picture taken.*

University of North Carolina at Charlotte, Atkins Library, Special Collections Unit

phone bills at the same window with them— no problem whatsoever. It was only when blacks sat down that there were problems. Therefore, Golden proposed the removal of all seats in public schools. *Time* magazine picked up the novel solution and soon the nation was chuckling over one man's witty approach to human folly. From all over the world, more than thirty thousand subscriptions to *Carolina Israelite* poured in. One note came from textile magnate Charles Cannon: "Dear Golden: Enclosed is $3 for renewal. Half your paper stinks, but the other half gives us all lots of pleasure."

Charlotte has never known quite how to take Harry Golden or others like him. He did not fit any pattern Charlotteans knew, so they decided to relax and enjoy him. And he in turn found amusement and grist for many columns by "watching the Christians chase a buck." In his house in the Elizabeth neighborhood, Golden continued adding to his twenty books of humor and wisdom. *Only In America* was his most popular book. That Golden stayed is a feather in Charlotte's cultural cap.

Literary efforts have a long but spotty history in Mecklenburg, going back to early preachers who did what writing or versifying was recorded. Charlotte's first poet was a highly literate blacksmith named Adam Brevard, whose rhymed couplets satirized local politicians in 1777. Charlotte's first novelist was a woman. Fanny Downing fled her Portsmouth, Virginia, home just ahead of Union troops in the 1860s and stayed in Charlotte to write poems and a novel and to contribute to the Southern literary magazine published in Charlotte by a former Confederate lieutenant-general and math professor, D. H. Hill. This magazine, *The Land We Love*, extolled the South—the land, legends, and heroes. In the early 1900s, John Charles McNeill, a *Charlotte Observer* columnist, wrote lyrical poems, both classical and in dialect, both humorous and formal, drawing inspiration from local folk and the rural countryside. McNeill wrote *Lyrics from Cotton Land* and *Songs Merry and Sad*. Erskine Caldwell's father was a Mecklenburg County native and brought his son to spend summers and visits. Erskine Caldwell later wrote about his experiences in *Deep South*.

W. J. Cash swung a sharp verbal sword as a brilliant North Carolina journalist. His mentor was H. L. Mencken. While Cash lived on North Church Street writing for the *Charlotte News*, he polished his acerbic essays published in Mencken's *American Mercury*. These were the kernels of his classic book, *The Mind of the South*. It won him a Guggenheim Fellowship and is still assigned reading on college and university campuses. Cash's book is a radical examination of Old and New South ideals. Prizewinning journalist Harry Ashmore wrote at the *News* under the tutelage of Brodie Griffith. Carson McCullers worked on the opening chapters of her first novel, *The Heart Is a Lonely Hunter*, as a bride in a Charlotte boardinghouse in 1938. Fiction writer Marian Sims was a friend of Cash and McCullers. Sims stayed on in Charlotte, writing stories for popular magazines as well as frank and incisive novels about 1940s urban Southern life (*Call It Freedom* and *City On A Hill*). For years, "Miss Patsy" Goodwin reviewed books by Charlotteans and national authors at public gatherings and book clubs, remarking with wit and unsparing judgment on the presence or absence of literary quality.

Dozens of published writers have lived and worked in Charlotte, but few have been as widely known as prolific novelist and biographer LeGette Blythe, or as provocative as poets T. J. Reddy, Paul Baker Newman, Julie Suk, Chuck Sullivan, and Marion Cannon, or as controversial as Charleen Swansea, teacher, author, and publisher of Red Clay Books. One prolific Charlotte native, Gail Haley, has won the prestigious Caldecott and Kate Greenaway awards for her children's books and illustrations (*A Story, A Story* and *The Post Office Cat*). Another native, Betsy Byars, writes children's favorites. Her *Summer of the Swans* won a Newberry Medal in 1971 and her *Night Swimmers* an American Book Award in 1981. Biographies and instruction books for children and young adults are the specialty of Elizabeth Simpson Smith.

W. J. Cash wrote his classic book, The Mind of the South,
while in Charlotte.

Charlotte Observer

Author LeGette Blythe wrote two dozen novels, drama,
and biography highlighting Carolina history.

University of North Carolina at Charlotte,
Atkins Library, Special Collections Unit

Provocative short stories and novels about the urban
South were Marian Sims's specialty.

University of North Carolina at Charlotte,
Atkins Library, Special Collections Unit

Marion Hargrove's *Charlotte News* columns were the foundation for the best-selling novel *See Here, Private Hargrove*, which later played on Broadway. Charles Kuralt, the deep-voiced journeyman of CBS television's "On the Road" and "Sunday Morning," began polishing his flawless sentences in high school for the *News* and WBT radio's sports department. Visiting Charlotte recently, he seemed puzzled by his airplane's swoop over downtown. "There's nothing there to recognize. But I remember tarpaper shacks and pellagra so I guess it's just as well." While he was here,

he autographed his latest books, *On the Road* and *North Carolina Is My Home*. The *News* was the launching pad also for Burke Davis, who went on to write more than fifty books of fiction and nonfiction, including his prizewinning biographies, *Old Hickory* and *They Called Him Stonewall*.

Ever since the *Catawba Journal*'s weekly appearance in 1824, Charlotteans have looked forward to the news. Usually, they got more than news in the subsequent *Charlotte Journal*, the *Whig*, the *Miners' and Farmers' Journal*, and numerous other short-lived papers. Besides

*In high school, Charlottean Charles Kuralt
wrote for the* Charlotte News *and broadcast sports for WBT radio.*
———
WBTV

ads for linament and notice of the latest cotton prices or railroad dividends, readers learned such details as those of the marriage of "the two beautiful and brilliant daughters of the late Confederate General Zollicoffer" in 1869, or those of another newsworthy marriage held on a tugboat in San Francisco Bay, in which the newlyweds successfully eluded the bride's outraged father.

Sentimental poetry appeared regularly in early newspapers. "Leonora's eye, swift as an eagle's, her heart grew hard as stone," one sample went. And the Mansion House hotel in a period of depression announced, "In consequence of the dull time and scarcity of money we reduce the price of the tableboard."

D. A. Tompkins changed the *Charlotte Chronicle* to the *Charlotte Daily Observer* when he purchased the Democratic paper in 1892. It later became today's *Charlotte Observer*, and after changing hands several times was bought by the Knight Publishing Company in 1954 from publisher Mrs. Curtis B. Johnson. Wade Hampton Harris founded the afternoon *Charlotte News* in 1888 and sold it in 1895 to William Carey Dowd, Sr., who also acquired the *Mecklenburg Times*. A lively competition existed between the *Observer* and the *News*, even though Knight also purchased the *News* in 1959. Subsequently, the *News* ceased publication. Two historic weekly newspapers that continue are the *Mecklenburg Times* and the *Charlotte Post*.

Charlotte's newspapers have often offered exceptional reading. George Stephens was so impressed that he published a book of Isaac Avery's columns in 1905. Another favorite writer beloved by the region was Lower Providence native H. E. C. "Red Buck" Bryant, who worked two months for no pay in 1895 until he could prove himself to editor Joseph Caldwell. Writing *Observer* columns for fifty years, Bryant got interviews no one else could—J. P. Morgan, for example. "The best training I had in newspaper work," wrote Bryant, "was in Providence Township on the farm learning human nature, mule tricks and the ways of wild life—rabbits, foxes. A party of Congressmen is very much like a pack of hounds. It is composed of leaders, babblers, wild runners who fly the track and break up the trace, workers and idlers." Following Bryant, *News* editor Perry Morgan, a Georgia farm boy, spread crystalline wisdom on many a disquieting afternoon in the late sixties and early seventies. Columnist Kays Gary, in his poignant human-interest stories, has long held a compassionate ear to Carolina clay with his edge-of-deadline writing. Former *Observer* journalists Jerry Bledsoe and Frye Gaillard have written important books, primarily nonfiction, about extraordinary Southerners and sensational Southern events. Bledsoe's *Bitter Blood* became a national bestseller. Patsy Daniels began her departure from *Observer* police writing with a biography of Ruth Bell Graham (Mrs. Billy Graham) and subsequent award-winning mysteries set in Richmond.

National anthologies of black and Southern literature carry Charlottean Diane Oliver's short stories, which detail growing up in a black neighborhood of Charlotte during the turbulent 1960s. The rise of the urban South has been chronicled and analyzed in numerous books by scholar and urban historian David Goldfield. Southern gardening classics are the work of Elizabeth Lawrence.

Playwrights have been scarce, while poets have proliferated in Charlotte, particularly since the 1970s. Novelists Bob Inman, Laurence Naumoff, Robin Hemley, Simmons Jones, Jonellen Heckler, Valerie Sherwood, and Peg Robarchek and short-story writer Ruth Moose continue to take strange truth and turn it into fiction. A book, *The Imaginative Spirit: Literary Heritage of Charlotte and Mecklenburg County*, published by the Public Library of Charlotte and Mecklenburg County, samples and surveys two hundred years of literary lore.

Traffic on South Tryon, looking north

El Grande Disco, *public art on the Square by Arnaldo Pomodoro,*
used to revolve until windy days on Charlotte's ridge line proved hazardous.

The Finer Things

Art traditionally fares better in Charlotte if it is something familiar and clearly recognizable, but art appreciation has clearly come of age. A stroll through uptown Charlotte is proof positive.

With recent legislation designating up to 1 percent of construction costs allowable for art in new public buildings, a proliferation of outdoor and lobby artworks are suddenly major attractions. One example is the water sculpture by Alfredo Halegua at the government center on East Fourth Street. Stunning new sculptures within and outside privately owned buildings uptown have created a stir of approval and controversy. Most notable are the Carillon Building's thirty-foot, seventeen-color outdoor sculpture by Jerry Peart and an astonishing interior kinetic sculpture by Jean Tinguely. Art critic Richard Maschal described Tinguely's *Cascade*: "Could it be the contents of some great, cosmic closet disgorged for all the world to see? . . . The work is full of references to Charlotte."

Frescoes by North Carolina artist Ben Long, trained in the European fresco tradition, celebrate the altar wall of Saint Peter's Catholic Church; another series of Long's remarkable frescoes punctuates the lobby of NationsBank Corporate Center at the Square. Two other singular pieces among Charlotte's growing array of public art are the stained glass at WTVI on Commonwealth Avenue and the clay wall mural *Water Cycle* by Cathy Triplett at the city waterworks on Belhaven Boulevard. To celebrate Charlotte's namesake, Queen Charlotte of England (the wife of King George III), two sculptures have reigned since the 1980s: one by Raymond Kaskey at the airport, where the wind-swept queen holds onto her ornate royal crown, and another by Graham Weathers, *Queen Charlotte*

Atop the tall, outdoor entrance fountain, Raymond Kaskey's bronze sculpture shows Queen Charlotte balancing her crown in airport winds.

1990 © Raymond Kaskey

Strolls in Her Garden, at East Fifth and College streets.

It has taken many decades for modern public art to be accepted locally. Charlotte was puzzled at first by some forms of art that arrived before she was ready. Arnaldo Pomodoro's metal *El Grande Disco* on the Square fared better because other large outdoor sculptures and murals had pioneered. *Kanturk* made its knotty statement at Saint Mary's Chapel on Third Street until public disapproval dispatched it to friendlier turf at a private corporation at Wendover and Monroe roads. Earlier, the angular, yellow *Sun Target* camped in the Mint Museum's front yard as long as neighbors could bear it. Then it was demoted to the rear meadow, then to the entrance of UNC-Charlotte, where it stayed briefly.

In a serene, wooded setting, the Mint Museum of Art nestles at 2730 Randolph Road, an eminent regional art center with a survey collection of European and American art, an important collection of pre-Columbian art, and one of the nation's foremost collections of pottery and porcelain, ranging in time from ancient Chinese dynasties to eighteenth-century Europe. The two-thousand-piece Auman Collection of North Carolina pottery is the state's most comprehensive historic pottery collection. The exhibited story of Carolina gold focuses on the historic United States branch mint at Charlotte. Part of the museum incorporates the handsomely relocated branch-mint building. The museum's permanent art collections are enhanced by temporary exhibitions organized by the museum and by major visiting exhibitions on national tour.

Romare Bearden, internationally known and widely exhibited collage artist, was featured in a one-man show at the Mint Museum of Art in 1980 and in subsequent exhibits at the Melberg Gallery. Bearden, who is known as the "dean of black American artists," is a Charlotte native, and some of his colorful works have a Mecklenburg County setting. They often recollect a city surrounded by cotton fields and flower gardens. A large mosaic of a work by Romare Bearden hangs in the main-floor entry area of the Public Library of Charlotte on North Tryon Street.

Several banks and businesses have undertaken the role of arts patron, affirming that good art is good business as well as interesting decor. They offer awards and purchase prizes and often loan their lobbies for exhibits. Springs Mills sponsors an open national art competition and a respected traveling art show.

Saving a Minor Landmark

A favorite choice for romantics is to marry at Saint Mary's Chapel, a quaint brick chapel that is ideal for weddings, small concerts, or other public or cultural events.

In 1887, five orphan children slept under quilts on the floor of a house. These were the first orphans cared for by Saint Peter's Episcopal Reverend Benjamin Bronson. Receiving sixty-three acres near the center of Charlotte from a defunct boys' school, Bronson and the church vestry organized an orphanage on the cottage plan for children ages two through eighteen. The children and teachers operated a farm, milked Holstein and Guernsey cows for ten thousand gallons of milk each year, and attended chapel exercises daily. The Thompson Orphanage under its first superintendent, E. A. Osborne, was the first orphanage in the state that was largely supported by a religious body. Its late-Victorian Gothic Revival chapel was built in 1892.

The farm, cottages, and chapel covered land now occupied by Midtown Square (formerly Charlottetown Mall), Cinema I and II, Third Street, and Independence Boulevard. When the property was leased, the orphanage moved to Margaret Wallace Road in 1970. All the orphanage buildings were removed except the chapel, which stood with its windows boarded and shrubbery overgrown.

Mary Froebe lived at Thompson Orphanage with her brother Henry. Mary married Mark Penny of Charlotte, and when their daughter was making plans for a wedding in 1974, they got permission to clean up old, forgotten Saint Mary's Chapel for the wedding. They unboarded the windows, cleared the yard, cleaned windows and pews. Mary scrubbed the floors and put snapdragons and daisies on the altar. After the ceremony, she reboarded and relocked Saint Mary's doors.

State Senator Fred Alexander, the man who pioneered blacks' reentry into politics in Charlotte, remembered Saint Mary's from his childhood in the adjacent neighborhood of Brooklyn. As city councilman and mayor pro tem, he pushed to save the chapel. A preservation committee was organized, and in 1976

Saint Mary's Chapel, popular wedding site, was at the center of the Thompson Orphanage and its working dairy farm until the 1960s, when its pastures became Charlottetown Mall and part of the Central Piedmont Community College campus.

the chapel became a public museum. "So many of our landmarks have disappeared," Alexander said. "Back in my day I could never go there—because I'm black. Now the little black boy from Brooklyn ends up preserving it for posterity." Alexander also presided over the end of another historic demarcation line between the races—the removal of the fence between Pinewood and Elmwood cemeteries in Fourth Ward.

The story of Saint Mary's Chapel is one small element of a national preservation movement, which has had moderate but impressive success in Mecklenburg County despite serious odds.

Arts and Science For the People

The stories behind the new downtown arts-and-science complex are better known. The congregation of First Baptist Church on North Tryon (established in 1832, built in 1908) moved to a new building near Marshall Park. The church's old domed, circular sanctuary and the adjacent educational building faced destruction. Gene Goldberg, Alex McMillan, Bill Williamson, Harriet Cuthbertson, C. C. Hope, and others dreamed it might escape demolition and gain new life somehow as an arts center for Charlotte.

Hotly pursued private and city funds made it possible. In 1976, the educational building (Phase I) opened as Spirit Square, with central arts offices, classrooms, display area, an entertainment hall, and restaurant. In 1980, the remodeled sanctuary opened as NCNB Performance Place. Funds donated by North Carolina National Bank made this possible. Joel Grey, Odetta, Carlos Montoya,

William Windom, plays, and a jazz band christened the hall with a sparkling parade of talent. It is a favorite hall among performers. One singer called it "a beauty, an intimate place to perform." A renovation in the late 1980s provided six art galleries, two additional small theaters with an ongoing performing-arts season, studios for classes, and a gift shop. The three-phase complex became Spirit Square Center for the Arts.

In the initial renovation, the original marble baptistry's face framed the ticket window in the foyer. When C. D. Spangler, Jr., attended opening shows at NCNB Performance Place in the 1980s, he could not help remembering when he and Carl McCraw, Jr., were immersed in the waters there. "It sure was cold. Dr. Luther Little dunked us right under. In those days he preached in tails every Sunday."

Discovery Place—directly across North Tryon's three-hundred block from Spirit Square—was the dream of director Russ Piethman and countless others. A hands-on science, technology, and natural-history museum for the Southeast, it is the strapping uptown son of the early Nature Museum at Freedom Park. Thousands of schoolchildren and visitors to the Nature Museum learned of muscles, snakes, and stars from the time Laura Owen began teaching there in 1947. The opening of Discovery Place put Charlotte on the national map, with one of the country's top-ten science-and-technology museums with hands-on activities for all age groups. The addition of the Omnimax Theater in 1991 expanded the dimensions of Discovery Place's exploratory journeys in science and adventure.

Another public outgrowth of a historic setting is the Afro-American Cultural Center, housed in the old Little Rock A.M.E. Zion Church (1911) on Seventh Street. It offers an art gallery, theater, classes, and exhibits and is a resource for research into Charlotte's black heritage. Adjacent to the center is an example of a common working-class house style—two original shotgun houses (c. 1898). When Seventh Street was widened, the church building was threatened. Protests caused the city to put a large curve in the formerly straight street. Those protests inspired what historian Dan Morrill called "the most sophisticated decision Charlotte has made in recent times."

Music's ardent fans are proud of Charlotte's big-city symphony. North Carolina's oldest, it offered in 1990–91 several concert series. The symphony's approximately 250 performances a year, some with guest artists, include educational and special performances, such as the Summer Pops at Freedom Park, a summer classical series, and a Fourth of July concert. The regional symphony in 1991 employed sixty full-time musicians and seven per-service players. Old-timers remember when the players were unpaid. In the early days, friends served free coffee in china cups at intermission of sparsely attended concerts. A recent labor dispute threatened to interrupt the symphony's long history; but after months of wrangling over contracts, the musicians and the symphony board reached an agreement late in 1991. The symphony in 1992 became the resident company of the new North Carolina Blumenthal Center for the Performing Arts in uptown Charlotte.

Beginning in 1948, opera subsisted faithfully for many years until enough money was

First Baptist Church was transformed internally to become part of Spirit Square Center for the Arts in 1980.

raised to bring professional touring stars. In 1990–91, Opera Carolina presented four productions with principal singers who perform on the professional regional and national circuit. An outreach program takes resident artists with one-act opera into rural communities of the Carolinas. The popular Singing Christmas Tree in 1990 celebrated its thirty-fifth year. An acclaimed array of theater groups, with Charlotte Repertory Theater in the forefront, spotlights exceptional actors of experimental and traditional works. This marks a solid new trend in Charlotte. Oratorio, dance, chamber music, and a wide range of other combined arts-and-crafts guilds enhance a growing cultural enrichment. Loonis McGlohan, talented composer-pianist, has long been Charlotte's "Super Music Man."

A wide variety of music draws large crowds to the Charlotte Coliseum (capacity 25,000), Ovens Auditorium, Spirit Square, and to local clubs and halls and two huge state-of-the-art outdoor amphitheaters, Blockbuster Pavilion (19,000) and Carowinds Palladium (15,000). In 1980, Paul Buck, manager of the old Charlotte Coliseum, proclaimed, "Rock is the biggest thing in town." As of 1992, country music was outstripping everything else in popularity. A Garth Brooks concert sold out 23,395 tickets in eighty minutes. When the Grand Ole Opry chose twenty cities for its limited national tour in 1991, Charlotte was one of them. Music historians trace Charlotte's history of bluegrass—Bill Monroe made early recordings here in 1936—and country music to the region's mill-town roots, to the many rural and Appalachian-born workers who had a yen for country songs. Charlotteans also go for big-name pop and rock performers, jazz, and round-the-clock radio jazz, news, and classical.

Once, Charlotteans clustered downtown to the Charlotte Opera House (1874) and later to live shows in the old Academy of Music

Renowned guitarist Carlos Montoya in town for his performance at Spirit Square

Courtesy of Elizabeth Ross

(1902)—jugglers, dancers, ladies on horseback, or the film *Birth of a Nation.* Subsequently, they listened to the likes of Enrico Caruso in 1920 in the Charlotte Auditorium at College and Fifth streets. Now, entertainment is widely scattered. Those uptown theaters—Bill Peter's Nickelodeon, the Casino, Princess, Amuzu, Alhambra, and later the Carolina and Imperial—surrendered to the country dinner playhouses, triple cinemas, commercial outdoor pavilions, and shopping-center concerts with magic acts, fireworks, and Indian dances. Shakespeare, fiddling, storytelling, and colonial reenactments at historic houses and in Charlotte parks delight lively good-weather gatherings. Charlotte's major special celebrations include Springfest, the International Festival, JazzCharlotte, the gala Festival in the Park, "Yiasou" Greek Festival, and the Fourth of July fireworks in the central city.

Tracing the City's Growth

Dome of the fourth courthouse, 300 South Tryon Street, rises behind a home on East Third Street. The courthouse was on this site from 1896 to 1928.

Courtesy of Mildred Morse McEwen

When Charlotte's sixth courthouse was dedicated on May 19, 1978, former Charlottean and North Carolina Supreme Court Chief Justice William H. Bobbitt gave the address. Tracing the city's growth, Bobbitt noted, "When I reflect that the years of my life are more than one-third of the life span of this nation, I realize that our experience in self-government has been brief, and that constant vigilance and dedication will be required if our present institutions endure."

Bobbitt was always a good storyteller. At the dedication, he traced the courthouse's purposeful trail around town.

In 1766, the earliest courthouse sat on pillars ten feet high right in the center of the road crossing at Trade and Tryon. Upstairs was the courtroom, with an open-air market below.

In 1809, a brick courthouse about the same size as the first sat in the middle of the crossroads and was described by a traveler as a "tolerably elegant Brick Courthouse with a cupola on top."

In 1845, the courthouse moved one block west on West Trade Street. It sat on the corner of Church and faced West Trade. Its predominant features were large white columns and two circular exterior staircases that wound up the front to the court and jury rooms on the second floor. Later, the Selwyn Hotel stood there.

In 1896, fifty-two thousand dollars built the fourth courthouse at the southeast corner of Tryon and Third streets, where Two First Union-Jefferson now stands. It was a massive building, a Victorian version of a European capitol building, and was certain to last forever. This was the courthouse E. D. Latta saw from his office across the street in the Latta Arcade.

In 1928, the courthouse moved to its fifth site, 610 East Trade, no longer in sight of the Square. The formal grandeur of the building's columns and brass doors contributed to a total cost of over one million dollars. Architect Louis Asbury, Sr., received an award for its design.

In 1978, Charlotte's sixth courthouse earned its Charlotte architect, Harry Wolf, an award for excellence in architectural design. It cost $5.3 million and was the first to contain only courtrooms and those offices directly related to judicial functions.

The fifth courthouse remains across the street from the newest one and is used for county offices, supplemental courtrooms, and the Mecklenburg County Law and Government Library.

The ever-growing courthouse is clearly visible evidence of a seam-bursting county whose population figures tell the story: 151,826 citizens in 1940; 197,052 in 1950; 272,111 in 1960; 354,656 in 1970; 404,270 in 1980; and 511,433 in 1990.

In 1990, the seven-county metropolitan statistical area surrounding and including Mecklenburg County numbered 1,162,093 persons.

East Trade Street looking west from Caldwell Street, c. 1949

Courtesy of Pat Morgan

A Racetrack of Pine and Cypress

The Charlotte Speedway was an incredible board racetrack of green pine and cypress that looped a 1.25-mile oval near Pineville in 1924. It was the South's ambitious answer to Indianapolis in the days before the city had any public arena, stadium, tennis courts, or swimming pools. Expert carpenters built it in forty long-houred days from four million feet of lumber, urged on no doubt by founders Osmond Barringer and B. D. Heath and other backers. In 1911, Barringer had attended the first Indianapolis 500 and brought the idea home. On the Charlotte Speedway's straightaway, Dunsenbergs and Miller Specials hit 150 miles per hour. The first race on the 282-acre site drew thirty thousand fans from all over the eastern seaboard. They parked their cars in the infield or rode special trains the 9-mile trip from the Square. After several years, crowds waned and weather took its toll on the planking. A newspaperman reported, "During action, dislodged boards would flip up like ground hogs from a hole. Dauntless spectators would dash to the rescue, pound a bobbing board into place and then leap back to safety." One police officer who risked his neck to nail a board back in place received a rousing ovation. The Depression prevented repair, and in 1942 salvageable lumber went to the war effort. Currently, Southland Industrial Park, including Lance, Inc., sits on the site just west of South Boulevard.

The Sporting Life

A look across Charlotte's life shows rapid change in every corner. The *Washington Post* noted in 1991, "Only the naive tell this city named for King George III's wife that it cannot be a player in major league sports." The subject of sports is a winsome and erratic example of Charlotte's forward-looking zeal, and the city's best chapter may be just around the corner.

A Southern city whose ardor leapt from baseball to ice hockey to auto racing in a generation was fickle at best. In early days, if someone called, "Baseball!" Charlotte dropped everything and hurried over. Baseball was magical even before 1900. Charlotte's Hornets reached their peak in the 1920s, playing teams like Charleston, Augusta, Macon, Savannah, and Knoxville. They were one of the founding teams in the class-B South Atlantic Baseball League.

Old Wearn Field was on South Mint Street. It was later named Robbie Field, then Hayman Field, after Felix Hayman. Hayman purchased the field, became president of the Hornets in 1919, and cultivated the club like a son. Hayman bought, sold, and traded players until his death in 1932, when the club was sold in turn to the Boston Red Sox, the Washington Senators, the Minnesota Twins, and the Baltimore Orioles. Successful games continued in Dilworth at Crockett Park (formerly Griffith Park) for the dynamic Charlotte O's as a Southern League farm team for Baltimore. Until the old coliseum on Independence Boulevard opened in 1955, Charlotte had few sports except minor-league baseball. Under the ownership of the Crockett family beginning in 1977, baseball drew greater crowds than ever before until Crockett Park burned and closed in 1985.

In the early days, the Twilight League marked a baseball heyday. Called "textile ball," it flourished in the twenties, forties, and fifties. Highland Park—one of Charlotte's largest mills—was known first for its cloth, then for baseball. After the war, many mills had teams, but Highland Park had a field and an exceptional team. Since there were no

The Charlotte Hornets made baseball a magical sport in the 1920s.

lights for night play, the semipro games began right after work at the mill and continued through twilight, until it was too dark to see. In 1941, Highland Park won the North and South Carolina championship and advanced to Battle Creek, Michigan. Gerard "Nig" Lipscomb, who had played with the Saint Louis Browns, joined Highland Park in 1941. In that same year, the team won the title and got ten light poles, and the wonders of night baseball began. On summer evenings, entire mill towns turned out to watch.

Pro football gained major impetus with the opening of Memorial Stadium in 1936. High-school teams from Central, Tech, and Harding played out fierce rivalries there. Then came the pros. Charlotte's Bantams and the incomparable Johnny Branch were followed by Floyd Summer and Gene McEver's Charlotte Clippers, a Southern League top team. During one Sunday-afternoon Clippers game, the Japanese attacked Pearl Harbor. Morris Field's Third Air Force team featured all-American Charlie Trippi of Georgia.

Hockey Pucks and Racecars

"It's a very fast, physical game," said Al Manch, owner of Fields Jewelers, Charlotte Hockey Club president, and prime mover of the Charlotte Checkers from 1961 to 1976. A year after Manch gave up the team due to a lack of financial support, the Checkers disbanded. "I miss it very much," said Manch. Before Manch took over the team, which was originally called the Charlotte Clippers, it had been playing in the Independence Boulevard coliseum almost since the building's opening. Minor-league ice hockey stayed in Charlotte for about twenty years,

often playing to sellout crowds and enjoying a brief reign of Carolina glory. It was a "socko" novelty that Southerners adopted on coliseum ice in 1956. Transported Northerners cheered. When tough French Canadian players like popular Mike Rouleau or André DeChamps were thrust into the penalty box, sedate Charlotteans discovered primitive urges they hardly knew existed. At first, crowds were sparse, but Charlotte rapidly clasped hockey to its heart. Many fans had to be turned away particularly in 1974, when the team won the Southern Hockey League championship. In the 1990s, ice hockey is scheduled to return to Charlotte in the reno-vated coliseum, now known as Independence Arena.

Charlotte golf made it onto the PGA circuit in 1944, when the prize was in war bonds. The Charlotte Open, held at Myers Park Country Club from 1945 to 1948, saw such winners as Byron Nelson, Bob Hamilton, and Cary Middlecoff. A win at the Charlotte Open was part of Nelson's never-equaled winning streak of eleven consecutive tourna-ments. The United States Women's Amateur was played at Myers Park in 1955. Pro golf did not return to Charlotte again until the Kemper Open in 1968 at Quail Hollow Country Club. Arnold Palmer's thirty-thou-sand-dollar win that year made him golf's first million-dollar winner. Charlotte sadly said farewell to the big names and social events the Kemper spawned when the tournament moved to Washington's Congressional in 1979 and later to Chicago.

The World Seniors Invitational (now the PaineWebber), open to golfers over age fifty, came to Charlotte in 1980, largely due to the efforts of PGA star Arnold Palmer. In 1972, the United States Men's Amateur golf tourna-ment was played at Charlotte Country Club, the oldest such club in the city. The assistant pro there one summer was Gene Sarazen.

Charlotte's climate has always encouraged

Al Manch, Charlotte Checkers club owner, poses with one of his players.
The Checkers ice-hockey team enjoyed a brief surge of spectator interest.

Courtesy of Al Manch

enthusiastic year-round tennis. In the twenties and thirties, Teddy Burwell, Bobby Spumer, and Julia Pickens were highly rated. In 1979, Bob Crosland was elected to the North Carolina Tennis Hall of Fame. An exhilarating glimpse of the big time occurred when the World Championship Tennis tournament was played at the five-thousand-seat Julian Clark Stadium at the Olde Providence Racquet and Tennis Club in the seventies. Davis Cup finals were held there also, and Chris Evert garnered early wins there. In 1968, the Davis Cup American-zone finals (United States versus Ecuador) took place in the coliseum. In 1990, the United States Clay Courts Tennis Championships were played in Charlotte.

Luke and Sol Tenner promoted boxing into a boom in the thirties and packed the old Armory Auditorium. The Golden Gloves Tournament (the oldest amateur boxing tournament in the Southeast) was started in 1933 by M. H. Brandon and Jake Wade of the *Charlotte Observer*. Fine boxers from Fort Bragg, Camp Lejeune, Cherry Point, and other military bases hurtled the event into popularity during World War II. But boxing faded in popularity.

Charlotte has long nurtured major football dreams but has relinquished them several times. In the 1970s, pro football exhibitions drew so poorly they were abandoned; semipro

*The first black high-school football team in the city represented Second Ward School.
They wore secondhand uniforms of Central High players.*

Courtesy of D. G. Burke

football failed twice. The death of the World Football League in 1975, the resultant demise of the WFL Hornets team, and the collapse of the initial plan for a proposed uptown stadium were punishing blows to fans' hopes for big-time Charlotte football.

Charlotte's most successful football story has been the popular Shrine Bowl games, begun in 1937 with a roar as high-school football all-stars squared off in a North Carolina versus South Carolina game before overflow crowds at Memorial Stadium. With Carolinians annually filling the twenty-five-thousand-seat outdoor stadium, millions of dollars in proceeds from Shrine Bowls over the years have fed into the Crippled Children's Hospital in Greenville, South Carolina. The game traditionally follows a colorful parade, with Shriners in full regalia marching with clowns and bands down Trade Street to the stadium.

In the past, Atlantic Coast Conference football was played in Memorial Stadium, particularly on Thanksgiving Day following a Christmas parade. Hopalong Cassidy, Fred Kirby, and other notables led Santa Claus into town. The Carousel Ball followed in the evening.

By 1992, Charlotte had acquired and cleared a large, complicated land package for a National Football League stadium between uptown and I-77. For construction to begin, what remained was for Charlotte to survive the competition with other cities and receive the NFL contract. This kind of heady optimism is typical of Charlotte's push in sports or other commercial endeavors.

Traveling Charlotteans are often surprised to learn abroad that their city has long been best-known for its racetrack. The first big automobile race at the Charlotte Speedway was a 250-miler in 1924. The 1.25-mile oval wooden speedway was built on 283 acres 9 miles south of town on the Columbia highway. It was one of Osmond Barringer's projects, aided by B. D. Heath, Lane Etheredge, Ira Triplett, and George Wadsworth.

Stock-car racing has flourished for decades at the Charlotte Motor Speedway, but Charlotte is known nationally for two annual NASCAR races at the current speedway. Race days make surrounding highways resemble a major migration. The National 500, sponsored by Mello Yello and held annually the first weekend in October, drew over 158,000 in 1991. Started in 1960, the Coca Cola 600, held every Memorial Day, attracted 160,000 fans in 1992. The Saturday preceding each race features the Busch Grand National 300. These roaring outdoor races have wide appeal and are unrivaled by any other event in Charlotte. The speedway sports an unparalleled track. The May race draws

the second biggest crowd in America for any event, trailing only the Indianapolis 500, which attracts about 400,000. The speedway, north of Charlotte on U.S. 29, is a year-round tourist attraction and is the nation's NASCAR capital.

Racecar stars like Kyle and Richard Petty are solid, longtime favorites. NASCAR's winningest driver, Richard Petty announced his intention to retire after the 1992 season following a thirty-five-year career of scrapes and escapes, two hundred wins, and seven championships. Wearing his trademark smile, sunglasses, and cowboy hat, Petty said he is grateful the Lord gave him twenty-five years of good luck. Avid racing fans and tourists have made Petty memorabilia a large spin-off industry, with lucrative sales of Petty clocks, bottles, phones, books, jackets, and tiny racecar replicas.

Above:
Richard Petty

Left and top left:
Crowds and cars roar at popular Charlotte Motor Speedway races. On Memorial Day 1992, 160,000 fans cheered their favorites in the Coca Cola 600.

Charlotte Motor Speedway

George Shinn,
owner of the Charlotte Hornets NBA basketball team
and the Charlotte Knights baseball team

Charlotte Hornets

Big-Time Basketball

Great news for Charlotte basketball is the new Charlotte Coliseum and a man named George Shinn. Completed in 1988, the 23,900-seat coliseum was welcomed with ovations because North Carolina has long been basketball country, and Charlotte wanted her share. The Eastern Regionals of the NCAA tournament and other important games were played in the city for several years successfully, but cities with larger facilities consistently gathered the plums. Sportswriter Ron Green applauded Shinn: "Against long odds, he sought an NBA franchise for the city and in 1987, it was awarded. That franchise vaulted the city into the major leagues and changed the nation's perceptions of the area. TV sports announcers in Duluth, Minn., or Seattle no longer had to add 'North Carolina' after 'Charlotte' on the evening news." The team took a popular, familiar name, the Charlotte Hornets. Since 1987, Shinn also has acquired the Charlotte Knights and Gastonia Rangers minor-league baseball franchises and promoted other events in the region.

Another prominent local hero with star talent as a developer-entrepreneur-sports supporter is businessman Johnny Harris. A Charlotte native who makes key changes happen, Harris has "worked behind the scenes," according to Green, "influencing people to bring events to Charlotte or to support those already in place." Harris headed the successful campaign to bring the 1994 Final Four tournament to Charlotte, served as chairman for the Kemper Open and the PaineWebber World Seniors Invitational, and spearheaded the drive for the new coliseum. Harris and Shinn provided leadership to swerve Charlotte from being a poor sports town to becoming a sizzling sports city.

It is not surprising that basketball made it happen. North Carolina's ACC teams have long been among the country's finest. Davidson College's Wildcats and UNC-Charlotte's Forty-niners have performed well nationally and are extremely promising college teams. When the Hornets and a regular basketball lineup moved into the new coliseum in 1988 with big-time entertainment glitz, suddenly everything changed.

Why was it so hard? What happened to change a town that for decades had a reputation for supporting only wrestling and stock-car racing? Green, in a look at Charlotte sports in the *Charlotte Observer,* credited a steady population growth and large-market ticket potential, as well as progressive, energetic leadership and citizens willing to spend money on sports events for entertainment. Many newcomers to Charlotte had moved from major-league cities. Green noted that "they had a taste for caviar and wouldn't settle for tuna."

Left:
Charlotte Hornets game in the new Charlotte Coliseum

Charlotte Hornets

Going and Growing

Herbert Baxter always had a list in his pocket, a string of ideas for a better Charlotte. The city's mayor in 1943 and subsequently a councilman, he had a fifteen-point plan (1958), a ten-point plan (1959), and at age seventy, the former Bostonian pulled out his fourteen-point plan. He was a prodder, an irritant, an idea man. Columnist Kays Gary wrote, "Everytime he reached inside his coat pocket, folks would flinch." He could not have said, "Let's get going!" at a better time, because postwar Charlotte needed an itch to scratch. During Baxter's active career, he and numerous other leaders worked on an amazing checklist for a modern city—smoke abatement, city planning, slum clearance, redevelopment, hospital, airport, and bus-service improvement, construction of Ovens Auditorium and the Independence Boulevard coliseum, annexation, rezoning, perimeter parks, and Sugar Creek improvements. In 1956 when Charlotte had 160,000 people, he urged, "We have to get in the 200,000 class. Blue chip companies say, 'Let's open up 15 new plants somewhere' and then they bring out all the facts on cities over 200,000 in size."

Editorial writer Hal Tribble of the *Charlotte Observer* noted, "Baxter neglected his business to promote his public dreams. In a community that had penny-pinched its way to a state of threatened stagnation, Baxter cajoled the voters into investing $12 million in a mammoth 'Program for Progress.' "

Former Mayor Stan Brookshire considered the transportation thoroughfare plan in the early sixties, the Odell Master Plan in 1965, and urban renewal with the cooperation of Southern Railway as key ventures in the city's physical progress.

In 1980, Mayor Eddie Knox broke ground for a $55.6-million Douglas Municipal Airport terminal, which was completed in 1982. Expansion in 1990 opened four international gates and twenty commuter gates, with concourse extensions and additions to meet the needs of increased overseas flights and growth by USAir, which merged with Piedmont Airlines in 1989. With 250 foreign firms located in Charlotte, the Charlotte/Douglas International Airport in 1991 originated nearly five hundred flights daily as a major transportation facility for cargo and passengers. That same year, more than eight million passengers boarded in Charlotte. Business experts looking for the why of Charlotte's growth credit the new airport, a huge amount of modern warehouse space, and rail and highway connections accessible for the distribution of goods.

Former Mayor John Belk said, "What the railroad was to Charlotte 100 years ago, the airport is today." He recalled that the first plane to take off on the new 1979 runway was a cargo jet carrying tobacco to Saudi Arabia. The city's regional leadership in manufacturing and trade has attracted large companies such as Celanese Corporation, IBM, Textron, and Phillip Morris. Each week's newspapers announce other firms opening offices in Charlotte. "Without the airport," said former city manager Bill Veeder, "they probably would not have located here."

Charlotte is a major trucking center and has the largest trucking employment in the Southeast. D. J. Thurston helped Charlotte become a trucking center. In 1932, he was unable to find work as an electrical engineer, so he hauled peaches from South Carolina orchards to Richmond. Night after night, he hauled anything he could find to carry in his 1931 Chevrolet truck. His small company, Thurston Motor Lines, has expanded and is now one of more than thirty husky trucking firms that list Charlotte as headquarters.

Standard and piggyback rail-freight busi-

Douglas Municipal Airport, c. 1950s

Outgoing Mayor Stan Brookshire swears in John Belk in 1969. Brookshire and Belk were the only Charlotte mayors to serve four terms. Charlotte freeways bear their names.

Belk Archives

ness also operate extensive services in Charlotte. Lately, railroad passenger service is on the upswing. Charlotte is on the New York to New Orleans route of that famous lady, the Silver Crescent, who now answers to the name of Amtrak. A popular revitalized route is the daily Carolinian from Charlotte to Raleigh, which connects with north-south Amtrak service between New York and Florida.

Charlotte's hospitals have long set her apart. She is a regional medical center with three major hospitals—one a prestigious medical teaching facility—and numerous hospitals and private clinics for specialty patient care. Satellite hospitals in the city's expressway perimeters burgeoned in the 1980s. Charlotte's Memorial Hospital underwent major expansion and became the Carolinas Medical Center in 1991.

The recent strong resurgence of Mecklenburg County's five major colleges and universities is one of Charlotte's happiest stories. The University of North Carolina at Charlotte, Davidson College, Johnson C. Smith University, Queens College, and Central Piedmont Community College offer an exceptional range of educational and trade opportunities.

Business aces like Hugh McColl, Ed Crutchfield, John Stedman, Rolfe Neill, and Bill Lee lent vigorous influence to the colleges to raise public interest and funding. Queens College initiated an executive MBA program. The University of North Carolina at Charlotte's creative energy flowed into the nearby twenty-six-hundred-acre University Research Park, where faculty and students work closely with industry. An example of academic subtlety is the boulevard named J. M. Keynes Drive in University City— Keynes was a British economic theorist. The University City–area concept was a radical idea for Charlotte. Strangled by a century of growth southeastward, Charlotte was desper-

Bill Lee

Duke Power Company

ate for change. The redirected growth north of the city in the 1970s and 1980s was chronicled in a book, *University Research Park, The First Twenty Years*, by Dean Colvard, Douglas Orr, and Mary Dawn Bailey.

Johnson C. Smith University launched 1992 with a fifty-million-dollar capital campaign. Because it lacks space, the 125-year-old historically black institution turns away hundreds of students. In its Advanced Technologies Center, Central Piedmont Community College offers advanced training in partnership with the region's most prestigious businesses and industries. Small but savvy and sophisticated, Davidson College regularly stars in national ratings of private liberal-arts colleges.

A Treasure to Preserve

Vernon Sawyer remembers the unhappiness of early urban renewal. In 1959, he began Charlotte's redevelopment program that cleared Brooklyn slums from Second Ward. In their place are pristine Marshall Park, the Education Center, the governmental plaza, and the John Belk Freeway link of the connector to I-77. The redevelopment program also cleared away black churches including Friendship Baptist and the United House of Prayer for All People, as well as homes and corner grocery stores. With it also went the rats. "They were everywhere and I was afraid for my babies," remembered one mother. Without housing plans for those people to be displaced, this first removal was a major lesson for all concerned and has not been repeated. Baseball player Bishop Dale was the first black member of Charlotte's Redevelopment Commission in 1965. Earlier, he served as the first black justice of the peace in Mecklenburg since Reconstruction, ran unsuccessfully for city council three times, and worked with black and white community interests through his American Legion, baseball, and business

efforts since the 1930s.

Cecilia Jackson Wilson, a longtime public-school teacher, grew up in the Brooklyn neighborhood. She lived there as a child and now goes to the dentist in the building on Alexander Street at Independence where her home sat. "My mother was a seamstress with customers in Dilworth," she said. "We'd go with her on the streetcar to carry dresses to her customers. We couldn't go to the park in Dilworth, but we could go to Lakewood. Our father took us to shows down the alley from Trade Street. I remember seeing *Smiling Through* and we went to the armory for programs. We thought Wachovia Bank belonged to our father, Oscar Jackson. He was a messenger there for 50 years and broke ground for their new building.

"We had no idea we lived in a ghetto. It was where most of the black people lived. Some of the best leaders lived there and businesses too, like the African Methodist Episcopal Zion Publishing House."

Housing at East Twelfth and Brevard streets, c. 1950, with Alpha Cotton Mill, built in 1901, in the background

*The Independence Building (above right) sagged
into dust one Sunday morning in 1981.*

*Smoke lingered in the skyline after the demolition,
viewed from East Trade Street.*

The Masonic Temple was among the other landmarks that disappeared, though protesters rallied to try to save the building in the late 1980s.

Cecilia Wilson taught English thirty-eight years in Mecklenburg schools at Second Ward, South Mecklenburg, West Charlotte, and Fairview. She regrets the loss of large, gracious homes in that most beautiful section near the YMCA on East Morehead Street.

Mrs. Wilson has company. "Where is everything?" people often ask in downtown Charlotte—newcomers who wonder what happened to Charlotte's urban past, old-timers who wonder now why no one saved the opera house, the Selwyn Hotel, the Phifer House, the Colonel William Johnston House, the Ezekiel Wallace Rock House, the

McIntyre Cabin, or the Dewey Bank. Major, controversial battles swirled around the Independence Building and the Masonic Temple. Both were lost. Such was the outcry for these that subsequently, in the dark of a single night, a small architectural jewel on South Church Street vanished—the Industrial Loan and Investment Bank, with its temple facade of carved limestone designed by Martin Boyer in 1929. Seven uptown buildings designated as historic sites were lost between the 1988 publication of a walking tour and its reprinting in 1990. During 1991, three more were destroyed.

Preservation has proved much more successful in the city's perimeter neighborhoods such as Myers Park and Dilworth, and in singular homes, churches, and schools

After the fuss over the Masonic Temple, the uptown Industrial Loan and Investment Bank vanished overnight.

The hornets' nest symbol appears on designated historic landmarks in Mecklenburg County.

Nancy Reid House in Matthews,
a preservation success

throughout the county. The organized muscle of neighborhood groups armed with lawyers, chiefly the Myers Park Homeowners Association and the Dilworth Community Development Association, proved so formidable in the 1980s that it changed the face of city politics and media coverage. A 1991 bond election approved for the first time a revolving preservation fund to purchase endangered structures. Perimeter towns are claiming small treasures such as the Nancy Reid House in Matthews, a Victorian charmer that was the village doctor's residence. The college town of Davidson, with its delightful abundance of nineteenth-century buildings, has strong support to maintain its authentic character. The Historic Landmarks Commission works vigorously on the present with a view to the significant past, giving annual awards for exceptional preservation efforts. During twenty years since its organization in 1972, the commission's patient but vigorous work led to historic-site approval for 179 properties in Charlotte-Mecklenburg.

In 1950, there were few, if any, public historic sites restored or open for visiting within the county. Particularly since 1975, impressive preservation efforts have enabled these sites to open regularly or by appointment: Afro-American Cultural Center (1911); J. S. Dowd House (1879); Hezekiah Alexander Homesite (1774); Latta Place (1800); James K. Polk Homesite (1795, reconstructed); Saint Mary's Chapel (1891); Spirit

A prime rural preservation is Latta Place, an 1800 Catawba River home located in Latta Plantation Park.

Another example of successful preservation is
The Homeplace at 5901 Sardis Road.

James K. Polk Memorial,
a North Carolina State Historic Site in Pineville,
consists of reconstructed log buildings on
lands where the eleventh president of
the United States spent his childhood.

Square (1909); Mint Museum of Art (1835, relocated with additions); Rosedale (c. 1815); and Hugh Torance House and Store (1770s).

Fred Bryant, a longtime member of the Charlotte Planning Commission staff, offered one explanation for what has often been an amazing demolition derby. "Charlotte never has had a concentrated historical area. It has gone piece by piece." Many of the finest homes were frame and unfortunately stood on commercial streets, particularly Trade, Tryon, Brevard, McDowell, College, and Church. Rather than preserve the large, rambling homes and the pedestrian-friendly two- to three-story commercial buildings, the overall

practice has been to clear or to build new structures. Bryant sees great value in coming back and using those passed-by areas.

The idea for the preservation of Fourth Ward was in the 1960 general development plan for Charlotte. It was a crazy idea. Bryant remarked, "It took real guts at first."

In 1884 when Charlotte had eight thousand citizens, John Newcomb built a house at 324 West Ninth Street in the prestigious downtown neighborhood of Fourth Ward. His brother George built next door. Together, the brothers ran a bellows factory. Their wives were partners in the S&C Newcomb millinery shop and sold hats to the town's well-to-do ladies. A Newcomb daughter married Ernest Berryhill, and they lived in the house on West Ninth, which remained in family hands. More recently, it became a four-unit apartment until it was purchased by the Charlotte Junior League in 1975 as a courageous bid to get the restoration ball rolling in the deteriorating downtown neighborhood—a crazy idea. But with money, enthusiasm, and low-cost loans, the idea is working.

The Charlotte Junior League in November 1975 took an option on the Berryhill House, a fallen queen of Fourth Ward, one of the homes that remained. The league invested and secured help from Knight Publishing Company, Exxon Corporation, and Ivey's to purchase and refurbish the house for fifty thousand dollars. Dennis Rash asked Hugh McColl for North Carolina National Bank's help in revitalizing Fourth Ward. He got it. This courageous pilot project, government renewal funds to encourage land accumulation, and special bank-loan conditions were the three catalysts that made it possible. Those who bought the first houses were pioneers of the first order.

The once-elegant in-town section was bereft of many of its finest homes. What few remained were often overgrown and unpainted. Empty lots attracted derelicts. Since 1975, houses have been remodeled, and some have been moved in from other neigh-

Rebuilding Fourth Ward, city workers lay a new sidewalk past the historic Overcarsh House (1880).

Charlotte Observer

borhoods. At least thirty charming houses now shine with attention in a neighborhood with a park, new and old condominiums, shops, apartments, a home for the elderly, and a large day-care center. Residents walk to work, to the library, or to plays, jog in Elmwood and Pinewood cemeteries, and enjoy sunsets reflected in the city's skyline. On their way to work, they can read the bronze sidewalk markers noting historic events and sites.

One of the most colorful, hardest-won dreams involving uptown preservation is the work by Dan Morrill and Charlotte Trolley, Inc., a private foundation. They raised $220,000 to restore two streetcars to run regularly on existing track in uptown Charlotte between Dilworth's Tremont Avenue on the south and Twelfth Street on the north, carrying tourists and Charlotteans just as the popular streetcar used to do. The route easily connects the convention center and hotels with Charlotte's uptown stars: the Square and Polk Park, Discovery Place, Spirit Square, the Performing Arts Center, the spacious public library, the government center, and restaurants and shops. One restored streetcar was built in 1927 to run in Dilworth and retired in 1938 when streetcars yielded to city buses. The second is an 1896 English streetcar that operated in Athens, Greece, after World War II. Why is the revived streetcar service important? It's lively, useful, authentic Charlotte history, and, as Morrill said, "It's fun!"

The sudden spurt of change in Charlotte's leisurely skyline has occurred since 1980, when a spate of familiar buildings was razed to provide space for tall new office buildings, banks, hotels, and other upstart symbols of the city's ambition and achievement. E. D. Latta would like knowing that hotels have finally found the vicinity of South Tryon and College to be prime hotel space. He bet on it long ago.

Uptown is Charlotte's healthy heartbeat. The planning proposals in 1965 and the consultants' plan for 1995, formulated by RTKL Associates of Baltimore, have invested heavily in the center city. Many of the 1965 proposals have been accomplished by way of Charlotte's responsive political process. The far-reaching 2005 plan addresses the problem of managed growth in a soon-to-be thoroughly urban county. Future planning hopefully will include continued preservation of interesting storefronts on Trade and Tryon, as well as preservation of rural sites important to Charlotte's historic character.

Preservationists hope for, and visitors enjoy, a colorful and careful blend of old and new. The three handsome sisters—Dilworth, Elizabeth, and Myers Park—are invaluable jewels in Charlotte's crown. The designated streetcar neighborhoods of Dilworth (1891), Elizabeth (c. 1891–1915), and Myers Park (1911) are on the National Register of Historic Districts. Unexcelled as places to live and to show off to visitors, they suggest Charlotte's rich textile past and the vitality of her present. The mill-village area of North Charlotte that arose from three mills (1903–15) was recently added to the National Register of Historic Districts.

Richard Vinroot, lawyer, council member, and mayor in 1992, considers Charlotte's history as that of "a middle class community by and large." Because of this, he believes the city lacks the scale and wealth of the many grand mansions of Charleston and Richmond. But, Vinroot added, "we have a more democratic past."

In her most gracious spaces, Charlotte is strong but vulnerable. She shows a pragmatic tendency to nibble at her past in favor of shiny, new uncertainty. To preserve the quality of life that is currently her best asset, her leaders must exhibit independent thinking and do what it takes to hold onto these places and the conscience that protects them.

Preservationist professor Dr. Dan Morrill and a restored Charlotte streetcar are ready to get on track.

Charlotte Observer

Above and right: The 1980s were uptown Charlotte's decade of constant construction, as shown here on Tryon Street.

Leather Walls and Poolside Parties

One wonders what Blanche would think of her house now. Villa Square, the European-style shopping plaza at 715 Providence Road, owes its unique Tuscan Revival sophistication to the artistic taste of Blanche Reynolds, the widow who built it as a home in 1926. She inherited wealth from her husband, William A. Reynolds of Southern Cotton Oil Company. While traveling in Italy, she met and married Alexis Gourmajenko, a refugee from the Russian Revolution. They returned to live in Charlotte in grand style—a leather-walled séance room at the top of the house, frescoes on the bedroom ceiling, hand-carved Belgian fireplaces, Cuban roof tiles, entrance fountain, piazzas, and, under tall cedars in the rear garden, Charlotte's first swimming pool. The couple gave lavish poolside parties and drove their Daimler automobile flamboyantly through the Square on Sundays with two Dalmatians in the back seat. Well-known New York architect William L. Bottomly designed the home. It was purchased by developers in 1976 for conversion into the Villa Square shops, with both courtyard and interior dining. In 1977, it was awarded designation as a Charlotte-Mecklenburg Historic Property.

Ornamental Details from Historic Landmarks of Charlotte

Benevolent angel from Elizabeth College

Detail from the Overcarsh House in Fourth Ward

Earthquake bolt from the Bagley-Mullen House at 129 North Poplar Street, built in 1895

Facade of the Southern Bell building

Tombstone at Elmwood Cemetery

Spire of First Presbyterian Church

Facade of Belk's

Of The People and For The People

"**H**ighly visible" aptly describes government in Charlotte. Newspapers insist on it. The public requires it. Not much gets by undetected in a city with so many active neighborhood groups and so many people who are conscience-bound to write letters to the editor. Occasionally, not much gets accomplished either.

Whether Charlotte has been kept honest by her heritage, her acumen, or her provincial naivete is debatable. But the effect is open, responsive, and often feisty government. She operates on the city-manager system, with a mayor and eleven elected members of the city council. Not until 1977 did district representation occur—seven members chosen from districts, four at large. Before district representation, the city council was primarily a group of "older white men from the Central Business District," according to UNC-C political scientist Ted Arrington. They very effectively ran Charlotte "like a small town. You had government by a kind of an anointed few who were in the business community." The path to politics required "moving through the chairs" of the United Way, the chamber of commerce, the arts, the church. District representation and the neighborhood movement changed all that. The *Charlotte Leader* described local government in 1991: "The mayor is a woman from outside the traditional establishment, and the council is peopled with lawyers and professional women and blacks from every part of the city." Partisan local elections began in 1975. Mecklenburg County is governed by a county commission of seven elected members in districts and at large (since 1986), with a full-time county manager. Consolidation of the two bodies has been argued periodically, was defeated once,

and is being accomplished haltingly by stages. Certain areas were consolidated years ago: public schools, the planning commission, the tax department, libraries, and utilities.

Since 1970, local government has been consistently biracial. Blacks and women comprise a consistent minority in elective office. Gone are the days recalled by Pat Locke, the second woman elected to city council, when she was omitted from the invited list of the new council for a fishing trip sponsored by one of the city's banks. She called to ask where her invitation was. Her call cancelled the trip.

Charlotte's first black mayor, architect Harvey Gantt, served first as councilman beginning in 1974 and as mayor in 1983, with a second term in 1985. Gantt subsequently ran for the United States Senate in 1990 against North Carolina's senior senator, Republican Jesse Helms, and was defeated despite a strong showing in the urban Piedmont. As an architecture student, Gantt in 1963 was the first black to be admitted to Clemson University. It took a federal court

Harvey Gantt

order to accomplish this, and South Carolina officials appealed the decision to the United States Supreme Court. Charlotte's first female mayor, Sue Myrick, with her personal and professional advertising savvy, followed Gantt and rode to victory on the old but urgent Mecklenburg issue of road improvement. New residents in traffic-strangled southeast Charlotte lined up to register Republican and elect her. Often in Charlotte, a Republican mayor is offset by a Democratic council and vice versa, but issues frequently override party lines.

Charlotte-Mecklenburg for most of its history has been an independent-thinking Democratic town with persistent Republican bastions. But Charles R. Jonas, elected with Eisenhower in 1954, captured the Ninth Congressional District seat for the Republicans and refused to let go, as did his successor, Republican James G. Martin, and Martin's successor, Alex McMillan of Charlotte. Martin, a Davidson College chemistry professor who began his political career on Charlotte's county commission, served two

terms as governor of North Carolina beginning in 1985.

Statewide, Charlotte-Mecklenburg exerts far less power than her size and population would indicate. Charlotte is the largest city in the Carolinas. But since earliest days when the Piedmont was regarded as ragtag back country, the power lay with the eastern gentry. Charlotte was cut off geographically and politically from the beginning. Not even the rivers connected her with eastern counties. Modern-day elected representatives, being true Mecklenburgers, have often tended to disagree among themselves, diluting their power. In Raleigh, she is referred to with some petulance as "the Great State of Mecklenburg," but she is gradually gaining long-sought respect for her muscle, if not for her manners.

One of the longest-fought and most locally desired laws to be enacted by the state legislature was the liquor-by-the-drink bill, passed on September 9, 1978. Until that time, liquor could only be served legally in private clubs in North Carolina. Restaurants across the line

Liquor battle: Nondrinkers, shown here at a neighborhood rally (tea and sandwiches), put up a good fight throughout the early 1900s.

Courtesy of Mary Cato

The Charlotte Observer

It Passes!
68% Of Voters Say 'Yes' To Mixed Drinks

A liquor-by-the-drink bill liberalized North Carolina in 1978, and Charlotteans then had the option to pass or reject it locally. They passed it.

in more liberal South Carolina welcomed heavy traffic from their northern neighbor. Prior to the bill's passage, customers carried their own liquor in bottles wrapped in brown paper bags. The odd custom of "brown bagging" was noted with amazement by visitors. The battle to prevent serving mixed drinks in the state and county caused a moral and religious war and was hotly debated in the media. Some thought passage of the bill would propel Charlotte's rapid growth and diminish the quality of life.

Since the bill's passage, the number and variety of restaurants in Charlotte have increased markedly. One of the chief local arguments in favor of the bill was that it would encourage convention business and hotel construction.

A Hurricane Named Hugo

Since 1989, September 22 never comes around in Charlotte without a collective shudder from everyone who remembers when Hurricane Hugo came through in the night. Dawn found residents trapped in their homes, barricaded in driveways, with huge trees across hundreds of rooftops and blocking major and minor roads. Yards that had been clear and grassy the afternoon before were head-high with snapped-off treetops and limbs as far as residents could see. In some city neighborhoods, power was out for weeks. Crews of tree-removal workers came hundreds of miles to clear the wreckage. Charlotte's proud legacy of huge trees and their dense canopy changed beyond recognition. But national attention was focused on Charleston, South Carolina, where (like the gale-force storm of 1916 that swept northwest to batter Charlotte and flood the Catawba) the storm came inland. Charlotteans who were fortunate enough to have operable televisions were astonished to see national news coverage focus on Charleston while the havoc of comparable wind damage filled Charlotte roads, yards, and rooftops. Hurricane winds in Charlotte measured up to eighty-seven miles per hour. People who fled from inland South Carolina to the perceived safety of Charlotte relatives wished they had stayed home. If one house on a street had a generator or electricity, a soup kitchen quickly opened for neighbors.

In addition to a long swath of South Carolina damage, Hugo mangled 2.7 million acres of North Carolina woodland, damaging timber worth an estimated $250 million. Charlotte, about two hundred miles inland from Charleston, never dreamed she could be in the path of such a storm. A forgotten account by W. M. Bell in 1916 captured what Charlotteans also saw in 1989: "Awnings [were] torn from buildings, signs ripped from their holdings, plate glass store fronts smashed, roofs blown away, homes and stores flooded, beautiful trees uprooted and those that remained standing shorn of their limbs in many instances and strewn along the streets for blocks. Next morning the city looked like a cyclone had struck it." That was Saturday morning, July 15, 1916.

Charlotte has more in common with Charleston than just the resemblance of their names. Not only have Charlotte's worst storm-related catastrophes come through Charleston, but even Charleston's devastating earthquake of 1886 rumbled this way. Charlotte received four shocks, enough to tumble children from their beds and scare folks out of the opera house and the Baptist church and crying into the streets. It was enough to make Charlotte greatly compassionate toward Charlestonians. The city of Charlotte authorized a thousand-dollar donation sent to Charleston "for sufferers from the earthquake."

Hurricane Hugo left a wake in Charlotte neighborhoods in September 1989.

Courtesy of
Pat and Molly Brugh

A Tradition from the Earliest Times

Charlotte has always loved rousing preachers and had more than her share of good ones. Word spreads in drugstores and markets and over lunches that someone is especially gifted, and a following begins. Such historic groundswells of area religion have been incredibly diverse and have regularly reached national proportions.

Back in the 1930s, an itinerant evangelist named A. G. Garr began a highly successful revival in Irwin's pasture on the outskirts of town. In the fall of 1930, he and his supporters built a wooden tabernacle to seat twenty-five hundred; they put sides on it in the winter. In 1932, when the old city auditorium at College and Fifth streets was put up for sale, Garr bought the structure and had it taken apart and reassembled by church members, who transported it at night, piece by piece, to the three-acre tract at Tuskaseegee Road and Duckworth, where it became Garr Auditorium. After his death, his wife and son continued the ministry on radio shows throughout the South and abroad. Garr's followers were innovative community savers who finished their church's interior with materials from demolished local institutions, such as the paneling from the early courthouse on West Trade Street.

During the 1950s, nearly 450,000 persons attended W. E. "Billy" Graham's Charlotte Crusade for Christ in the coliseum, accompanied by a 1,750-voice choir from area churches. Graham was born and grew up on his father's Charlotte dairy farm, which encompassed what is now Park Road Shopping Center. He rose from local tent revivals to become a worldwide evangelist and preacher to presidents. He practiced his

Billy Graham, shown above in his graduation photograph from Sharon High School and below as a worldwide evangelist

B.G.E.A. Photo

Dr. Carlyle Marney

Myers Park Baptist Church

Dr. James A. Jones

Myers Park Presbyterian Church

preaching on a creek bank and occasionally on the Saturday-afternoon uptown steps of Spirit Square (old First Baptist Church).

In the 1960s, interest ranged from the rapid institutional growth and fundamentalist fervor of Jack Hudson to the provocative intellectual gymnastics and poetics of Carlyle Marney, an ecumenist who lectured at Princeton and Yale universities and to air-force troops in the Orient. Both were Baptists.

In the 1970s, the erudite good humor of James A. "Jazz A." Jones and Warner Hall pleased the Presbyterians immensely. But Bishop C. M. "Daddy" Grace's annual arrival in Charlotte for Grace Holy Convocation eclipsed everything in town. Nationwide

Bishop C. M. "Daddy" Grace

Charlotte Observer

followers of the 180 United Houses of Prayer for All People attended the parades, which were preceded by baptism at the outdoor United House of Prayer pool. Many uniformed black followers and local string, brass, and "shout" bands followed, and in 1947 over twenty-five thousand stood in the streets to watch. When in town, Daddy Grace stayed at the United House of Prayer residence, where flags were draped on each side of the door and a large neon sign said, "Welcome, Daddy Grace." Grace's headquarters were in Washington, but he considered the Charlotte church one of his strongest houses.

The most recent flamboyance reached national proportions. Television's most boyish religious fund-raiser, Jim Bakker, succeeded in his once-tiny television ministry in Charlotte to such a degree that the state-of-the-art television studio on Park Road Extension became far too small for the thousands of pilgrims who poured into the studio and mailed their donations to the PTL Club. In

Jim Bakker

The House of Prayer for All People, Bishop C. M. "Daddy" Grace's church on North McDowell Street, was razed by urban renewal for Marshall Park.

Public Library of
Charlotte and Mecklenburg County

1975, televangelist Bakker broke ground for Heritage Village, which included a hotel, television studios, homes, campsites, a water slide, and other recreational and worship facilities on a large site south of Charlotte near Fort Mill, South Carolina. Bakker's rise and fall are the subject of a book, *Forgiven*, by *Charlotte Observer* investigative reporter Charles E. Shepard. Bakker's conviction in 1989 for mail fraud and wire fraud resulted in a forty-five-year sentence, which in 1991 was reduced to eighteen years. Bakker was accused of fraud to the extent of $150 million. Bakker's trial in Charlotte was one of the most curious and widely publicized events in recent history. Shepard's reporting led to an exposé of Bakker that won a Pulitzer Prize in public service for the *Charlotte Observer*. Heritage Village was put up for sale. The complex was described by Frye Galliard in his book, *Southern Voices*, as "a $170 million Lego land for the Lord."

Julia Mauldin, Charlotte director for Habitat for Humanity, and national founder Millard Fuller pause for a break in construction of homes for the working poor.

A couple watches home being built by Habitat for Humanity volunteers and future residents.

With such a diverse past, Charlotte wears an ecumenical atmosphere to a remarkable degree for a Southern city on the edge of the Bible Belt. Some of the city's best work for positive social change arises from churches; Habitat for Humanity is a prime example. Habitat for Humanity helps low-income working people who could never hope to own a home do so with their own "sweat equity." Since 1983, 133 houses have been built by Habitat for Humanity with local and national volunteers and future homeowners. Churches in Charlotte know how to get important things done. The question put to newcomers, "Where do you go to church?" is a long-standing regional expression that goes back to the importance of church in the lives of Southerners. It is a traditional, courteous inquiry that used to be about the safest social question one could ask in order to open a conversation.

Charlotte in the mid-1900s was known as a city of beautiful churches. Throughout her history, she has had not only an unusually large number and variety of churches, congregations, and colorful preachers, but also consistently thirsty listeners. Their religious appetites have varied widely according to current personalities and the times.

Of Banks and Buildings

Anyone who has not seen downtown Charlotte since 1970 will rub his eyes in disbelief. James Batten, who was an *Observer* reporter in the mid-1970s, remembers uptown "as a pretty forgettable, down-at-the-heels sort of place. It was really at a low ebb." Coming back periodically, Batten now stands "slack-jawed anew" at the physical changes.

Since 1975, Charlotte has reinvented herself to become a new city visibly, even though she is far older than Durham or even Atlanta. Except for her churchyards, Charlotte's cityscape in no way resembles earlier photographs. It is as though Queen Charlotte has thrown off her cape and tossed aside her petticoats in sudden preference for modern clothing. Hotels, office buildings, and competing bank towers built since 1980 offer new variety in building styles and exhibit distinctive architecture. Some are by Charlotte architects, others by national stars. Appropriately, the major transformation has occurred on the corners of the four blocks that touch Charlotte's central Square, the ancient crossroads site at the intersection of Trade and Tryon streets.

Longtime observers attribute this "zoom factor" to the groundwork laid twenty years before—urban renewal, the government center, the airport—so that when the nation turned toward service industries rather than manufacturing, Charlotte was ready with exceptional financial, transport, and distribution capabilities. In the 1980s, Charlotte also spent millions in public monies for very visible cultural assets: Mint Museum and Discovery Place expansion, Spirit Square renovation, main-library expansion, and a new Performing Arts Center. These were sparked by energetic volunteer efforts and supportive private and corporate funding, as well as public bond issues for construction. The "new city" is no accident. It has meant twenty years of hard labor.

Charlotte's perimeters during that time have leapt across what is sometimes called the "Textile Highway" (I-85) and sprawled past Eastland Mall, South Park, Carolina Mall, Carowinds, University Research Park, and the UNC-C campus and into extensive residential expansion within surrounding counties. Statesville, Rock Hill, Salisbury, and Gastonia are closely linked neighbors, rather than the far country. In 1980, the Champion Map company decreased Charlotte's map scale 35 percent to take care of new growth, and within the decade of the eighties added five hundred to a thousand new streets annually to county-map revisions. I-77, which follows the river basin, brings to commuters the pleasure of Lake Norman and Lake Wylie, with a combined 847 miles of shoreline. Newcomers with their sailboats praise sparkling Lake Norman, while old-timers recall their farmhouses and family fields, which now lie beneath the blue waters.

The rapid population growth includes transplants not only from the North and West, a stream of West Virginians down the "Hillbilly Highway," and newcomers from the Midwest and lower South, but also an influx of immigrants from foreign countries. The number of Asian residents in Charlotte tripled between 1980 and 1990. The mixed languages in shopping malls and markets commonly include German, Japanese, and Asian Indian speech.

Business writer M. S. Van Hecke and urban historian David Goldfield agree that Charlotte as we know it in the 1990s began in the 1880s, with the New South's rise in manufacture and commerce so visible in the D. A. Tompkins era. And what a rise it has been. *Fortune* magazine in 1991 placed Charlotte seventh among the country's top-ten

---

Left:
The Garden, *outdoor sculpture by Jerry Peart*

Sailing on Lake Norman

Charlotte Chamber of Commerce

The Mint Museum of Art's modern entrance and plaza are at 2730 Randolph Road. The mint's historic face is visible from Hempstead Place.

Charlotte Convention and Visitors Bureau
Photo by Mark Fortenberry

cities for business: "What this upstart North Carolina city lacks in polish it makes up for in one all-important intangible: pro-business attitude, a category in which it ranks first, even ahead of Atlanta." The *Los Angeles Times* agreed: "No longer a sleepy mill town dependent upon the fortunes of the surrounding textile and furniture industries, Charlotte . . . is a dynamic financial, manufacturing and transportation center." Van Hecke sees banks as the glamour industry, but the underlying strength is in distribution. "These," said Van Hecke, "are the people you never see."

Charlotte's "entrepreneurial pluck," as described in *Management Review* in 1989, has long been the prime mover for change. Businesses or institutions sparked recent bank expansion, the arrival of newcomers like IBM, Royal Insurance, and Hearst Corporation, and the expansion of the airport. Individuals spearheaded other major advances, such as grocer W. T. Harris's leadership toward the creation of University Research Park. Grocer Ralph Ketner, wrote Van Hecke, "came to the old Manger Motor Inn in uptown Charlotte with his calculator and determined he could lure more customers to his Food Town stores [Food Lion] if he cut the price on every item." Pat Hall combined forces with Crescent Land and Timber Company and Wachovia to launch Carowinds. Commercial developer Henry Faison pushed Eastland, the Independence Tower, the Interstate Tower, and other widespread office towers and centers in Charlotte and on the East Coast. Faison and others began to seek a departure from the architectural styles to which Charlotteans were accustomed. Faison's Interstate Tower was designed by Kohn Pedersen Fox, currently thought to be one of the hottest office-tower designers in the country. The regional and local influence of John Crosland and developer Johnny Harris show an exceptional talent for property and land development. Historian David Goldfield said, "Charlotte has been especially blessed with these entrepreneurs. Tompkins in the 1880s initiated and led the cotton mill campaign—in a wider region, but based in Charlotte. This is how Charlotte began to build a base as the administrative and financial center for industry."

NationsBank Chairman Hugh McColl "is in that mold," said Goldfield. "What he did was parlay Charlotte's financial importance in the Carolinas into a broader regional and national prominence. He shares, particularly with Tompkins, a vision that goes considerably beyond Charlotte, both for its city and its people."

McColl in some ways is the archetypal New South entrepreneur. From a small Carolina town—Bennettsville, South Carolina—he came to the city young and tough and educated. He worked extremely hard at Commercial National Bank/NCNB and climbed, even ran, to the top. McColl admitted, "I like challenge. . . . I like competition. But what I like most of all is winning." He was especially proud of NCNB's ability to "quickly adapt our vision to seize a huge and

fruitful opportunity." The strength of his drive and NCNB's aggressiveness led to the acquisition of banks in Texas and Florida. Then in 1991, the merger of NCNB with C&S/Sovran of Atlanta created a giant of approximately $118 billion in assets and $6.8 billion in shareholders' equity. The new bank, headquartered in Charlotte, is NationsBank, third nationally in terms of banking assets. This change made Charlotte the third-largest banking center in the nation, exceeded only by New York and San Francisco.

Charlotte is headquarters of First Union National Bank, a strapping competitive local son and vital presence in the Southeast. A strong third member in the triumvirate is Wachovia, based in Winston-Salem. Mecklenburg County has seventeen banks. Six of the nation's top two hundred banks operate in Charlotte. Banks in Mecklenburg County beginning in 1992 had more than 8 billion in deposits.

Hugh McColl

NationsBank

Financial genealogy is a local labyrinth, but the family patriarch is Commercial National Bank, the oldest national banking institution in North Carolina (1874). Others began earlier but fell by the wayside. Commercial National Bank merged with several other banks to become North Carolina National Bank (NCNB) in 1960. Charlotte National (1897) merged twice before becoming Wachovia in 1939. Union National, which the steely eyed H. M. Victor steered through the Depression, merged to become First Union National Bank in 1959.

Strong competition continues among the banks, the big guys and the small. Mutual Savings and Loan goes back to 1881 and has claimed three generations of the Keesler family's leadership. Sam Wittkowsky's Mechanics and Perpetual Building and Loan Association (1883) has a new name—Home Federal. The Federal Reserve Bank of Charlotte has been a key factor in the city's early and continued growth.

Architecturally, the banks compete to command the skyline. With perfect timing, NationsBank's $150-million, sixty-story corporate center opened in 1992. Designed by Cesar Pelli, one of America's most renowned architects, on what Pelli described as "a fantastic site," it crowns the antique crossroads. Visible for miles, it stretches with its peers to achieve Louis Sullivan's definition of a skyscraper, "a proud and soaring thing." Part of a complex, it includes the Performing Arts Center, Founders Hall, and shopping and dining. It shares the vista with the singular rose-granite and glass-arched tower of forty-two-story One First Union Center (1988), designed by JPJ Architects of Dallas in association with FWA Group of Charlotte. First Union's complex incorporates the Charlotte Omni Hotel, the uptown YMCA, and a second office building with a $3-million park designed by M. Paul Friedberg and Partners, whose work includes the Olympic

Plaza for the 1988 Winter Olympics in Calgary, Alberta, Canada. The park encompasses the corner once occupied by the controversial Masonic Temple, which was razed. Wachovia's sleek, white thirty-two-story Wachovia Center on South Tryon was designed by Little and Associates Architects of Charlotte and built in 1974.

Financially and physically, Charlotte is riding a growth spurt. "The economic mix," said UNC-C geographer Dr. Jim Clay, "is beginning to have a dynamic of its own." Lenoir Keesler reported in 1980, "It took Mutual [Savings and Loan] 92 years to accumulate its first $100 million in savings deposits, but only five years to accumulate the second $100 million."

As these healthy financial giants rub tall, monied elbows along South Tryon and elsewhere, the competition is tangible and constant. Vague stories of competition and disagreement enliven the smooth face of success. One such story, unearthed by the Historic Landmarks Commission's research on downtown, tells of the early days of the Realty Building, which Julian Little always called the Independence Building on the Square. Little resigned as president of Charlotte National in 1912. Soon afterwards, he opened the Independence Trust Company in the basement of the Independence Building, right under the feet of the tellers of Charlotte National. When Woodall and Shepherd Drugstore upstairs moved out, Little moved upstairs to share the first floor of the Independence Building.

Competition extended to other levels also. About this same time, builder James A. Jones vacated his offices in the Independence Building, which he had built in 1908. A construction contract for adding two floors to the building had been awarded to another firm. Jones reportedly refused to endure some competing contractor hammering over his head.

City of Stories

Charlotte has a serious case of contagious ambition. Between 1955 and 1990, she sped gaily along like a sled with its runners waxed. Somewhere on the slope, she lost her hardy naivete; but with the hustle and bustle around her, it was no wonder.

She gained big-time sports and auditoriums and coliseums along with a sudden thicket of skyscrapers, malls, and sparkling hotels.

She became Asian and German and Middle Eastern.

She attracted prestigious industry, and transferring south suddenly became respectable.

Culture became her. Then she dreamed theater and a science museum and stunning libraries and an arts district, and clasped a neighborhood (once lost) and reclaimed it with joy, paint, and children.

She found whimsy at last—a giant yellow balloon and yo-yos for the arts suspended from a bank roof, and questionable dinosaur bones unearthed at a museum groundbreaking.

She created restaurants and markets where folks could buy things that Charlotte in 1980 had never heard of.

She built an airport and built more airport and still more to become a travel and transport hub.

Marathon runners captured her heart. She cheered them at every wintry corner.

Mecklenburg's windy lakes tilted white regattas, while crowds at the World 600 ached for any breeze.

People began to wonder at the newness of the city. When old-time pictures were gathered for display, unexpected crowds came to see what or who might be remembered. They reminisced, laughed, and marveled.

Charlotte is her people:

Mary Froebe Penny scrubs the old Saint Mary's Chapel floor she remembers from childhood.

Bill Lee, third-generation engineer, builds the Piedmont's future from the rich legacy of her past.

Elizabeth Randolph, educator, collects historic photographs of Charlotte faces and neighborhoods for *An African-American Album*.

Thomas Moore sings with and teaches the city's children.

Ron Leeper and friends band together to protect a new generation from violence and drugs.

Hugh McColl challenges Charlotte to regain her sensitivity to the "have-nots," to be inclusive toward all races, to find a common purpose for the greater good.

Frye Galliard, journalist and author, wonders aloud, "In the push to become a major-league city, will Charlotte lose something rare, the quality of civility and neighborliness, her sense of the common good, of doing right by all her citizens?"

A woman moves to the city, comes to the downtown library asking, "What is this town? Where did it come from?" So the city begins once again with the question, the journey, the land, the river, and the spirit moving among her people.

Right:
Charlotte's new skyline

Photo by Donna Bise

Ballet in Charlotte

Charlotte Chamber of Commerce

Charlotte Motor Speedway

Charlotte Motor Speedway

Carowinds

Carowinds Theme Park

Above:
One of the most popular physics exhibits
at Discovery Place, "Sparks, Anyone?" really
makes your hair stand on end.

Left:
Biology specialist Tammy Remsburg shows a Girl
Scout the wonders of snakes.

Discovery Place

Charlotte's dogwoods in bloom

A Bridge to the Future

In the days of Catawba Indians along the river or those days of settlers clattering down the path, the town clung inextricably to the road. It is still her lifeline.

Charlotte straddles the twentieth-century trading path, the crossing of the textile and river highways, and claims both the future and the past. United States Senator Terry Sanford is right—Charlotte is "a can-do city." She is, as she has always been, a confident and believing town, a practical, ambitious city.

Clearly, Charlotte has sought growth. But with it has come radical change. The familiar society that Charlotte knew for generations, two-thirds white, one-third black, almost all Southern in origin, has altered rapidly. Better than one in three residents were not here ten years ago. Charlotte is now a city of many values, with many voices, here at this antique crossroads. A partner to the towns and small cities of her region, Charlotte is at a new crossroads in her existence. Who will her leaders be? How will she strive? What will be her song?

Looking out upon Charlotte near the close of the century, it is clear she has paved her mud, outdone herself with classy spires. The people on her avenues are vigorous and diverse. Art and music spill into her streets, parks, and buildings. Trees have grown to grace her blemishes, and except for unrelieved prairies of concrete, she aspires to be more beautiful. Dogwoods sprawl on lush lawns in city neighborhoods and deep in lonely woods. These are valued. On a Saturday in spring, something involuntary causes people of the Piedmont to buy azaleas when all they intended was a loaf of bread or a newspaper. The dogwood and azalea are tangible investments in the land, as visible as the taut financial muscle of diverse industry and progress.

But there are other bridges to the future. The street names recall Freedom, Independence, Camp Greene, Mint, Church, and College. They recall people whose fiber carried Charlotte forward—Caldwell, Vance, Hill, Alexander, McDowell, Graham, Phifer, Davidson, and Brevard—such a stalwart, feisty clan. What power these old names gathered and relinquished, what perseverance and gifts they left behind!

There is a choice to be made in this "delicious country." As new migrations arrive and elbow us toward change, Charlotte can choose to affirm what she is known for: an unusual degree of fairness and equal opportunity for all the people who live here.

Charlotte has her flaws, said newspaperman James Batten, "but the spirit, the leadership, the quality of life, the value systems one finds in Charlotte, most American communities would love to have.

"Charlotte in a lot of ways is an embodiment of the best of what the New South might aspire to."

Selected Resources

Abbott, F. C. *Fifty Years In Charlotte Real Estate, 1897–1947*. Charlotte: 1947. Pamphlet in Carolina Room, Public Library of Charlotte and Mecklenburg County.

Adair, James. *History of the American Indians*. Edited by Samuel Cole Williams. Johnson City, Tenn.: The Watbaugh Press, 1930.

Alexander, J. B. *History of Mecklenburg County, 1840–1902*. Charlotte: Observer Printing House, 1902.

Avery, Isaac Erwin. *Idle Comments*. New York: Publishers Printing Company, 1905.

Avery, Waightstill. "Diary of Colonel Waightstill Avery, 1769." The Avery Papers are among the North Carolina Papers in the Draper Manuscript Collection at the History Society of Wisconsin. A Microfilm copy is in the Carolina Room at the Public Library of Charlotte and Mecklenburg County.

Blythe, LeGette, and Charles R. Brockman. *Hornet's Nest: The Story of Charlotte and Mecklenburg County*. Charlotte: McNally Publishing Co., 1961.

———. *William Henry Belk*. Chapel Hill: University of North Carolina Press, 1950.

Boger, Mary Snead. *Charlotte 23*. Bassett, Va.: Bassett Printing, 1972.

Brown, Douglas Summers. *The Catawba Indians:The People of the River*. Columbia: University of South Carolina Press, 1966.

———. *A City Without Cobwebs*. Columbia: University of South Carolina Press, 1953.

Brown, Henry S., and Mary Hoffman. *Gold Mining on the Rudisill Lode and the Development of Charlotte, N.C.* Charlotte: City of Charlotte Community Development Department, 1978.

Byrd, William. *William Byrd's Histories of the Dividing Line Betwixt Virginia and North Carolina*. Edited by William K. Boyd. Raleigh: North Carolina Historical Commission, 1929.

Carson, James H. "A Tale of the Sixties." From the papers of Mrs. J. A. Fore, Carolina Room, Public Library of Charlotte and Mecklenburg County.

Claiborne, Jack. *The Charlotte Observer: Its Time and Place, 1869–1986*. Chapel Hill: University of North Carolina Press, 1986.

———. *Jack Claiborne's Charlotte*. Charlotte: Charlotte Publishing Company, 1974.

Clay, James W. *Atlas of Charlotte-Mecklenburg*. Charlotte: UNC-Charlotte, 1978.

Clay, James W., and Douglas M. Orr. *Metrolina Atlas*. Chapel Hill: University of North Carolina Press, 1972.

Davidson, Chalmers Lee. *Piedmont Partisan: The Life and Times of Brigadier General William Lee Davidson*. Davidson, N.C.: Davidson College, 1951.

———. *The Plantation World Around Davidson.* Davidson, N.C.: Briarpatch Press, l982.

Dowd, Jerome. *Sketches of Prominent Living North Carolinians.* Raleigh: Edwards and Broughton, 1888.

Duke Power News. Special edition, January 1980. In Duke Power Archives.

Eaton, Clement. *A History of the Southern Confederacy.* New York: Macmillan Co., 1954.

Evans, Eli. *Judah P. Benjamin.* New York: Free Press, 1988.

Foote, William Henry. *Sketches of North Carolina.* New York: R. Carter, l846.

Galliard, Frye. *The Dream Long Deferred.* Chapel Hill: University of North Carolina Press, 1988.

———. *Southern Voices.* Asheboro, N.C.: Down Home Press, 1991.

Golden, Harry. *Only in America.* Cleveland and New York: World Publishing Co., 1958.

Goldfield, David R. *Cotton Fields and Skyscrapers: Southern City and Region, 1607– 1980.* Baton Rouge: Louisiana State University Press, 1982.

———. *Promised Land: The South Since 1945.* Arlington Heights, Ill.: Harlan Davidson, Inc., 1987.

Graham, William A. *General Joseph Graham and his Papers on North Carolina Revolutionary History.* Raleigh: Edwards and Broughton, 1904.

Hale, P. M. *Industries of North Carolina in the Coal and Iron Counties of North Carolina.* New York: E. J. Hale and Son, 1883.

Hall, Jacquelyn Dowd, James Leloudis, Robert Korstad, Mary Murphy, Lu Ann Jones, and Christopher B. Daly. *Like a Family: The Making of a Southern Cotton Mill World.* Chapel Hill: University of North Carolina Press, 1987.

Ivey, J. B. *My Memoir.* Greensboro, N.C.: Piedmont Press, 1940.

Jenkins, John Wilbur. *J. B. Duke, Master Builder.* New York: George H. Doran Co., 1927.

Kratt, Mary. *The Imaginative Spirit: Literary Heritage of Charlotte and Mecklenburg County.* Charlotte: Public Library of Charlotte-Mecklenburg, 1988.

———. *A Little Charlotte Scrapbook.* Davidson, N.C.: Briarpatch Press, 1990.

———. *Marney.* Charlotte: Dowd Press, l980.

Kratt, Mary, and Thomas W. Hanchett. *Legacy: The Myers Park Story.* Charlotte: Myers Park Foundation, 1986.

Lawson, John. *A New Voyage to Carolina.* Edited by Hugh Talmadge Lefler. Chapel Hill: University of North Carolina Press, 1967.

Lefler, Hugh T., and Albert Ray Newsome. *North Carolina: The History of a Southern State.* Chapel Hill: University of North Carolina Press, 1983.

Leyburn, James. *The Scotch-Irish: A Social History.* Chapel Hill: University of North Carolina Press, 1962.

Lossing, Benson J. *Pictorial Field Book of the Civil War.* Vol. 3. Hartford, Conn.: T. Belknap, 1866.

———. *Pictorial Field Book of the Revolution.* Vol. 2. New York: Harper and Brothers, l860.

McCrorey, H. J. "A Brief History of Johnson C. Smith University." *Johnson C. Smith University Bulletin 1* (May 30, 1935).

McEwen, Mildred Morse. *Growing Up in Fourth Ward.* Charlotte: Heritage Printers, 1987.

———. *Queens College Yesterday and Today.* Charlotte: Heritage Printers, 1980.

Making a Difference: Women of Mecklenburg. Charlotte: American Association of University Women, 1980.

Mitchell, Miriam Grace, and E. S. Perzel. *The Echo of the Bugle Call.* Charlotte: Heritage Printers, 1979.

Ovens, David. *If This Be Treason.* Charlotte: Heritage House, 1951.

Pardee, J. T., and C. F. Park, Jr. *Gold Deposits of the Southern Piedmont*. U.S. Geological Professional Paper 213, Department of the Interior. Washington, D.C.: U.S. Government Printing Office.

Parker, Inez Moore. *The Biddle–Johnson C. Smith Story*. Charlotte: Charlotte Publishing House, 1975.

Pope, Liston. *Millhands and Preachers*. New Haven, Conn.: Yale University Press, 1942.

Powell, William S. *The North Carolina Gazetteer*. Chapel Hill: University of North Carolina Press, 1968.

Preyer, Norris W. *Hezekiah Alexander and the Revolution in the Backcountry*. Charlotte: Heritage Printers, 1987.

Records of the Moravians in North Carolina. Vol. 2. Winston-Salem, N.C.: Moravian Archives, 1775.

Reynolds, D. A., ed. *Charlotte Remembers*. Charlotte: Community Publishing Co., 1972.

Rights, Douglas L. *The American Indian in North Carolina*. Winston-Salem, N.C.: John F. Blair, Publisher, 1957.

———. "The Buffalo in North Carolina." *North Carolina Historical Review* 9 (1932): 242–49.

———. "The Trading Path to the Indians." *North Carolina Historical Review* 8 (1931): 403–26.

Romine, Dannye. *Mecklenburg: A Bicentennial Story*. Charlotte: Independence Square Associates, 1975.

Saunders, William L., ed. *Colonial Records of North Carolina*. Vol. 5. Raleigh: P. M. Hale.

South, Stanley A. *Indians in North Carolina*. Raleigh: North Carolina Department of Archives and History, 1959.

Speizman, Morris. *The Jews of Charlotte*. Charlotte: McNally and Loftin, 1978.

Spratt, Thomas Dryden. "Recollections." 1875. Papers in Carolina Room, Public Library of Charlotte and Mecklenburg County.

Springs, Katherine Wooten. *The Squires of Springfield*. Charlotte: William Loftin Publishers, 1965.

Stenhouse, James. "Exploring Old Mecklenburg." 1952. Typescript in Carolina Room, Public Library of Charlotte and Mecklenburg County.

Thompson, Edgar T. *Agricultural Mecklenburg and Industrial Charlotte*. Charlotte: Chamber of Commerce, 1926.

Tompkins, D. A. *History of Mecklenburg County from 1740–1903*. Charlotte: Observer Printing House, 1903.

Washington, George. *Diaries of George Washington*. Vol. 4. Edited by J. C. Fitzpatrick. Boston: Houghton Mifflin Co., 1923.

Wheeler, John Hill. *Historical Sketches of North Carolina from 1584–1851*. Baltimore: Regional Publishing Co., 1964.

Wilkinson, Henrietta H. *The Mint Museum of Art at Charlotte: A Brief History*. Charlotte: Heritage Printers, 1973.

Wilson, Edith Bolling. *My Memoir*. New York: Bobbs-Merrill Co., 1938.

Winston, George Tayloe. *D. A. Tompkins: A Builder of the New South*. New York: Doubleday, 1920.

Work Projects Administration for the State of North Carolina. *Charlotte, A Guide to the Queen City of North Carolina*. Charlotte: Charlotte News Printing House, 1939.

Additional Sources

Microfilm records of Charlotte newspapers in the Carolina Room at the Public Library of Charlotte and Mecklenburg County: *Catawba Journal* (1824–28); *Miners' and Farmers' Journal* (1830–35); *Charlotte Journal* (1851); and *Charlotte Daily Observer/Charlotte Observer* (1892–1992)

Index

Abbott, F. C., 164, 201
Academy of Music, 177, 238
Adair, James, 10
Aderholt, D. A., 185
Afro-American Cultural Center, 236, 257
Alexander, Abraham, 15
Alexander, Adam, 27
Alexander, Annie Lowrie, 160
Alexander, David, 105
Alexander, Fred, 234
Alexander, Hezekiah, 22, 27, 37, 42
Alexander, Isaac, 51
Alexander, J. B., 25, 42, 44, 60, 160
Alexander, John McKnitt, 22, 25–27, 37
Alexander, Julia, 121
Alexander, Nathanael, 153
Alexander, Samuel C., 78
Alexander, Sydenham "Syd", 138–39, 143, 152
Alexander, William, 22
Alexander, Wm B., 51
Alexander Hotel, 194
Allison, Margaret, 44
AME Zion Publishing House, 94, 253
American Cotton Manufacturers Association, 193
American Revolution, 30–36, 39, 40
American Tobacco Company, 82
American Trust Company, 164
Andrews, Mildred, 108, 136
Armory Auditorium, 182, 216, 245
Arrington, Ted, 264
Arrowood, 215
Asbury, Louis, Sr., 195, 239
Ashmore, Harry, 226
Atherton Mill. See Cotton mills
Avery, Isaac Erwin, 134, 135, 229
Avery, Waightstill, 22, 27

Back Creek Associate Reformed Presbyterian Church, 209
Bagge, Traugotte, 26
Bailey, Mary Dawn, 252
Bakker, Jim, 270
Banks, Dick, 44
Barber-Scotia College, 127
Barnett, Susan (Susannah). See Smart, Susan (Susannah) Barnett
Barnhardt, Thomas M., 108, 109
Barnhardt Manufacturing Company, 204
Barringer, Osmond, 137–38, 192, 242, 247
Barringer, Paul, 160
Barringer, Rufus, 76, 138
Barringer Hotel, 204
Batten, James, 273, 282
Baxter, Herbert, 250

Bearden, Romare, 234
Beauregard, Pierre G. T., 65–67
Beaver Dam, 42
Bechtler, Christopher, 58
Belk, Henderson, 215
Belk, John, 250
Belk, Tom, 209
Belk, William Henry, 91–92, 214
Bell, Spencer, 192
Bell, W. M., 148, 267
Belmont Abbey College, 127
Benjamin, Judah P., 69, 70
Bennett Gold Mine, 189
Berryhill House, 259
Bickett, Thomas, 152
Biddle, Mrs. Henry, 78
Biddle Institute, 78–81, 127
Biddle University. See Biddle Institute
Bigger, Richard, 183
Big Ore Bank, 40
Billy Graham Crusade, 215
Bissell, Humphrey, 55–56
Bland, Mrs. M. A., 216
Bledsoe, Jerry, 229
Blockbuster Pavilion, 238
Bluegrass Boys, the, 210
Blumenthal, I. D., 203
Blythe, Legette, 216, 226
Bobbitt, William H., 214, 239
Bottomly, William L., 262
Boyer, Martin E., 192, 255
Brandon, M. H., 245
Branson's North Carolina Business Directory, 76
Brem, Walter, 164
Brevard, Adam, 226
Brevard, Alexander, 40
Brevard, Ephraim, 27, 29
Brevard, Harriet, 41
Briarhoppers, 210
Brick Store House, 52
Bronson, Benjamin, 234
Brooklyn 78, 217, 253
Brookshire, Stan, 223, 250
Bryant, Fred, 258
Bryant, "Red Buck", 100, 104, 138, 229
Buck, Paul, 238
Buford, A. S., 194
Buford Hotel, 92, 127, 191, 194
Bull, William, 10
Burns, Robert, 153
Burnside, J. Ed, 223
Burwell, Armistead, 214
Burwell, Mrs. Robert, 51
Burwell, Robert, 51
Busch Grand National 300, 247
Busing, 223–25
Byars, Betsy, 226

Bynum, William Preston, 214
Byrd, William, 8

Caldwell, Erskine, 226
Caldwell, J. P., 104, 229
Calhoun, John C., 100
Camp Greene, 73, 142–46, 160, 204, 215
Camp Sutton, 200
Cannon, Charles A., 85
Cannon, James W., 82, 108
Cannon, Marion, 226
Cannon Mills. *See* Cotton mills
Cape Fear Mercury, 26
Capps Hill Mine, 55
Carillon Building, 195
Carolina Isralite, 203, 225
Carolina Theater, 182, 211
Carolinas Medical Center, 78, 86, 252
Carowinds, 215, 238, 273, 276
Carson, J. H., 68, 73
Carter Family, 210
Caruso, Enrico, 180, 238
Carver College, 206
Cash, W. J., 226
Catawba Indians, 3, 5–8, 10, 20, 22, 39, 44, 69
Catawba Journal, 228
Catawba River, 3, 5–6, 13; battle of Cowan's Ford on the, 35–36, 143; camp meetings near the, 53; flooding of the, 149; homesites along the, 40–41, 42; mills and power plants located on the, 63, 65, 82, 104; supplied Duke's fountain, 86
Cedar Grove, 42, 43–44, 58
Central High School, 182, 206
Central Hotel, 92, 127, 188, 194, 216
Central Piedmont Community College, 177, 182, 190, 206, 252
Charles II, 5, 12
Charles R. Jonas Federal Court Building, 190
Charlotte and South Carolina Railroad, 48
Charlotte Auditorium, 238
Charlotte Chamber of Commerce, 73, 180
Charlotte Checkers, 244
Charlotte Chronicle, 104, 229
Charlotte City Club, 104, 194
Charlotte Clippers. *See* Charlotte Checkers
Charlotte Coliseum, 238, 249
Charlotte College, 206, 207
Charlotte Country Club, 73, 169, 244
Charlotte Daily Observer, 229
Charlotte/Douglas International Airport, 199, 250
Charlotte Female Academy, 51
Charlotte Female Institute, 51, 127
Charlotte Hornets (baseball), 243
Charlotte Hornets (basketball), 249
Charlotte Hornets (football), 246
Charlotte Hotel, 73, 182
Charlotte Journal, 46, 50, 60, 228

Charlotte Junior League, 259
Charlotte Knights, 249
Charlotte Leader, 264
Charlotte Male Academy, 51
Charlotte-Mecklenburg School Board, 206, 225
Charlotte Memorial Hospital, 78
Charlotte Mint, 59–61, 63, 68, 70, 73, 190–92
Charlotte National Bank, 104, 188
Charlotte News, 180, 191, 226, 228, 229
Charlotte Observer: employees of, 87, 134, 225, 226, 229, 245, 249, 250, 270; ownership of, 100, 104, 169
Charlotte Open, 244
Charlotte Opera House, 238
Charlotte O's, 243
Charlotte Post, 229
Charlotte, Queen, 17, 233
Charlotte Repertory Theater, 238
Charlotte Speedway, 138, 242, 246
Charlotte Symphony, 192, 237
Charlotte Women's Club, 191, 202
Chavis, D. W., 58
Cherokee Indians, 5, 6, 9, 22, 44
Citizens Advisory Group, 224
Civil War, 52–53, 63–70, 76, 77, 105
Claiborne, Slug, 223
Clarkson, Edwin, 144
Clarkson, Heriot, 153, 214
Clay, Jim, 277
Clayton Hotel, 194
Clemson University, 104
Clinton, Henry, 32
Coca Cola 600, 247
Cochrane, Elam, 209
Coddington, C. C., 210
Cohen, Hermann E., 203
Cole, E. A., 216
Cole, Grady, 210
Colonel William Johnston House, 255
Colonial Records of North Carolina, 9, 15
Colvard, Dean, 252
Commercial National Bank, 127, 188, 204, 276, 277
Commercial National Bank Building, 202
Cone, Bonnie, 206
Confederate Navy Yard, 64, 74, 78, 215
Confederate States Acid Works, 65
Cook's Inn, 194, 195
Coolidge, Calvin, 216
Coon, Charles, 102
Cornwallis, Charles, 30–36, 39, 143
Cotton Mill Campaign, 100, 276
Cotton mills, 100–111, 135, 161, 192, 276; Ada, 108; Alpha, 108; Atherton, 100, 101, 108, 120; Cannon, 85, 183, 204; Chadwick-Hoskins, 136, 193; Cramerton, 138; Glenroy, 105; Gosset, 193; Highland Park, 108, 136, 243–44; Loray, 185; Monbo, 149; Mountain Islands, 105; Stowe, 105; Victor, 108; Woodlawn, 105
Courthouses, 139

Cowan's Ford, 35, 36
Craighead, Alexander, 16, 19, 26, 160
Cramer, Stuart, 108, 136
Crockett Park, 243
Crosland, Bob, 245
Crosland, John, 276
Crump, Russell, 203
Crutchfield, Charles, 210
Crutchfield, Ed, Jr., 252
Cunningham, John, 223
Cuthbertson, Harriet, 236

Dale, Bishop, 253
Daniels, Patsy, 229
D. A. Tompkins Company, 100
Davidson, Chalmers G., 36, 43, 52
Davidson, John, 40
Davidson, Nancy, 44
Davidson, William Lee, 30, 35–36, 41
Davidson College, 36, 51–52, 127, 134, 160, 249, 252;
    endowment of, 86, 87, 92; experimentation with x-ray at,
    137; first president of, 53, former students and professors
    of, 151, 161, 265; students join Revolutionary War, 63
Davie, William R., 30
Davis, Burke, 228
Davis, Jefferson, 66, 68–70
Davis, Jimmie, 210
Davis, Varina (Mrs. Jefferson), 67
De Soto, Hernando, 5
Dewey, T. W., 68
Dewey Bank, 68, 255
Dilworth, 101, 118–20, 169, 180, 202, 253; baseball in, 243;
    fire station serving, 177; mills near, 108; preservation in,
    255; trolleys in, 191, 260
Dilworth Community Development Association, 257
Discovery Place, 236, 260, 273
Doak, Samuel, 32
Dobbs (governor), 14, 15
Douglas, Ben, 198–99, 201, 217
Douglas Aircraft Company, 215
Douglas Municipal Airport. See Charlotte/Douglas
    International Airport
Dowd, Clement, 104
Dowd, James C., 143
Dowd, Mrs. W. Carey, 216
Dowd, W. Carey, 216
Dowd, William Carey, Sr., 229
Dowd farmhouse, 146
Downing, Fanny, 226
Draper, Earl, 85, 86, 138, 164, 185, 216
Duke, James B. "Buck," 81–87, 108, 111, 121, 149, 165,
    202
Duke Endowment, 86, 87
Duke Power, 82, 85
Duke University, 86
Dumbell, Jim, 188
Duncan, Buell, 223

Dunhill Hotel, 195
Dunn's Mine, 54
Dwelle, Mary Myers, 192

Eastover, 192
Edison, Thomas, 190–91
Edison General Electric Company, 191
Efird, J. B., 92, 185
Eisenhower, Dwight D., 220
Elizabeth College, 92
Emergency Bank Bill, 185, 189
Enderly, 138
Erwin, John R., 137
Etheredge, Lane, 247
Exxon Corporation, 259
Ezekiel Wallace Rock House, 255

Faison, Henry, 276
Federal Reserve Bank of Richmond, 182
Ferguson, Patrick "Bull Dog," 32–33
Festival in the Park, 238
Field, Robbie, 243
Fields Jewelers, 244
First Baptist Church, 236, 269
First National Bank, 76, 127, 180, 185
First National Bank Building, 182
First Presbyterian Church, 53, 78, 121, 128, 142, 194
First Union National Bank, 188, 276, 277
Flood of 1916, 148–50
Foote, William Henry, 16, 53
Ford Motor Company, 138, 182, 201
Forney, Daniel, 41
Forney, Peter, 40
Fortune, 273
Founders Hall, 277
4C's, 118–120, 191, 202
Fourth Ward, 128, 215, 236, 258–59
Fox, Kohn Pedersen, 276
Freedmen, 74, 75, 78
Freedom Park, 169, 206, 220, 236, 237
Frew, Archibald, 41
Frew's Folly, 41
Friendly Relations Committee, 220
Friendship Baptist Church, 217, 253
Froebe, Mary. See Penny, Mary Froebe
Frohock, John, 15
Furman University, 86

Galliard, Frye, 210, 224, 229, 270, 278
Gantt, Harvey, 264
Garinger, Elmer, 206
Garr Auditorium, 268
Gary, Kays, 229, 250
Gastonia Rangers, 249
Gautier-Gilchrist House, 202
George II, 13
George III, 17, 24, 243

Gibbon, Robert L., 137
Gittlin, Sam, 203
Goldberg, Gene, 236
Golden, Harry, 95, 203, 225–26
Goldfield, David, 217, 229, 273, 276
Good Samaritan Hospital, 78
Goodman, Arthur, 203
Goodwin, "Miss Patsy" Harry, 220, 226
Gossett, Ben, 193
Gourmajenko, Alexis, 262
Grace, C. M. "Daddy", 269–70
Grace African Methodist Episcopal Zion Church, 94
Graeber, Eugene, Jr., 206
Graham, George, 51
Graham, Joseph, 30, 36, 40
Graham, Maggie, 64
Graham, Ruth Bell (Mrs. W. E. "Billy"), 229
Graham, W. E. "Billy", 268
Graniteville Manufacturing Company, 46
Great Depression, the, 183–98, 242, 277
Great Wagon Road, 13
Greek Orthodox Cathedral, 203
Green, Ron, 249
Greene, Nathanael, 35–36, 39, 143
Greensboro Daily News, 148
Greenwood, Janette, 63
Griffith, Brodie, 226
Griffith, E. C., 192

Habitat for Humanity, 271
Hagler (Indian king), 8–10
Haile Gold Mine, 191
Halegua, Alfredo, 233
Haley, Gail, 226
Hall, James, 53
Hall, Pat, 214, 215, 276
Hall, Warner, 223
Hall House, 204
Hanchett, Tom, 211
Harding, Harry, 188
Harding, Irving. *See* Johnson, Irving Harding
Hargett, Edna, 136
Hargrove, Marion, 228
Harris, Johnny, 249, 276
Harris, W. T., 275
Harris, Wade Hampton, 216, 229
Harshinger, Jay, 203
Hawley, F. O., 161
Hayes, Kathleen, 78
Hayman, Felix, 243
Hayman Field, 243
Heath, B. D., 242, 247
Heckler, Jonellen, 229
Heineman, Dannie, 203
Helms, Jesse, 264
Helper, Hinton Rowan, 43
Helper Hotel, 52

Hemley, Robin, 229
Heritage Village, 270
Hermitage Court, 169
Hezekiah Alexander Homesite, 257
Hill, D. H., 63, 76, 77, 226
Historic Landmarks Commission, 257, 277
Holly Bend, 42
Holt, William E., 136
Home Federal Savings and Loan, 73, 277
Hood, Ralph E., 150
Hook, C. C., 121, 202
Hoover, Herbert, 193, 214
Hope, C. C., 236
Hopewell Presbyterian Church, 43, 50
Horner Military School, 166, 180
Hotel Charlotte, 121, 194
Hudson, Jack, 269
Hugh Torance House and Store, 37, 44, 258
Hunter, Lester Walker, 161
Hurricane Hugo, 266

Independence Building, 102, 180, 255, 277
Independence National Bank, 188
Independence Park, 135, 169
Industrial Loan and Investment Bank, 255
Ingleside, 41, 42
Inman, Bob, 229
International Festival, 238
Irwin, John, 53
Ivey, J. B., 91–92
Ivey's, 259

Jack, James, 25, 194
Jack, Patrick, 194
Jackson, Andrew, 49, 50, 53, 59
Jackson, Mary Anna Morrison (Mrs. Stonewall Jackson), 76
Jackson, Oscar, 253
Jackson, Stonewall, 76
J. A. Jones Construction Company, 204
James I, 12
James K. Polk Homesite, 257
JazzCharlotte, 238
Jefferson Standard Broadcasting Company, 210
Jenkins, Snuffy, 210
Johnson, Curtis B., 87
Johnson, Irving Harding (Mrs. Curtis B.), 87, 149, 229
Johnson, R. D., 76
Johnson, Samuel, 55
Johnson C. Smith University, 78, 80, 81, 86, 220, 252
Johnson Family singers, 210
Johnston, C. W., 108–9, 136
Johnston, Joseph E., 69
Johnston, William, 68, 104
Johnston Building, 108, 109, 180
Jonas, Charles R., 244, 265
Jones, Hamilton C., 104

Jones, J. A., 102, 120, 203, 277
Jones, James A. "Jazz A.," 269
Jones, Simmons, 229
J. S. Dowd House, 257
J. T. Williams Junior High School, 94

Kahn, Aaron, 95
Kahn, Max, 95
Karnazes brothers, 190
Kaskey, Raymond, 233
Keesler, Lenoir, 277
Kemper Open, 244
Kennedy, "Woody," 206
Kerry, Coleman, 224
Ketner, Ralph, 275
King, Martin Luther, Jr. 223
Kings Mountain, 32–34, 40
Kings Mountain National Military Park, 33
Kirby, Fred, 210, 246
Kirkpatrick, T. L., 139, 151–52, 216
Knight Publishing Company, 259
Knox, Eddie, 250
Knox, John, 12, 16
Kokenes, Constantine, 190, 203
Kokenes, Steve, 190
Kress's, 185, 220
Kuester, Clarence, 180, 215–16
Kuralt, Charles, 210, 228

Lake Norman, 273
Lake Wylie, 273
Lakewood Park, 143, 182, 189, 253
Lance, Inc., 242
Land We Love, The, 226
Latrobe, Benjamin, 60
Latta, E. D., 101, 118–121, 169, 191, 194, 202, 239, 260
Latta, James, 43, 44, 118
Latta, Mary, 44
Latta Arcade, 120, 121
Latta Park, 118
Latta Place, 42, 169, 257
Lavitan, Gladys Kahn, 95
Lawrence, Elizabeth, 229
Lawson, John, 5–8
League of Women Voters, 185
Lee, Robert E., 68
Lee, W. S. (Bill), Jr., 198, 252, 278
Lee, William S., 82, 149
Leeper, Ron, 278
Levine, Al, 203
Levine, Leon, 203
Liberty Hall. See Queens Museum
Lincoln, Abraham, 68
Lineberger, A. C., 108
Lineberger, Caleb, 108
Lineberger, Lewis, 108
Lipscomb, Gerard "Nig", 244

Little, Julian, 277
Little, Luther, 216, 236
Little Rock A.M.E. Zion Church, 236
Little Theater, 192
Locke, Pat, 264
Logan, James, 13
Lombardo, Guy, 195
Long, Ben, 233
Loray Mill. See Cotton mills
Lords Proprietors, 5, 13
Los Angeles Times, 275
Lossing, Benson, 82

McAden, R. Y., 108
McColl, Hugh, 252, 259, 276, 278
McComb, Samuel, 44, 54, 60
McComb's Mine, 55
McCraw, Carl, Jr., 236
McCrorey, Henry L., 81
McCullers, Carson, 226
McCulloch, Henry, 14–15
McGill, Ralph, 217
McGinnis, Mary, 209
McGlohan, Loonis, 210, 238
McIntyre Cabin, 31, 255
McKinley, William, 94, 100
McKnight, C. A., 223
McLaughlin, Maude, 209
McManaway, C. G., 73, 137
McManaway-Wittkowsky House, 166
McMillan, Alex, 236, 265
McMillan, James B., 223–24
McNeill, John Charles, 226
McNinch, Frank, 143
Macon, Uncle Dave, 210
Mallonee-Jones House, 202
Management Review, 275
Manch, Al, 244
Mansion House, 50, 92, 194, 229
Marney, Carlyle, 269
Martin, James G., 192, 265
Martin, Josiah, 25–26, 30
Maschal, Richard, 233
Masonic Temple, 255, 277
Matoon, Mary, 81
Matoon, Stephen, 81
Mechanics and Farmers Bank, 188
Mecklenburg College, 206
Mecklenburg Declaration of Independence, 25–27, 37, 70, 88, 102, 151, 194, 215
Mecklenburg Flour Mills, 76
Mecklenburg Hotel, 194
Mecklenburg Iron Works, 63, 67, 76, 128
Mecklenburg Resolves, 27–29
Mecklenburg Times, 229
Mello Yello National 500, 247
Memorial Hospital, 161

Memorial Stadium, 244, 246
Mencken, H. L., 226
Merchant and Farmers National Bank, 127
Mercy Hospital, 161
Miller, Harris H., 95
Miller, Willis L., 80
Mills, Robert, 60
Miners' and Farmers' Journal, 55, 56, 228
Mint Museum of Art, 192, 233–34, 258, 273
Misenheimer, C. A., 137
Mitchell, Miriam, 142
Monroe, Bill, 210, 238
Montoya, Carlos, 236
Moore, Thomas, 278
Moose, Ruth, 229
Morgan, Daniel, 35
Morgan, J. P., 77, 229
Morgan, Perry, 229
Morrill, Dan, 136, 237, 260
Morris, William C., 199
Morris Field, 199, 201, 244
Morrison, Cameron, 139, 143, 152, 153, 214
Morrison, Robert Hall, 53
Morrocroft, 153
Morse, Samuel F. B., 56
Mount Mourne, 42
Mount Tirzah Forge, 40
Munroe, John P., 160
Mutual Savings and Loan, 277
Myers, John Springs, 152, 164
Myers, William R., 78
Myers Park, 73, 85, 142, 164–169, 180, 182, 255, 260
Myers Park Country Club, 166, 180, 244
Myers Park Homeowners Association, 257
Myers Street School, 92
Myrick, Sue, 265

Nancy Reid House, 257
Nation's Ford, 5, 7, 20, 44, 65, 68, 69
NationsBank, 46, 164, 188, 233, 276
Nature Museum, 236
Naumoff, Laurence, 229
Neill, Rolfe, 252
New Deal, 189, 217
Newcomb, George, 258
Newcomb, John, 258
Newell, L. B., 161
Newman, Paul Baker, 226
Nolen, John, 164, 169
North Carolina Blumenthal Center for the Performing Arts, 237
North Carolina College for Negroes at Durham, 153
North Carolina Jewish Home for the Aged, 203
North Carolina Medical College, 160, 161
North Carolina Military Institute, 63, 64, 77
North Carolina National Bank (NCNB), 164, 236, 259, 277. *See also* NationsBank

North Carolina Powder Manufacturing Company, 65
North Carolina Provincial Assembly, 25
North Carolina Railroad, 48
North Charlotte, 108, 260

Oates, R. M., 105
Odell Master Plan, 250
Old Settlers Cemetery, 53
Olde Providence Racquet and Tennis Club, 245
Oliver, Diane, 229
Olmstead, Frederick Law, Jr., 169
Olmsted, Denison, 54
Opera Carolina, 238
Orr, Douglas, 252
Osborne, E. A., 234
Osborne's Corner, 190
Ovens, David, 92, 143, 180, 188
Ovens Auditorium, 238, 250
Overmountain Men, 32
Owen, Laura, 236

Palmer, Arnold, 244
Pardo, Juan, 5
Parker, Inez Moore, 80
Parker, John J., 214, 216
Parks, Wilson, 105
Peart, Jerry, 233
Peeps, William, 120
Pelli, Cesar, 277
Penman, John, 60, 61
Pennsylvania Packet, 31
Penny, Mary Froebe, 234, 278
Performing Arts Center, 260, 273, 277
Perkins, William R., 87
Perzel, Ed, 142
Petty, Kyle, 247
Petty, Richard, 247
Phifer, Martin, 18, 66
Phifer, William F., 66–67, 69–70
Phifer House, 255
Piedmont and Northern, 109
Piethman, Russ, 236
Plank Road, 138
Poe, William, 224
Polk, James K., 49, 59
Polk, Thomas, 13–18, 25, 27, 29, 30, 34, 39, 42, 50, 53
Polk Park, 260
Pomodoro, Arnaldo, 233
Presbyterian College for Women, 51, 67, 81, 160, 166. *See also* Queens College
Presbyterian Hospital, 92, 161
Presbyterian meeting houses: Centre, 16; Hopewell, 16; Poplar Tent, 16; Providence, 16; Rocky River, 16; Steele Creek, 16; Sugaw Creek, 16
Presson, Mrs. Sam, 95, 120
PTL Club, 270

Quail Hollow Country Club, 244
Queens College, 24, 37, 51, 92, 165, 166, 252
Queens Museum, 25, 39, 49

Radiator Specialty Company, 203
Randolph, Elizabeth, 278
Rash, Dennis, 259
Ray, Margaret, 224
Realty Building, 102
Reddy, T. J., 226
Reed, Conrad, 54
Rehoboth Furnace, 40
Reid, Thomas Neely, 161
Reynolds, Blanche, 262
Reynolds, William A., 262
Rights, Douglas, 8
Rivafinoli, Vincent de, 56, 58, 60
Roads campaign, 152–53
Robarchek, Peg, 229
Robert Potts House, 42
Rock Creek Camp Grounds, 53
Rock Island Manufacturing Company, 105
Rock Island Woolen Mill, 63, 76, 104
Rock Springs Campground, 53
Roosevelt, Eleanor (Mrs. Franklin D.), 194
Roosevelt, Franklin D., 189, 193–94
Roosevelt, Theodore, 100, 135
Rosedale, 41, 258
R. S. Dickson Company, 183
Rudisill Gold Mine, 56, 58, 60, 192
Rudisill's Hill, 55
Ruger, Thomas, 73
Runyan, Morris, 73
Rural Hill, 40

Saint Catherine Mine, 56, 60
Saint Mary's Chapel, 234, 236, 257, 278
Saint Mary's Seminary, 127
Saint Peter's Catholic Church, 233
Saint Peter's Episcopal Church, 234
Saint Peter's Home and Hospital, 77, 78, 161
Salem Academy, 44
Salem Diary, 26
Sample, Mary, 37
Sanders, D. J., 81
Sanders House, 194
Sanford, Terry, 282
Sawyer, Vernon, 252
Schenck, Michael, 104
Seaboard Passenger Depot, 202
Second Ward High School, 206
Selwyn, George Augustus, 14–15
Selwyn Hotel, 194, 239, 255
Sharon Church, 134
Shepard, Charles E., 270
Sherman, William Tecumseh, 64, 65, 67, 69
Sherwood, Valerie, 229

Shinn, George, 249
Shuford, Alex, 215
Silverstein, Benjamin, 95
Sims, Marian, 226
Singing Christmas Tree, 238
Slavery, 42–43, 64, 67
Smart, Susan (Susannah) Barnett, 25, 31, 50
Smith, Arthur, 210
Smith, Elizabeth Simpson, 226
Smith, H. L., 137
Smith, Hubert, 199
Smith, James S., 220
Smith, Jane Berry (Mrs. Johnson C.), 81
Smith, M. B., 95
Soper, Morris A., 214
South Atlantic Baseball League, 243
Southern Cotton Oil Company, 101, 262
Southern Manufacturers' Club, 104, 137, 142
Southern Power Company, 82, 85, 177
Southern States Trust Company, 164
Southland Industrial Park, 242
Spangenberg, August Gottleib, 13
Spangler, C. D., Jr., 209, 225, 236
Speizman, Morris, 95, 203–4
Speizman Industries, 105, 204
Spencer, J. S., 136
Spirit Square Center for the Arts, 236, 238, 257, 260, 269, 273
Spratt, Susannah, 13
Spratt, Thomas, 14
Spratt, Thomas Dryden, 8, 20, 25, 69
Springfest, 238
Springfield Plantation, 44, 67
Springs, John, 42, 44, 48
Springs, Katherine Wooten, 48
Springs, Leroy, 76
Springs Mills, 48, 234
Star Lunch, 190
Statesville Landmark, 104
Stedman, John, 252
Steere, J. E., 192
Stephens, George, 152, 164, 165, 166, 169, 229
Stephens Company, 164, 169
Stevenson, Adlai, 216
Stewart, Ivey, 203
Stoneman's Raiders, 68
Stowe, Harriet Beecher, 62
Stowe, R. L., 108
Stowe, S. T., 108
Strickland, William, 60
Stringfield, Lamar, 216
Sugar Creek, 5
Sugaw Creek Presbyterian Church, 24, 37, 41, 51
Suk, Julie, 226
Sullivan, Chuck, 226
Sullivan, Louis, 277
Swann v. Charlotte-Mecklenburg Board of Education, 223

Swansea, Charleen, 226

Taft, William Howard, 216
Tarleton, Banastre, 30, 31–32, 35
Tate, Thad, 188
Taylor, Z. V., 85, 143
Temple Beth El, 203
Temple Israel, 203
Tenner, Luke, 245
Tenner, Sol, 245
Thies, Ernst, 190
Thies, Oscar J., 190
Thompson Orphanage, 234
Thurston, D. J., 250
Thurston Motor Lines, 250
Time, 185, 225
Tinguely, Jean, 233
Tompkins, D. A., 50, 64, 76, 100–104, 108, 194, 229, 273, 276
Tompkins tower, 134
Torance, Hugh, 37, 44
Torrance, James G., 44, 58
Trading Path, 7, 11, 13, 14, 19, 20, 39, 49, 92, 194
Trenholm, George A., 69
Tribble, Hal, 250
Triplett, Cathy, 233
Triplett, Ira, 247
Trippi, Charlie, 244
Trotter, John Scott, 210
Trust Building, 177, 202
Tryon (governor), 24
Tuscarora Indians, 5, 8, 22

Umstead, William B., 220
Union National Bank, 188. *See also* First Union National Bank
United House of Prayer for All People, 253, 270
University of North Carolina at Chapel Hill, 153
University of North Carolina at Charlotte (UNC-C), 207, 209, 233, 249, 252, 273
University of North Carolina at Greensboro, 153
University Research Park, 252

Van Every, Phillip, 220
Van Hecke, M. S., 273, 275
Vance, Zebulon B., 70, 73, 76, 153
VanLandingham, John H., 108
Veeder, Bill, 250
Vesuvius Furnace, 40, 44
Victor, H. M., 188, 277
Villa Square, 262
Villalonga-Alexander House, 202
Vinroot, Richard, 260

Wachovia Bank, 188, 253, 276, 277
Wade, Jake, 245
Wadsworth, George, 247

Walker, Charles E., 161
Walker, Platt D., 214
Wall Street Journal, 224
Walter Brem House, 202
Warlick, Absalom, 104
Warner Hall, 269
Washington, George, 30, 34, 35, 39, 40, 143, 194–95
Washington Post, 243
WBT radio, 180, 210–11
W. Duke and Sons, 81
Wearn Field, 243
Weathers, Graham, 233
Western Democrat, 64, 95
Wheeler, John Hill, 61
Whig, 228
White Oaks, 85, 86, 202
Wicker, Tom, 211
Wildacres, 203
Wilkes, Jane, 67, 76–78
Wilkes, John, 76
Wilkinson, Henrietta, 61, 150
Williams, J. T., 92, 94
Williamson, Bill, 236
Wilson, Cecilia Jackson, 253, 255
Wilson, James, 51
Wilson, Woodrow, 151
Wittkowsky, Samuel, 70, 73, 203, 277
Wolf, Harry, 239
Wood, Jack, 182, 188
Wood, Leonard, 142
Wood, Word, 164, 169
Woodall and Shepherd Drug, 104
Woolen Act, 13
World War I, 142–46, 169, 199, 204
World War II, 199–201, 203–4, 214, 220, 245
Wyatt, Henry I., 63
Wylie, W. Gill, 82

Yadkin River, 6
Yarborough, J. A., 216
"Yiasou" Greek Festival, 238